Essentials

of WISC-III and WPPSI-R Assessment

Alan S. Kaufman and
Elizabeth O. Lichtenberger

 John Wiley & Sons, Inc.

NEW YORK • CHICHESTER • WEINHEIM • BRISBANE • SINGAPORE • TORONTO

"WISC-III" and "WPPSI-R" are registered trademarks of The Psychological
Corporation.

This publication is designed to provide accurate and authoritative information in
regard to the subject matter covered. It is sold with the understanding that the
publisher is not engaged in rendering professional services. If legal, accounting,
medical, psychological or any other expert assistance is required, the services of
a competent professional person should be sought.

Library of Congress Cataloging-in-Publication Data:
Kaufman, Alan S.
    Essentials of WISC-III and WPPSI-R assessment / Alan S. Kaufman and
Elizabeth O. Lichtenberger.
        p.   cm. — (The essentials of psychological assessment series)
    Includes bibliographical references (p.   ) and index.
    ISBN 0-471-34501-6 (pbk. : alk. paper)
    1. Wechsler Intelligence Scale for Children.   2. Wechsler Preschool and
Primary Scale of Intelligence.   I. Lichtenberger, Elizabeth O.   II. Title.
III. Series
    BF432.5.W42K36   2000
    155.4'1393—dc21   99-31561
                                                                        CIP

Printed in the United States of America.
10 9 8 7 6 5 4 3

To the wonderful support group of family members that has provided Nadeen and me with consistent love and nurturance every step of the way (by age, youngest first, spanning four generations): Nicole, James, David, Jennie, Hannah, Seymour, Blanche

And to our poodle support group: Muffin, Disco, and Figaro
—ASK

To Mike, and our new little wonder, Hannah, for providing support, love, and inspiration during this work and all my endeavors
—EOL

CONTENTS

SERIES PREFACE

n the *Essentials of Psychological Assessment* series, we have attempted to provide the reader with books that will deliver key practical information in the most efficient and accessible style. The series features instruments in a variety of domains, such as cognition, personality, education, and neuropsychology. For the experienced clinician, books in the series will offer a concise yet thorough way to master utilization of the continuously evolving supply of new and revised instruments, as well as a convenient method for keeping up to date on the tried-and-true measures. The novice will find here a prioritized assembly of all the information and techniques that must be at one's fingertips to begin the complicated process of individual psychological diagnosis.

Wherever feasible, visual shortcuts to highlight key points are utilized alongside systematic, step-by-step guidelines. Chapters are focused and succinct. Topics are targeted for an easy understanding of the essentials of administration, scoring, interpretation, and clinical application. Theory and research are continually woven into the fabric of each book, but always to enhance clinical inference, never to sidetrack or overwhelm. We have long been advocates of "intelligent" testing—the notion that a profile of test scores is meaningless unless it is brought to life by the clinical observations and astute detective work of knowledgeable examiners. Test profiles must be used to make a difference in the child's or adult's life, or why bother to test? We want this series to help our readers become the best intelligent testers they can be.

In *Essentials of WISC-III and WPPSI-R Assessment*, the authors have attempted to provide readers with succinct, straightforward methods for competent clinical interpretation and application of these popular instruments. These two latest versions of Wechsler's children's scales are linked by history, as both are descendants of the 1946 Wechsler-Bellevue, Form II, and the 1949 WISC. Taken together, they can be used to assess children and adolescents across the broad range of 3 to nearly 17 years. They both reflect Wechsler's approach to intellectual assessment, yielding Verbal, Performance, and Full Scale IQs, and offering profiles of about a dozen scaled scores. Yet despite their common history, goals, and framework, no previous work has integrated the two tests thoroughly by providing analogous guides and guidelines to facilitate their interpretation and clinical application. This book has done just that, enabling practitioners to better understand the continuum that binds the preschool and primary-age test battery (WPPSI-R for ages 3–0 to 7–3) with the instrument designed for elementary and high school–age students (WISC-III for ages 6–0 to 16–11).

Alan S. Kaufman, Ph.D., and Nadeen L. Kaufman, Ed.D., Series Editors
Yale University School of Medicine

One

OVERVIEW

There are a plethora of IQ tests available for psychologists to use today, but the Wechsler instruments are the most widely used measures of intelligence for children, adolescents, and adults. Much has been written on these measures over the years, from clinical use of the scales to diverse research using the scales. Our goal for this book is to provide an easy reference for those who use the Wechsler Preschool and Primary Scale of Intelligence–Revised (WPPSI-R; Wechsler, 1989) and the Wechsler Intelligence Scale for Children–Third Edition (WISC-III; Wechsler, 1991). The book was developed for those who test children within the 3 to 16 year age range and wish to learn the essentials of the WPPSI-R and WISC-III in a direct, systematic manner. The reader will find that the book is easy to read. The main topics include administration, scoring, interpretation, and clinical use of the instruments. Important points are highlighted by "Rapid Reference," "Caution," and "Don't Forget" boxes. Each chapter contains a set of questions that are intended to help you consolidate what you have read. After reading this book you will have, at your fingertips, in-depth information on the WPPSI-R and WISC-III that will help you to become a competent examiner and clinician.

CONTROVERSY OF PROFILE INTERPRETATION

The measurement of intelligence and the process of profile interpretation that are advocated in this book and others (e.g., Kaufman, 1994a; Kaufman & Lichtenberger, 1999) have long been debated. We present a structured approach to WISC-III and WPPSI-R profile interpretation that has both a clinical and empirical foundation. Some argue that interpreting the profile of subtest scores should not be done (Glutting, McDermott, Prifitera, & McGrath, 1994; McDermott, Fantuzzo, & Glutting, 1990). These authors base their opposition to profile interpretation primarily on psychometric analyses, which lead them to conclude that the three Wechsler IQs are worthy of keeping, but not the subtest profile. Another team that opposes not only profile interpretation but also the notion of Verbal and Performance IQs is Macmann and Barnett (1994). Their argument is that the Wechsler scales only measure general intelligence (*g*). Therefore, they say, the Verbal and Performance IQs are not worthy of interpretation because the IQs are, in effect, general factors that have been both truncated and degraded. They advocate alternative methods of assessment, as their view is that even measuring general IQ (e.g., the Full Scale IQ) does not serve a constructive purpose.

MacMann and Barnett (1994) rely on their empirical acumen to provide "psychometric proof" that Verbal-Performance differences on Wechsler scales are not meaningful. Their advice to professionals is to not administer conventional intelligence tests because all that is gained is a sense of a child's general intelligence. Kaufman (1994b) recognizes that Macmann and Barnett used sound statistical methods to arrive at their conclusions, but he notes that their dismissal of IQ tests was hasty in light of clinical practice. Kaufman argues that viewing IQ tests simply as a measure of *g* neglects empirical and clinical data with various populations such as brain-damaged individuals, bilingual individuals, and delinquent individuals, as well as striking differences between Verbal IQ and Performance IQ in terms of how they change during the normal aging process. Among clinical populations, for example, multiple Wechsler studies have shown that patients with right-hemisphere brain damage have Performance IQs that are 8 to 10 points lower than their Verbal IQs (Kaufman, 1990a). Many studies with Hispanic and Native American samples have shown that these individuals' Performance IQs, on average, are significantly higher (by 10 to 15 points) than their Verbal IQs. Studies of the Wechsler tests across the adult life span have shown that the Verbal IQ remains relatively constant across the age range (through age 89) but the Performance IQ decreases rapidly between ages 20 to 24 and ages 84 to 89 (Kaufman & Lichtenberger, 1999). If one only focuses on *g* (or the Wechsler Full Scale IQ), the many noted differences between the Verbal and Performance scales in a number of populations are ignored. The WISC-III, WPPSI-R, and other Wechsler instruments are not one-factor tests, and to interpret them as such is not clinically beneficial.

Other opponents of profile interpretation (McDermott, Fantuzzo, Glutting, Watkins, & Baggaley, 1992) have based their arguments on psychometric analysis of group data. McDermott et al. insist that ipsative assessment, or the interpreting of strengths and weaknesses relative to the child's own level of ability, be evaluated in a manner similar to norm-based scores. They argue that the ipsative process fails to improve prediction and removes the test's reliable variance (McDermott, Fantuzzo, Glutting, Watkins, & Baggaley, 1992). However, Kaufman (1994a) disagrees, saying that their arguments are based on psychometric analyses of group data that are "irrelevant for individualized profile interpretation" (p. 30). It is inappropriate to subject the ipsative scores for each individual child to procedures meant for group data. In an ipsative comparison (described in detail in Chapter 4), the mean subtest score for an individual child is simply shifted up or down to provide a more even set of hypotheses about the child's cognitive assets and deficits. The process of ipsative comparison is not intended to be the ending of profile interpretation; rather, it is just the beginning point for practical, clinical analysis. From the ipsative comparison, hypotheses are generated and then may be supported or disconfirmed with further information.

The sophisticated statistical methods employed by McDermott and Glutting to oppose ipsative comparison have also been used to develop core profiles (Glutting, McDermott, Prifitera, & McGrath, 1994). Although the core profile search is an important line of study, it is important that examiners looking for core profiles through group data also investigate each child's profile to see what is unique to that particular child.

Ultimately, we strongly agree with Anastasi and Urbana's (1997) perception of the critics of profile interpretation: "One problem with several of the negative reviews of Kaufman's approach is that they seem to assume that clinicians will use it to make decisions based solely on the magnitude of scores and score differences. While it is true that the mechanical application of profile analysis techniques can be very misleading, this assumption is quite contrary to what Kaufman recommends, as well as to the principles of sound assessment practice" (p. 513).

HISTORY AND DEVELOPMENT

Interest in testing intelligence developed in the latter half of the 19th century. Sir Francis Galton (1869, 1883) developed the first comprehensive test of intelligence (Kaufman, 1983) and is regarded as the father of the testing movement. Galton theorized that because people take in information through their senses, the most intelligent people must have the best developed senses; his interest was in studying gifted people. Galton's scientific background led him to develop tasks that he could measure with accuracy. These were sensory and motor tasks, and although they were highly reliable, they proved ultimately to have limited validity as measures of the complex construct of intelligence.

Alfred Binet and his colleagues developed tasks to measure the intelligence of children within the Paris public schools shortly after the end of the 19th century (Binet & Simon, 1905). In Binet's view, simple tasks like Galton's did not discriminate between adults and children and were not sufficiently complex to measure human intellect. In contrast to Galton's sensory-motor tasks, Binet's were primarily language oriented, emphasizing judgment, memory, comprehension, and reasoning. In the 1908 revision of his scale, Binet (Binet & Simon, 1908) included age levels ranging from 3 to 13 years; in its next revision in 1911, the Binet-Simon scale was extended to age 15 and included five ungraded adult tests (Kaufman, 1990a).

The Binet-Simon scale was adapted and translated for use in the United States by Lewis Terman (1916). Binet's test was also adapted by other Americans (e.g., Goddard, Kuhlmann, Wallin, and Yerkes). Many of the adaptations of Binet's test were of virtual word-for-word translations; however, Terman had both the foresight to adapt the French test to American culture and the insight and patience to obtain a careful standardization sample of American children and adolescents (Kaufman, in press). Terman's Stanford-Binet and its revisions (Terman & Merrill, 1937, 1960) led the field as the most popular IQ test in the United States for nearly 40 years.

The assessment of children expanded rapidly to the assessment of adults when the United States entered World War I in 1917 (Anastasi & Urbina, 1997) The military needed a method by which to select officers and place recruits, so Arthur Otis (one of Terman's graduate students) helped to develop a group-administered IQ test that had verbal content quite similar to that of Stanford-Binet tasks. This was called the Army Alpha. A group-administered test consisting of nonverbal items (Army Beta) was developed to assess immigrants who spoke little English. Ultimately, army psychologists developed the individually administered Army Performance Scale Examination to assess those who simply could not be tested validly on the group-administered Alpha or Beta tests (or who were suspected of malingering). Many of the non-verbal tasks included in the Beta and the individual examination had names (e.g., Picture Completion, Picture Arrangement, Digit Symbol, Mazes) that may look familiar to psychologists today.

David Wechsler became an important contributor to the field of assessment in the mid-1930s. Wechsler's approach combined his strong clinical skills and statistical training (he studied under Charles Spearman and Karl Pearson in England) with his extensive experience in testing, which he gained as a World War I examiner. The direction that Wechsler took gave equal weight to the Stanford-Binet/Army Alpha system (Verbal Scale) and to the Performance Scale Examination/Army Beta system (Performance Scale). The focus that Wechsler had in creating his battery was one of obtaining dynamic clinical information from a set of tasks. This focus went well beyond the earlier use of tests simply as psychometric tools. The first in the Wechsler series of tests was the Wechsler-Bellevue Intelligence Scale (Wechsler, 1939). In 1946 Form II of the Wechsler-Bellevue was developed, and the Wechsler Intelligence Scale for Children (WISC; Wechsler, 1949) was a subsequent downward extension of Form II that covered the age range of 5 to 15 years. Ultimately, the WISC became one of the most frequently used tests in the measurement of preschool functioning (Stott & Ball, 1965). Although the practice of using tests designed for school-age children in assessing preschoolers was criticized because of the level of difficulty for very young children, the downward extension of such tests was not uncommon prior to the development of tests specifically for children under age 5 (Kelley & Surbeck, 1991).

The primary focus of the testing movement until the 1960s was the assessment of children in public school and adults entering the military (Parker, 1981). However, in the 1960s the U.S. federal government's increasing involvement in education spurred growth in the testing of preschool children. The development of government programs such as Head Start focused attention on the need for effective program evaluation and the adequacy of preschool assessment instruments (Kelley & Surbeck, 1991). In 1967 the Wechsler Preschool and Primary Scale of Intelligence (WPPSI) was developed to meet the growing need of evaluating programs such as Head Start. The WPPSI was developed as a downward extension of certain WISC subtests but provided simpler items and an appropriately aged standardization sample. However, because the WPPSI accommodated the narrow 4 to 6.5 year age range, it failed to meet the needs of program evaluations because most new programs were for ages 3 to 5 years.

Public Law 94-142, the Education for All Handicapped Children Act of 1975, played an important role in the continued development of cognitive assessment instruments. This law and subsequent legislation (Individuals with Disabilities Education Act—IDEA of 1991 and IDEA Amendments in 1997) included provisions that required an individualized education program (IEP) for each disabled child (Sattler, 1988). A key feature of the development of the IEP is the evaluation and diagnosis of the child's level of functioning. Thus these laws directly affected the continued development of standardized tests such as the WPPSI and WISC. The WISC has had two revisions (1974 and 1991), and the WPPSI has had one (1989). The WISC-III is the great-

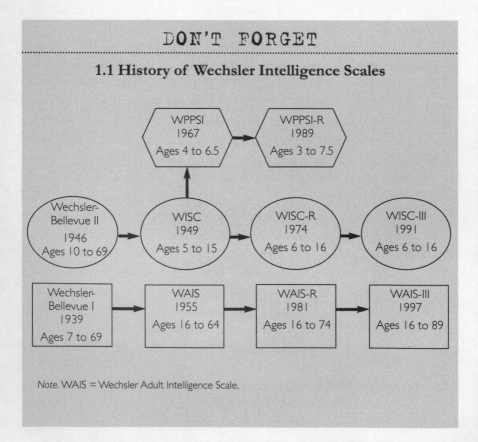

DON'T FORGET

1.1 History of Wechsler Intelligence Scales

WPPSI
1967
Ages 4 to 6.5

WPPSI-R
1989
Ages 3 to 7.5

Wechsler-
Bellevue II
1946
Ages 10 to 69

WISC
1949
Ages 5 to 15

WISC-R
1974
Ages 6 to 16

WISC-III
1991
Ages 6 to 16

Wechsler-
Bellevue I
1939
Ages 7 to 69

WAIS
1955
Ages 16 to 64

WAIS-R
1981
Ages 16 to 74

WAIS-III
1997
Ages 16 to 89

Note. WAIS = Wechsler Adult Intelligence Scale.

grandchild of the 1946 Wechsler-Bellevue Form II; it is also a cousin of the WAIS-III, which traces its lineage to Form I of the Wechsler-Bellevue. Don't Forget 1.1 shows the history of Wechsler's scales.

THEORETICAL FOUNDATION

The concept of intelligence has always been difficult to define, and the concept today remains elusive (Flanagan, Genshaft, & Harrison, 1997). Wechsler's view of intelligence as a person's "capacity to act purposefully, to think rationally, and to deal effectively with his [or her] environment" (1944, p. 3) provided the foundation for the current Wechsler tests. Practical and clinical perspectives were the cornerstone of these tests rather than theory per se (except perhaps on Spearman's *g*, or general intelligence, theory). The origin of each of the WISC-III and WPPSI-R subtests is shown in Rapid Reference 1.1. Wechsler believed that IQ tests offered a way to peer into an individual's personality. Since the development of the Wechsler scales, extensive theoretical speculations have been made about the nature and meaning of these tests and their scores (Kaufman, 1990a, 1994a), but originally the tests were developed without regard to theory. The Wechsler tests are strongly supported as measures of general *g* (e.g., Kaufman, 1994a; Sattler, 1988). However, as we will show throughout this book, much more can be gleaned from the Wechsler scales than simply an understanding of a child's level of *g*.

Wechsler made a major contribution to the field of cognitive assessment with his inclusion of both Verbal and Performance scales. The dual-scaled tests went against the conventional wisdom of his time, when most examiners were reluctant to administer a lengthy nonverbal subtest when (they thought) a quick verbal subtest could glean just as much data. However, most examiners now realize that Verbal and Performance have critical value for understanding brain functioning and theoretical distinctions between fluid and crystallized intelligence. In addition, because Wechsler stressed the clinical value of intelligence tests, this provided a new layer to the psychometric, statistical emphasis of testing that accompanied the use and interpretation of earlier tests such as the Stanford-Binet. Finally, Wechsler's inclusion of a multi-score subtest profile (as well as three IQs instead of one) met the needs of the emerging field of learning disabilities assessment in the 1960s to such an extent that Wechsler's scales replaced the Stanford-

≡ Rapid Reference

1.1 Origin of WPPSI-R and WISC-III Subtests

Verbal Subtest	Source of Subtest
Vocabulary	Stanford-Binet
Similarities	Stanford-Binet
Arithmetic	Stanford-Binet/Army Alpha
Digit Span	Stanford-Binet
Information	Army Alpha
Comprehension	Stanford-Binet/Army Alpha
Sentences	Stanford-Binet

Performance Subtest	Source of Subtest
Picture Completion	Army Beta/Army Performance Scale Examination
Coding	Army Beta/Army Performance Scale Examination
Block Design	Kohs (1923)
Picture Arrangement	Army Performance Scale Examination
Symbol Search	Shiffrin & Schneider (1977) and S. Sternberg (1966)
Object Assembly	Army Performance Scale Examination
Geometric Design	Gesell Copy Forms (Gesell, Ilg, & Ames, 1974)
Animal Pegs	Coding & Digit Symbol
Mazes	Army Beta

Binet as king of IQ during that decade. They have maintained that niche ever since.

PURPOSES OF ASSESSING PRESCHOOLERS, SCHOOL-AGE CHILDREN, AND ADOLESCENTS

Children are assessed for a variety of reasons, and thus the WPPSI-R and WISC-III may be applied in many different situations. Typically children are referred by a teacher for a psychological evaluation to determine if they have an educationally related disability and are eligible for special education or other special services. Many referrals seek assessment for developmental delay, learning disabilities, mental retardation, behavioral problems, neuropsychological impairments, or giftedness. Often the goal of a child's assessment is to provide effective interventions. The number of children in the United States between ages 6 and 16 who are diagnosed as educationally disabled and in need of special education is approximately 4.4 million (U.S. Department of Education, 1994). Assessments take place in psychologists' private practices, schools, clinics, hospitals, and research settings.

Although there are by now numerous measures of children's intelligence, the Wechsler scales remain by far the most popular (Daniel, 1997). For example, in a survey of school psychologists assessing children to identify mental retardation the Wechsler scales were reportedly the most frequently used tests for determining IQ (Woodrich & Barry, 1991). Even in assessing bilingual children and limited-English-speaking students, the WISC-R and WISC-III were reported to be the most frequently used tests (Ochoa, Powell, & Robles-Pina, 1996). In another study, school psychologists rated the Wechsler scales as most useful and as actually used the most (Giordano, Schwiebert, & Brotherton, 1997). In yet another survey of school psychologists, the WISC-III was reportedly used 10 times per month, whereas the next most frequently used test (of 11 listed) was only used twice (Wilson & Reschly, 1996). Because of their popularity throughout the years, the WISC, WISC-R, and WISC-III have remained staples of the batteries of most psychologists who test school-age children and adolescents. The WPPSI and WPPSI-R have also remained a strong force in the assessment of preschool-age children.

DESCRIPTION OF WPPSI-R

The WPPSI-R is a measure of cognitive functioning of children from ages 2 years 11 months to 7 years 3 months. The WPPSI-R comprises two scales: Verbal and Performance. Each provides standard scores with a mean of 100 and a standard deviation of 15. Mainly motor responses are required on the Performance Scale (pointing, placing, or drawing), and spoken responses are required on the Verbal Scale. The two scales each comprise five subtests, plus one optional subtest (see Figure 1.1, page 11). Each of the subtests provides

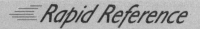

1.2 Description of WPPSI-R and WISC-III Subtests

Performance Subtests

WPPSI-R and WISC-III

Object Assembly. Child is required to fit puzzle pieces together to form a meaningful whole.

Block Design. On WPPSI-R, child reproduces patterns made from flat, red-and-white colored blocks. On WISC-III, child replicates geometric patterns with red-and-white colored cubes from both two-dimensional and three-dimensional models.

Mazes. Child solves paper-and-pencil mazes of increasing difficulty.

Picture Completion. Child identifies what is missing from pictures of common objects.

WPPSI-R Only

Animal Pegs. Child places pegs of the correct colors in the holes below a series of pictured animals.

Geometric Design. In the first part of the task, child must look at a design and point to a matching design from an array of four. In the second part, child copies a drawing of a geometric figure.

WISC-III Only

Coding. Child uses a key to write symbols below corresponding numbers.

Symbol Search. Child indicates, by marking a box, whether a target symbol appears in a series of symbols.

Picture Arrangement. Child rearranges a set of pictures into a logical story sequence.

Verbal Subtests

WPPSI-R and WISC-III

Information. On WPPSI-R, child must either point to a picture or verbally answer brief oral questions about commonplace objects and events. On WISC-III, child answers a series of questions tapping knowledge of common events, objects, places, and people.

Comprehension. On WPPSI-R, child verbally responds to questions about consequences of events. On WISC-III, child answers questions that require an understanding of social rules and concepts or solutions to everyday problems.

Arithmetic. On WPPSI-R, child demonstrates ability to count and solve more complex quantitative problems. On WISC-III, child mentally solves a series of arithmetic problems.

Vocabulary. On WPPSI-R, child names pictured items and provides verbal definitions of words. On WISC-III, child orally defines a series of orally and visually presented words.

Similarities. On WPPSI-R, child chooses which pictured objects share a common feature, or child completes a sentence that contains a verbal analogy. On WISC-III, child explains how two common words are conceptually alike.

WPPSI-R Only

Sentences. Child repeats verbatim a sentence that is read aloud.

WISC-III Only

Digit Span. Child repeats a list of orally presented numbers forward and backward.

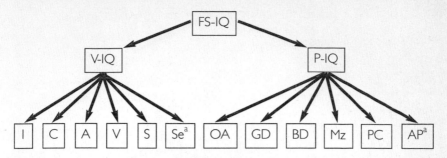

Figure 1.1 Building Blocks of WPPSI-R Structure

Note. FS-IQ = Full Scale IQ; V-IQ = Verbal IQ; P-IQ = Performance IQ; I = Information; C = Comprehension; A = Arithmetic; V = Vocabulary; S = Similarities; Se = Sentences; OA = Object Assembly; GD = Geometric Design; BD = Block Design; Mz = Mazes; PC = Picture Completion; AP = Animal Pegs.

[a]Sentences and Animal Pegs are optional subtests.

scaled scores with a mean of 10 and a standard deviation of 3. Rapid Reference 1.2 lists and describes each of the WPPSI-R subtests.

DESCRIPTION OF WISC-III

The WISC-III is an instrument for assessing the cognitive abilities of children and adolescents ages 6 years 0 months to 16 years 11 months. It has 13 subtests that yield three IQs (Verbal, Performance, and Full Scale) and four factor indexes (Verbal Comprehension, Perceptual Organization, Freedom from Distractibility, and Processing Speed). Figure 1.2 shows how the subtests are combined to form each of the IQ scales and factor indexes. Each of the IQs and factor indexes are standard scores with a mean of 100 and a standard deviation of 15. The subtests on the WISC-III provide scaled scores with a mean of 10 and a standard deviation of 3.

The five subtests that make up the Verbal IQ are Vocabulary, Similarities, Arithmetic, Information, and Comprehension. In addition to these Verbal subtests, a supplementary Verbal subtest (Digit Span) is administered and may substitute for other Verbal subtests if necessary. The five nonverbal subtests that make up the Performance IQ are Picture Completion, Picture Arrangement, Block Design, Object Assembly, and Coding. In addition, there are two supplementary subtests on the Performance Scale: Symbol Search (which may be used to replace Coding) and Mazes (an optional subtest that may be used to replace any Performance subtest). Because of the significantly

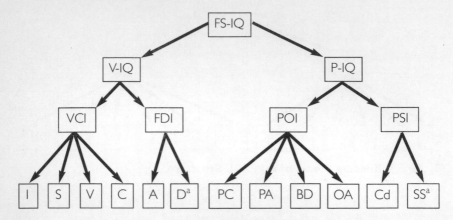

Figure 1.2 Building Blocks of WISC-III Structure

Note. FS-IQ = Full Scale IQ; V-IQ = Verbal IQ; P-IQ = Performance IQ; VCI = Verbal Conceptualization Index; FDI = Freedom from Distractibility Index; POI = Perceptual Organization Index; PSI = Processing Speed Index; I = Information; S = Similarities; V = Vocabulary; C = Comprehension; A = Arithmetic; D = Digit Span; PC = Picture Completion; PA = Picture Arrangement; BD = Block Design; OA = Object Assembly; Cd = Coding; SS = Symbol Search.

[a]Digit Span and Symbol Search are not used in calculation of the IQs.

stronger psychometric properties of Symbol Search in comparison to Coding, we recommend that Symbol Search be routinely substituted for Coding as part of the regular battery and in calculation of the Performance IQ (see Kaufman, 1994a, pp. 59–61, for a more detailed rationale). We also recommend that Mazes not be administered as a supplement, or used as a substitute for any Performance subtest, because of its faulty data (Kaufman, 1994a, pp. 61–62). Rapid Reference 1.2 describes each of the WISC-III subtests.

STANDARDIZATION AND PSYCHOMETRIC PROPERTIES OF WPPSI-R AND WISC-III

The WPPSI-R was standardized on a sample of 1,700 children who were chosen to closely match the 1986 U.S. Census data on variables of age, gender, geographic region, ethnicity, and parental education and occupation. The reliability and validity information are presented in the WPPSI-R manual (Wechsler, 1989). The average internal consistency coefficients are .95 for the Verbal IQ, .91 for the Performance IQ, and .96 for the Full Scale IQ. Internal consistency values for individual subtests across all ages range from .54 on Similarities and Object Assembly at age 7 to .93 on Picture Completion at age 4.5 (median = .81). The WPPSI-R is a fairly stable instrument with test-retest reliabilities of .90, .88, and .91 for the Verbal, Performance, and Full Scale IQs, respectively (see Rapid Reference 1.3 for a summary of reliability val-

≣Rapid Reference

1.3 Average WPPSI-R and WISC-III Reliability

	WPPSI-R		WISC-III	
WPPSI-R or WISC-III Scale, Index or Subtest	Split-Half Reliability	Test-Retest Reliability	Split-Half Reliability	Test-Retest Reliability
Verbal IQ	.95	.90	.95	.94
Performance IQ	.92	.88	.91	.87
Full Scale IQ	.96	.91	.96	.94
Verbal Comprehension Index	—	—	.94	.93
Perceptual Organization Index	—	—	.90	.87
Freedom from Distractibility Index	—	—	.87	.82
Processing Speed Index[a]	—	—	.85	.84
Verbal				
Information	.84	.81	.84	.85
Similarities	.86	.70	.81	.81
Arithmetic	.80	.71	.78	.74
Vocabulary	.84	.75	.87	.89
Comprehension	.83	.78	.77	.73
Digit Span	—	—	.85	.73
Sentences	.82	.79	—	—

continued

WPPSI-R or WISC-III Scale, Index or Subtest	WPPSI-R		WISC-III	
	Split-Half Reliability	Test-Retest Reliability	Split-Half Reliability	Test-Retest Reliability
Performance				
Picture Completion	.85	.82	.77	.81
Coding[a]	—	—	.79	.77
Picture Arrangement	—	—	.76	.64
Block Design	.85	.80	.87	.77
Object Assembly	.63	.59	.69	.66
Symbol Search[a]	—	—	.76	.74
Mazes	.77	.52	.70	.57
Geometric Design	.79	.67	—	—
Animal Pegs[a]	—	.66	—	—

[a]For the Processing Speed Index, Coding, Symbol Search, and Animal Pegs, only test-retest coefficients are reported because of the timed nature of the subtests.

ues). Construct validity of the WPPSI-R is supported by the factor analytic studies described in the manual that reveal the WPPSI-R to be a two-factor test; one is clearly identified as Verbal and the other as Performance. Validity is further supported by strong correlations with other instruments such as the Stanford-Binet–Fourth Edition. Chapter 5 presents a more detailed review of validity issues.

The WISC-III was standardized on 2,200 subjects grouped according to age, gender, race/ethnicity, geographic region, and parental educational level. This sample was selected to match basic demographic characteristics provided in the 1988 U.S. Census data. The excellence of the WISC-III's norms has been noted by several reviewers (e.g., Braden, 1995; Kaufman, 1993; Sandoval, 1995).

The reliability data for the WISC-III are strong. The average split-half reliability coefficients for individual subtests across the different age groups range from .69 to .87 (median = .78). The average reliability values for the IQs and indexes are .95 for the Verbal IQ, .91 for the Performance IQ, .96 for the Full Scale IQ, .94 for the Verbal Comprehension Index, .90 for the Perceptual Organization Index, .87 for the Freedom from Distractibility Index, and .85 for the Processing Speed Index (see Rapid Reference 1.3 for a summary of reliability values). Factor analytic studies were performed for four age groups: ages 6 to 7, ages 8 to 10, ages 11 to 13, and ages 14 to 16. The underlying four-factor structure of the WISC-III (corresponding to the four factor indexes) was validated (Wechsler, 1991) and provides evidence of the WISC-III's construct validity. The factor structure has also been cross validated with large representative samples in the United States (Roid, Prifitera, & Weiss, 1993) and Canada (Roid & Worrall, 1997); moreover, it has been validated for children with handicapping conditions such as mental retardation and learning disabilities (Konold, Kush, & Canivez, 1997). Substantial loadings on the large unrotated first factor also provide support for the construct of general intelligence (g) underlying the Full Scale IQ.

COMPREHENSIVE REFERENCES ON THE TESTS

The *Manual for the Wechsler Preschool and Primary Scale of Intelligence–Revised (WPPSI-R)* (Wechsler, 1989) provides detailed information about the development of the test, description of the subtests and scales, standardization, reliability, and validity. *Assessment of Children: WISC-III and WPPSI-R Supplement* (Sattler, 1992) presents an overview of what the test measures and an approach to interpretation. Gyurke's (1991) chapter on the WPPSI-R describes the subtests and scales, summarizes psychometric information, and provides steps for interpreting the test.

The *Manual for the Wechsler Intelligence Scale for Children–Third Edition (WISC-III)* (Wechsler, 1991) provides detailed information about the development of the test, description of the subtests and scales, standardization, reliability, and validity. Kaufman's (1994a) *Intelligent Testing With the WISC-III* explains how to interpret the WISC-III from a clinical and theoretical perspective and provides numerous case studies as examples. In a book edited by Prifitera and Saklofske (1998), *WISC-III Clinical Use and Interpretation*, diverse topics related to the WISC-III are discussed: gifted children, mental retardation, attention-deficit hyperactivity disorder, emotionally disturbed children, learning disabilities, language impairment, deaf children, neuropsychological bases, minority children, and more. Rapid Reference 1.4 provides basic information on the WPPSI-R, WISC-III, and their publisher.

≡ Rapid Reference

....

1.4. Wechsler Preschool and Primary Scale of Intelligence–Revised and Wechsler Intelligence Scale for Children–Third Edition

WPPSI-R

Author: David Wechsler

Publication date: 1989

What the test measures: Verbal, nonverbal, and general intelligence

Age range: 3 years to 7 years 3 months

Administration time: 60–75 minutes depending on the age of the child

Qualification of examiners: Graduate- or professional-level training in psychological assessment

Publisher: The Psychological Corporation
      555 Academic Court
      San Antonio, TX 78204-24988
      800-211-8378
      http://www.PsychCorp.com

Complete kit test price: $682.50 (1999 catalog price)

WISC-III

Author: David Wechsler

Publication date: 1991

What the test measures: Verbal, nonverbal, and general intelligence

Age range: 6 to 16 years

Administration time: 10 regular subtests take 50–70 minutes, and 3 supplementary tests take 10–15 more minutes

Qualification of examiners: Graduate- or professional-level training in psychological assessment

Publisher: The Psychological Corporation
      555 Academic Court
      San Antonio, TX 78204-24988
      800-211-8378
      http://www.PsychCorp.com

Complete kit test price: $621.00 (1999 catalog price)

⚓ TEST YOURSELF ⚓

1. **If you were a member of the McDermott and Glutting team who opposes profile interpretation, you might feel that the Verbal, Performance, and Full Scale IQs are worthy of keeping but that analysis of an individual's subtest profile is worthless.** True or False?

2. **Judging from the content of Binet's 1905 and 1908 scales of intelligence, he felt that measuring what types of abilities were important in estimating a person's intelligence?**
   (a) Sensory-motor
   (b) Visual acuity
   (c) Language
   (d) Olfactory

3. **What major event in world history impacted the development of intelligence tests?**
   (a) President Clinton's impeachment
   (b) The Vietnam War
   (c) Watergate
   (d) World War I

4. **Preschool assessment measures such as the WPPSI-R were developed as upward extensions of infant tests of intelligence.** True or False?

5. **Either the WPPSI-R or the WISC-III may be used when assessing a child in which age range?**
   (a) 4 to 5 years
   (b) 5 to 6 years
   (c) 6 to 7 years
   (d) 7 to 8 years

6. **The WPPSI-R and the WISC-III are quite comparable because they both have a four-factor structure (Verbal Comprehension, Perceptual Organization, Freedom from Distractibility, and Processing Speed).** True or False?

7. **You may use this WISC-III Performance Scale optional subtest to replace the Coding subtest, and we recommend that you do this routinely.**
   (a) Digit Span
   (b) Symbol Search
   (c) Object Assembly
   (d) Block Design

Answers: 1. True; 2. c; 3. d; 4. False; 5. c; 6. False; 7. b

Two

HOW TO ADMINISTER THE WISC-III AND WPPSI-R

Both standardized and nonstandardized procedures must be used in unison to uncover a child's true abilities and disabilities. Norm referenced tests such as the WPPSI-R and WISC-III provide information that compares an individual to a norm group. In order to obtain accurate scores from a norm referenced test, a standardized procedure must be followed under a set of standard conditions. When this is adequately done, the individual tested can be compared fairly to those who were assessed as part of the normative group. As will be discussed throughout this book, however, nonstandardized procedures such as interviews, behavioral observations, and informal assessments should be used together with standardized tests to provide an integrated and full picture of a child's abilities. Simply taking a snapshot of a child's abilities through a time-limited sample of performance, as is done during administration of the WISC-III and WPPSI-R, does not provide adequate information about the child for the purposes of making a diagnosis and recommendations.

APPROPRIATE TESTING CONDITIONS

Testing Environment

There are some issues regarding the testing environment that should be considered whether you are testing a young preschool child, a school-age child, or an adolescent. However, certain issues are unique to each of these age groups, and all these issues are presented in this chapter.

For a child of any age it is important that the testing environment be relatively free of distractions, both visual and auditory. The surroundings should not have too many toys and windows but likewise should not be too formal or adultlike. The testing environment should be comfortable for both you and the child. In most situations only you (the examiner) and the child should be present in the testing room. However, when testing a very young child (age 3 or 4) or when evaluating a child who is anxious about separating from a parent or caregiver, it may be necessary for the parent to accompany you into the testing room, at least for a brief period. We will expound further on this issue when we discuss establishing rapport.

A table is necessary for all testing situations. Ideally, when testing a pre-schooler or young child you should have an appropriately sized table and chairs (similar to those in a preschool classroom). If these are not available, then you should use a booster chair or high chair (with safety restraints) to raise the child to a comfortable level that is even with the table. In some cases when testing a highly energetic preschool child, it may be advantageous to move the testing materials to the floor if that seems to be the location at which the child will best attend to you. With some children it may be necessary to alternate between highly structured activities at a table and informal activities that can be done on the floor. In all cases, a clipboard provides a smooth writing surface and can be used on the floor if necessary.

Testing Materials

While the testing is taking place, we recommend that you sit either opposite the child or at a 90-degree angle from the child (kitty-corner) in order to most easily view the test-taking behaviors and manipulate the test materials (see Figure 2.1). The testing manual may be propped up on the table and positioned as a shield behind which the record form can be placed. This allows the examiner to easily read the directions, but it prevents the child from being distracted by what the examiner is writing on the record form. Only the testing materials that are immediately being used should be visible to the child. Young children can be easily distracted by stimulus materials if they are in view. We recommend that you keep other testing materials on the floor or on a chair beside you so that they are readily available.

Both the WPPSI-R kit and the WISC-III kit contain multiple pieces, and we recommend that you double-check that all elements are present and accounted for prior to beginning the testing. A young child is not likely to remain attentive while you search for a missing piece from an Object Assembly

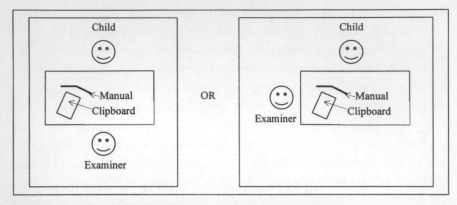

Figure 2.1 Alternative Seating Arrangements for Testing

puzzle item. A few materials are not contained within the testing kits, and you will need to bring these yourself: a stopwatch, clipboard, two No. 2 graphite pencils without erasers, and extra paper for taking notes. Don't Forget 2.1 summarizes the essential elements for administering the test.

RAPPORT WITH EXAMINEE

Establishing Rapport

When working with preschoolers, school-age children, or adolescents, building rapport is crucial to obtaining valid testing results. Even the most experienced examiners may find it challenging to juggle the maintenance of rapport with adherence to standardized procedures. When initially interacting with the child, it is important to allow him or her enough time to become accustomed to you and the testing situation before jumping into the evaluation. The manner in which a parent or caregiver has introduced their child to the testing situation

> **DON'T FORGET**
> ....
> ### 2.1 Keys for Preparing to Administer the Test
>
> - quiet, distraction-free room
> - table and chairs of appropriate size for the child
> - smooth writing surface
>
> Necessary materials not in the kit:
>
> - two No. 2 pencils without erasers
> - stopwatch
> - clipboard
> - extra paper and writing utensils (just in case)

can have effects throughout the evaluation. We encourage parents to explain to their children ahead of time what they may expect during the evaluation. For example, it is good to let the child know the examiner will be showing him or her some puzzles and blocks and will be asking some questions. We advise parents not to use the word *test* when introducing the situation to their child because the word has a negative connotation to many children and can even elicit a fear reaction. However, if a child directly asks "Am I going to do a test?" then it is best not to lie, but rather explain to the child, "Most of the things you are going to be doing are not like the tests you take at school. In fact, lots of kids think that these special kinds of tests are pretty fun."

It is important to gain information from the parents about how their child reacts to separating from them prior to bringing the child to the testing room. This information is especially relevant with preschool-age or young school-age children. If a parent indicates that the child is usually shy or upset upon separation from them, then it is advisable to ask the parent to accompany the child into the testing room until the child is comfortable with the examiner and the examination situation. It is important that the examiner be flexible in structuring the assessment sessions according to the child's needs. Some children may need their parents to accompany them at the beginning of each testing session, whereas others need only a brief 5 minutes with their parents in the testing room during the first evaluation session.

To ease into the testing situation, you may want to allow the child to remain standing until he or she is comfortable or less threatened by the testing situation. You should not talk too loudly or too formally, as your voice and intonation may startle a young child. However, it is also important not to talk down to younger children. Exam-

DON'T FORGET

2.2 Keys to Establishing Positive Examiner-Child Rapport

- Effectively introduce the child to the testing activities.
- Do not use the word *test*.
- Explain that many activities will be done: puzzles, blocks, drawing, answering questions.
- Allow the child ample time to adjust to the testing situation.
- If testing a very young child, allow a parent to accompany the child into the testing room.
- Achieve a balance between professional (formal) and friendly (informal) demeanor.
- Allow the child to stand if necessary until he or she is comfortable.

iners should try to adjust their vocabulary appropriately to the child's age level. Adolescents may become particularly uncooperative if they are treated like younger children. With teens, it is important to try to strike up a conversation that is interesting to the adolescent but does not appear overly invasive, showing a respect for the adolescent's boundaries. A balance between formality and informality—between being professional and friendly—should be achieved in testing a child of any age. Don't Forget 2.2 summarizes key points in establishing rapport.

Maintaining Rapport

Getting the attention of a child is often not as difficult as keeping the attention and motivation of a child. This is when the delicate balance between maintaining rapport and adhering to the standardized procedure becomes especially important. Providing frequent praise for a child's efforts is key in maintaining his or her motivation and attention. The examiner needs to watch vigilantly for signs of the child's attention waning or of the child becoming frustrated, tired, or unmotivated. Such signs may be verbal (e.g., "How much longer?" "These are too hard.") or nonverbal (e.g., increased fidgeting, sighing, grimacing). These are signals to the examiner to increase praise and encouragement or perhaps take a break. Caution 2.1 lists ways to give appropriate feedback and encouragement.

Encouragement and praise may be delivered in many different ways (an understanding smile, a pat on the hand, "We've got a lot more fun things to do," "You're working so hard," "Wow, you're a hard worker"). However, it is important that praise not be overly repetitive, as it will lose its reinforcing effects. Likewise, be careful not to give feedback about whether the child's responses are correct. Encouragement should be given throughout administration of the items, not just when a child is struggling or giving incorrect responses.

Some children may require more than verbal and nonverbal praise to maintain motivation. In these cases it may be useful to develop a reward system. For example, an agreement may be reached that the child can play with certain toys after a required number of tasks has been completed. Sometimes a small snack may be used as a reward, but you should always discuss this with the parent ahead of time (some parents disapprove of certain types of foods, don't want dinner spoiled, or will need to warn you about their child's food allergies).

Maintaining the child's motivational level requires consistent effort on the examiner's part. It is important to be able to remove materials skillfully and present the next task quickly, which creates a smooth and rapid transition between subtests. It is wisc to continue small talk while recording behavioral observations between subtests, as this helps maintain a child's attention. Keeping eye contact also helps maintain rapport; thus it is crucial to be familiar enough with the standardized instructions that you don't have to read them word for word with your head buried in the manual at the time of administration.

> # CAUTION
>
> ## 2.1 Appropriate Feedback and Encouragement
>
> - Praise frequently but don't be repetitive, which lessens the reinforcement value.
> - Be aware that encouragement/feedback may be verbal or non-verbal:
>   - Smile
>   - Pat on the hand
>   - "Good job," "You sure are working hard," etc.
> - Praise and encourage the child's level of effort.
> - Be careful *not* to give feedback on whether a particular response is right or wrong.
> - Give encouragement throughout items, not just when the child is struggling.

Children may occasionally refuse to cooperate, be easily fatigued, or become too nervous to continue. In such situations it is appropriate to give several breaks throughout the testing or to reschedule the testing for another day. However, examiners should be aware that many children are skilled in "testing the limits" and may try to distract the examiner from the task at hand. Being alert to such behavior helps keep the testing flowing. When children indicate that they do not want to go on with a subtest (perhaps a challenging subtest), it is advisable to provide encouragement such as "Just try your best" or "Give it your best shot." To prevent undue frustration during timed subtests, it may be useful to allow a few extra seconds past the time limit to work if the child is actively involved in the task. Although any response given after the time limit has expired is not counted toward the score, allowing the few extra seconds may lessen discouragement.

Don't Forget 2.3 summarizes various ways of maintaining rapport.

DON'T FORGET

2.3 Keys to Maintaining Rapport

- Provide frequent praise and encouragement.
- Set up a reward system if necessary.
- Give frequent breaks if necessary.
- Reschedule testing if the child is too tired, anxious, or uncooperative.
- Give eye contact; don't bury your head in the manual.
- Make smooth transitions *between* subtests. Move rapidly and use some small talk.
- Avoid small talk *during* a subtest.
- Familiarize yourself ahead of time with test directions and test materials.
  - Use precise wording of questions and directions.
  - Be aware that only the mildest of paraphrasing is acceptable occasionally.
- Be subtle, not distracting, when using a stopwatch.
- Use abbreviations when writing down the child's responses.

TESTING INDIVIDUALS WITH SPECIAL NEEDS

Children with special needs may require certain modifications during an evaluation in order for the assessment to be accurate. Special needs may include speech, language, or hearing deficits, visual impairment, mental retardation, neurological impairments, physical handicaps, or behavioral disorders. It is crucial to obtain thorough information about any disability from the caregiver prior to beginning the assessment. The caregiver may be able to make suggestions about the best way for the child to respond to verbal or nonverbal stimuli and may give clues about special accommodations that are made for the child in other structured settings, such as school.

Children with impairments and those with multiple handicaps challenge the examiner to find the best means of expression while minimizing the impact of their handicapping conditions. Depending on the child's particular special needs and the severity of the problem, various strategies may be employed during assessment procedures. Examiners should always be prepared to be flexible and should have heightened awareness of factors such as fatigue, which may arise more quickly when testing a child with special needs. The bottom line is that the child should not be penalized because of the effects of his or her sensory or motor deficits.

When modifications are made to the standardized procedure to accommodate children with special needs, these changes may impact test scores or invalidate use of the norms. Clinical judgment must be employed to determine whether the modifications or the level of impairment prevent obtaining valid scores on all or part of the test. (See Caution 2.2 for the main issues relating to modification of standardized procedures.) Modifications may include some of the following:

- Administer only the Verbal Scale subtests to a child with visual impairment.
- Administer the test in American Sign Language (if you are specially trained) or allow the child to lip-read if he or she is deaf or hard of hearing.
- Extend or eliminate the time limits for children who have motor difficulties or neurological impairments.
- Allow a nonverbal (nodding or pointing) or a written response for a child who has severe expressive difficulties.
- Provide translation for a child for whom English is a second language.
- Extend the testing over more than one session for any child with special needs.

The suggestions presented here are clearly not an exhaustive list and should not be considered rigid rules. Successful evaluation of a child with special needs may also require supplemental instruments or another instrument altogether. Careful consideration, coupled with

CAUTION

2.2 Modifying Standardized Procedure

- Modifications to the standardized procedure to accommodate a child's limitations may invalidate the scores on the test.

- Clinical judgment is key in determining what quantitative and qualitative data are interpretable from the test administration.

- If adaptations are made in the time limits allowed on timed subtests, this will invalidate the use of the norms.

- Translating the test into another language may also cause problems in interpreting the scores.

astute observation of the child, will help to determine which types of modifi-cations are best.

ADMINISTRATION CONSIDERATIONS

Special Considerations for 6- and 7-Year-Olds

Either the WPPSI-R or the WISC-III may be administered to children who are ages 6 years to 7 years 3 months. Examiners must decide which instru-ment is the most appropriate for any particular child being assessed. The fol-lowing factors should be taken into consideration: the reliability of each sub-test, the floor of each subtest, the ceiling of each subtest, and the recency of the test's norms. On the basis of these considerations, we make the recom-mendations outlined in Table 2.1 when assessing children who fall in this overlapping age range.

Children ages 6 to 7 with Below Average cognitive ability may not be ca-pable of achieving above the level of the floor on the WISC-III and may better demonstrate what they are capable of answering on the WPPSI-R. However, if a child in this age range is estimated to be functioning in the Above Average range, he or she may not be able to achieve a ceiling on the WPPSI-R but will likely be properly assessed with the more difficult items on the WISC-III. For children who are functioning in the Average range of cog-nitive ability, the WISC-III is preferred for several reasons. First, the norms are more recent. Flynn (1987) has demonstrated that norms in the United States become outdated by about 3 points per decade. Thus newer norms are generally preferable to older norms. Second, the WPPSI-R has weaker IQ and subtest reliability values at age 7. For example, at age 7 the reliability val-ues for the WISC-III Verbal and Performance IQs are .92 and .90, but for the WPPSI-R they are only .86 and .85. Third, the WISC-III provides additional information from the four factor indexes that can be especially helpful in referrals for children with learning disabilities and attention-deficit disorders.

There is a benefit to the overlap in tests at ages 6 and 7 in cases of retest-ing. If a child who was recently tested on the WPPSI-R needs to be re-assessed, he or she may be retested on the WISC-III if he or she is in the 6- to 7-year, 3-month-old age range. The reverse is also true for a child who has recently been evaluated with the WISC-III. The WPPSI-R may be ad-

Table 2.1   Deciding on the WPPSI-R Versus the WISC-III for Children Ages 6–0 to 7–3

Estimated Ability Level of Child	Wechsler Test to Administer
Below Average	WPPSI-R
Average	WISC-III
Above Average	WISC-III

ministered rather than reusing the WISC-III and increasing the risk of practice effects.

Starting and Discontinuing Subtests

The administration rules of both the WPPSI-R and WISC-III are listed in their respective manuals and record forms. In this section we highlight the general overall rules.

On both tests some of the subtests start at predetermined items according to the child's age, whereas other subtests begin at item 1 regardless of age. Rapid Reference 2.1 identifies subtests that have age-based starting points and those that require all children to start at item 1. Subtests with the age-based starting points allow examiners to shorten the testing times for most children but yet also allow easier items to be administered to children who cannot answer items correctly at the designated starting point.

Specific rules are employed that enable examiners to go back to easier items if the first set of items causes the child difficulty. There are two ways in which the WPPSI-R and WISC-III instruct examiners to go back to earlier items; one is in "reverse sequence" and the other is in "normal sequence." Administering items in reverse sequence requires a child to return to earlier items in reverse order until a perfect score is obtained on two consecutive items. For example, if an 8-year-old child begins the WISC-III Picture Completion subtest at item 5, as suggested by the record form, but misses either items 5 or 6, then that child must be administered item 4, item 3, item 2, and so on until two consecutive correct responses are given. Sample items are not part of the reversal procedure. The other method for returning to easier items

≡ Rapid Reference

2.1 Starting Points and Reverse Rules of Subtests

Subtest	Age-Based Starting Point		Start Point at Item 1	
	WPPSI-R	WISC-III	WPPSI-R	WISC-III
Information		✓ Reverse	✓	
Similarities			✓	✓
Arithmetic	✓ Normal	✓ Reverse		
Vocabulary		✓ Reverse	✓	
Comprehension			✓	✓
Digit Span				✓
Sentences	✓ Reverse			
Picture Completion	✓ Normal	✓ Reverse		
Block Design	✓ Reverse	✓ Normal		
Object Assembly			✓	✓
Mazes	✓ Normal	✓ Normal		
Geometric Design			✓	
Animal Pegs			✓	
Picture Arrangement		✓ Normal		
Symbol Search				✓
Coding				✓

Note. Reverse = items on this subtest are administered in reverse sequence (e.g., 4, 3, 2 . . .) if a child misses the first item(s); Normal = items on this subtest are administered in normal sequence (e.g., 1, 2, 3 . . .) if a child misses the first item(s).

is normal sequence. An example can be seen on the WISC-III Block Design subtest. If a 9-year-old child misses the first item administered (the designated start point is item 3), that child must return to the very beginning of the subtest and be administered item 1 and then item 2. Rapid Reference 2.1 lists the reverse rules (normal vs. reverse sequence) of subtests that require children to begin at an item other than 1. The WISC-III manual provides examples of reverse-sequence administration procedures (Figures 3.2, 3.3, and 3.4 on pp. 40–42 of Wechsler, 1991).

Occasionally when administering a subtest, you may find that you are unsure of how to score a response and therefore whether a subtest should be discontinued. Most often this uncertainty arises during subtests that involve a degree of subjectivity in scoring, such as Vocabulary, Similarities, and Comprehension. If it is not possible to quickly determine whether a response is correct, it is best to continue administering additional items until you are certain that the discontinue rule has been met. This procedure is the safest because the scores can always be reviewed later and items that are passed after the discontinue criterion has been met must be excluded from the child's raw score on the subtest. However, the information obtained on the items that were accidentally administered beyond the discontinue criterion may provide valuable *clinical* information. If you do not follow the procedure described here and later note that items should have been administered beyond where the subtest was ended, it will be too late and the test may be unscorable. (See Caution 2.3 for common general errors in test administration.)

CAUTION

2.3 Common General Errors in Administration

- forgetting that if the child gets the second item administered *partially* correct you may have to apply the "reverse rule" (even though the child got the first item administered correct)

- forgetting that when applying the reverse rule you administer until *two* consecutive perfect scores are obtained, *including* previously administered items

- forgetting to administer enough items to meet the discontinue rule

Recording Responses

The manner in which responses are recorded during administration of the WPPSI-R and WISC-III is very important. Examiners should be careful to write down responses for all items administered or attempted. This is especially important for the Vocabulary, Similarities, Information, and Comprehension subtests, which tend to elicit a good amount of verbiage from children. However, even when only a brief verbal response is given by a child, such as during Arithmetic, Digit Span, or Picture Completion, it is wise to record these responses as well. It is tempting for some examiners to write down only a child's score rather than the child's exact response, but this practice is discouraged. If only a 0 or 1 is recorded on the record form, then irretrievable clinical information may be lost. Writing down all responses affords the examiner an opportunity to note useful patterns in responding and subtle clinical information. For the same reasons it is crucial to attempt to capture most of what is said verbatim. This can be quite a challenge with extremely verbose children. The use of abbreviations makes the process of recording information easier and also helps balance the maintenance of rapport with the gathering of essential information. (Rapid Reference 2.2 shows a list of commonly used abbreviations.)

In addition to recording what a child says, you may need to record your own statements. For example, if you probe to clarify an answer by saying "Tell me more about that," you should always record the letter Q in parentheses on the record form directly after the response that you queried. During the process of interpretation of a child's performance, it may be of clinical interest to note whether many of the responses were elicited by querying or whether the child produced them spontaneously. Beyond noting the level of prompting required for a child, it may be useful to determine whether the quality of response improved after the child was queried. Some children may not add anything to their first response, "I don't know"; other children elaborate a great deal after a query but do not necessarily improve their score.

Timing

Precision is necessary for administration of subtests that require timing. Examiners must be prepared to utilize a stopwatch for about half the WPPSI-R

≡ Rapid Reference

2.2 Abbreviations for Recording Responses

@	at
B	both
DK	don't know
EO	everyone
F	fail (child responded incorrectly)
INC	incomplete (response wasn't completed within the time limit)
LL	looks like
NR	no response
OT	overtime
P	pass (child responded correctly)
Prmt	prompt
PC	points correctly
PPL	people
PX	points incorrectly
Q	question or query
R	are
Shd	should
SO	someone
ST	something
↓	decrease
↑	increase
U	you
w/	with
w/o	without
Wld	would

and WISC-III subtests. All the Performance subtests and one Verbal subtest (Arithmetic) require a stopwatch during administration. Its use should be unobtrusive so that it is not distracting to the child. If possible, use a stopwatch that does not make beeping sounds. If children ask whether they are being timed, you may want to respond "Yes, but you don't need to worry about that." The WISC-III record form shows a clock icon at the top of each subtest that requires a stopwatch; however, this reminder is not provided on WPPSI-R record forms, so you must be careful not to forget.

As you are giving the directions to the timed subtests, you should have your stopwatch out and ready for use. This level of preparation is especially important when testing children who are impulsive, because they tend to jump into the testing earlier than you would expect and therefore you must be ready to time them immediately. Although beginning the timing can be tricky, knowing when to stop timing can be even more complicated. It is important to note that even if a child asks for clarification or repetition of an item, the timing of the item must continue once it has begun. Although on many of the timed subtests the directions ask the child to tell you when he or she has finished, often the child does not give a clear indication that he or she is done. In such cases if it appears that the child has completed working on an item, ask "Are you done?" and immediately record the time. On the other hand, if you have stopped timing the child because you thought he or she was finished and then the child continues working, be sure to restart the stopwatch and count the entire time during which the child was working. In cases where the stopwatch was restarted, you need to estimate the number of seconds that the stopwatch was off and add that to the total completion time.

Querying

Examiner judgment often comes into play during subtests that allow a wide variety of responses, as many of the Verbal subtests do. If a child's response is too vague or ambiguous to score, examiners must decide whether to query or prompt the child for clarification. The administration manuals of the WPPSI-R and the WISC-III both list responses to Vocabulary, Similarities, and Comprehension items that should be queried. However, the responses in the manual are only illustrative, leaving the examiner to decide whether to query other responses not presented in the manual's scoring system. The key to deciding whether to query a response is ambiguity or incompleteness. A child's nonverbal cues, such as tone of voice or facial expression, may indicate that a response should be queried.

The manner in which children are queried may strongly impact how they respond. Therefore it is crucial that querying be done with neutral, nonleading questions as suggested in the manuals. Good queries are "Tell me more about that" and "Explain what you mean." Examiners should avoid providing hints or clues to the answer and should attempt to use the queries listed in the manuals. Also, don't ask "Can you tell me more?" A possible answer to that question is "no." When a query is made, this should be noted in the record form with the letter Q in parentheses, as mentioned earlier. Querying should not be done with spontaneously produced responses that are completely incorrect.

Repeating Items

Occasionally a child may not completely hear or understand the instructions or a question that has been read. In some cases the child may ask you to repeat the question. Generally it is okay to repeat a question or instructions; however, for WISC-III Digit Span a number sequence may not be repeated, for WPPSI-R Sentences a sentence may not be repeated, and during Arithmetic a question may be repeated only one time. It is important to remember to repeat the entire question, not just a portion of it, if there must be a repetition.

A pattern of responding in which the child provides answers to difficult items after providing "I don't know" responses to earlier, easier items may be worth further examination. In your judgment, if you believe that a child knows the answer to earlier easier items, it may be worth readministering them. Factors such as anxiety or insecurity can interfere with a child's initial response on easier items, leading to quick "I don't know" responses. However, you may not readminister timed items or items on the Digit Span and Sentences subtests.

SUBTEST-BY-SUBTEST RULES OF ADMINISTRATION

Rules for administering each of the WPPSI-R and WISC-III subtests are presented in their respective manuals (each of the record forms also highlights the starting and discontinue rules). In this section we present important reminders for competent administration of each subtest. This section will be especially useful to new users of the tests but may also refresh your memory if you have already learned the details of test administration. We list the Verbal subtests and then the Performance subtests for both tests. Along with carefully following standardized procedures during administration, examiners must be astute observers of children's behavior. Obtaining detailed behavioral observations during testing can give insight into how to interpret a particular subtest score, and linking patterns of behavior across multiple subtests may provide additional interpretive information. Therefore for each subtest we also identify key behaviors for which you may want to watch.

WPPSI-R and WISC-III Verbal Subtests

Information

For items 1 through 6 of Information on the WPPSI-R, the stimulus booklet is needed for administration; but for the last WPPSI-R items and all the WISC-III items, only the manual with the questions and the record form are needed for administration. On the first six items of WPPSI-R Information, the child is urged to point to the correct answer in the stimulus booklet. If the

≡ Rapid Reference

2.3 Behaviors to Note on Information

- Make note of any observable pattern in a subject's responses. Patterns of responding such as missing early, easy items and having success on harder items may suggest anxiety, poor motivation, or retrieval difficulties.

- Observe whether items on which errors are made are related to the child's cultural background (e.g., questions about a character in U.S. history at a certain time or about the geography of a specific location). Such observations should be incorporated in interpretation.

- Note whether children provide unnecessarily long responses. Long responses filled with excessive detail, may be indicative of obsessiveness or a desire to impress the examiner.

- Note whether the content of failed items is consistently owing to lack of knowledge in a certain area (e.g., numerical information, history, or geography).

- Be aware that inhibited children or children with speech difficulty may be inclined to respond by gesturing or pointing. This behavior may be noted more often on the WPPSI-R, which begins with items that call for pointing to the correct response.

child does not respond to the first item correctly (either verbally or by point-ing), the examiner demonstrates the correct answer by pointing to the correct picture. Similarly, for the youngest age group on the WISC-III Information subtest, if a child does not give a correct response to item 1, the examiner demonstrates the correct verbal answer for the child. On none of the other items on the WPPSI-R and WISC-III Information subtest is the examiner al-lowed to give help. Each question may be repeated once if a child does not understand or is not paying attention. Words should not be spelled for a child, and when a question is repeated it should be done so verbatim. Throughout the subtest on both tests, there are specific queries on certain re-sponses of which the examiner should be aware (i.e., on WPPSI-R items 11, 17, 19, 20, 23, 26, and 27, and on WISC-III items 4, 8, 9, 16, 18, 19, 24, 26, 28, 29, and 30). Querying a child's response with neutral prompts is also accept-able. Rapid Reference 2.3 lists telling behaviors to watch for and note during administration of Information.

Comprehension

Only the manual and record form are needed to administer the WPPSI-R and WISC-III Comprehension subtest. On both tests all children begin with item 1. Questions should be read at such a pace that children find it easy to follow the examiner but do not become distracted because of the speed. If a ques-tion needs to be repeated, it should be reread in its entirety without abbrevia-tion. On the first two WPPSI-R items and the first WISC-III item, if a child does not give a 2-point response the examiner is to illustrate with a 2-point answer. This is done in order to teach the child the type of response desired during the task. Additionally, on one WPPSI-R question (item 11) and eight WISC-III questions (items 2, 6, 7, 11, 12, 15, 17, and 18) the child is required to give two general concepts in response to the question in order to receive 2 points credit. Thus on these items the examiner is required to prompt the child for another response (e.g., "Tell me another reason why . . .") if only one general concept is reflected in the child's response. However, if the child's first spontaneous response on these items is incorrect, the examiner is not to prompt for a second response. In addition to prompting these specified items, it is acceptable to query with a neutral probe those responses that are unclear or ambiguous. Rapid Reference 2.4 lists telling behaviors to watch for and note during administration of Comprehension.

≡ Rapid Reference

2.4 Behaviors to Note on Comprehension

- Observe whether unusually long verbal responses are an attempt to "cover up" for not actually knowing the correct response, or an indication that the child tends to be obsessive about details.

- Be aware that Comprehension requires a good amount of verbal expression; therefore word-finding difficulties, articulation problems, and circumstantial or tangential speech may be apparent during this subtest.

- Be aware that some Comprehension questions have rather long verbal stimuli. Note whether inattention is impacting the child's responses to such items. For example, only part of the question may be answered.

- Note whether defensiveness is occurring in responses to some Comprehension items. For example, when asked about seatbelts, if the child's response doesn't really answer the question and is something like "We shouldn't have to wear seatbelts," this may be defensive responding.

- Note whether children require consistent prompting for a second response or whether they spontaneously provide enough information in their answer.

- Observe children's responses carefully to determine whether poor verbal ability is the cause of a low score or whether it is more caused by poor social judgment.

- Note how children respond to queries. Some may be threatened or frustrated with the constant interruption, and others may seem comfortable with the extra structure. Some children, when asked for another reason, simply restate the first reason in different words or otherwise do not give a second "idea."

Arithmetic

The WPPSI-R and WISC-III each require a stimulus book with picture items for administration of various items on this subtest (WPPSI-R items 1–7 and WISC-III items 1–5 and 19–24). Additional materials needed to administer the subtest include nine WPPSI-R Block Design blocks, a WISC-III blank card, a stopwatch, and the tests' respective manuals. The Arithmetic subtest incorporates three means of administration for both the WPPSI-R and the WISC-III. On WPPSI-R items 1–7 a child points to an object in a visually presented array of objects that illustrates a quantitative characteristic; on items 8–11 the child demonstrates numeric knowledge by counting and manipulating

≡ *Rapid Reference*

2.5 Behaviors to Note on Arithmetic

- Observe children for signs of anxiety. Some children who view themselves as "poor at math" may be anxious during this task. Be aware of statements such as "I was never taught that in school" or "I can't do math in my head."
- Be aware that focusing on the stopwatch may be a sign of anxiety, distractibility, or competitiveness. Watch for statements such as "How long did that take me?"
- Watch for signs of distractibility or poor concentration, which are usually noticeable during Arithmetic.
- Be aware that counting on fingers may occur in children of any age. This may be indicative of insecurity about math skills or may an adaptive problem-solving tool for younger children.
- Note when a child asks for repetition of a question, as it may indicate several things, including poor hearing, inattention, and stalling for more time.
- Take note of whether children respond quickly, are impulsive, or are methodical and careful in their processing of the information.

blocks; and on items 12–23 the child solves arithmetic problems that are read aloud by the examiner. For the first 11 WPPSI-R items there are no time limits, but for items 12–23 there is a 30-second time limit, so the examiner must be prepared to use a stopwatch. On WISC-III items 1–5 the child responds to questions posed by the examiner that are related to pictures in a stimulus book; on items 6–18 the child solves problems that are read aloud by the examiner; and on items 19–24 the child reads problems aloud that are printed in a stimulus book and then solves the problems. Rapid Reference 2.5 lists telling behaviors to watch for and note during administration of Arithmetic.

Vocabulary

Administration of the Vocabulary subtest requires the stimulus book plus the manual and record form for the WPPSI-R, but only the manual and record form for the WISC-III. The first three items of the WPPSI-R Vocabulary subtest are pictures that the child has to name (identify). On only the first item if the child does not produce the correct response, the examiner is to give the child the correct answer. The remaining WPPSI-R Vocabulary items (4–25) and all the WISC-III Vocabulary items are words that the examiner reads aloud and the child is asked to define. It is important that the examiner pronounce all words carefully and correctly. The first item of the WISC-III Vocabulary subtest, similar to that of the WPPSI-R, requires the examiner to say a correct response if the child does not spontaneously give a 2-point response.

Children sometimes respond by defining a homonym of a word. If this occurs, the examiner is required to ask "What else does _____ mean?" Definitions of such homonyms are not given credit. Children sometimes also respond with a regionalism or slang response not found in dictionaries. If you are unsure about the acceptability of a response involving a colloquialism, you should ask the child for another meaning. Children never receive credit for simply pointing to an object, so if a child responds nonverbally he or she should be encouraged to give a verbal response ("Tell me in words what a _____ is."). Occasionally it is apparent that children have misheard the word you asked them to define (e.g., a child defines *concise* instead of *precise*); in such a case you should say "Listen carefully, what does _____ mean?" However, you should never spell the word you are asking the child to define. As with other Verbal subtests, if a child's

≋Rapid Reference

2.6 Behaviors to Note on Vocabulary

- Note whether children have difficulties pronouncing words or whether they seem uncertain about how to express what they think. Some children supplement what they say with gesturing; others rely on nonverbal communication more than verbal expression.

- Make note of "I don't know" responses, as they may indicate word retrieval problems. Word fluency can impact an individual's performance as much as his or her word knowledge.

- Note that hearing difficulties may be apparent on this test. The Vocabulary words are not presented in a meaningful context. Note behaviors such as leaning forward during administration to hear better, as well as indications of auditory discrimination problems (defining *confine* rather than *confide*).

- Note children who are overly verbose in their responses. They may be attempting to compensate for insecurity about their ability, or they may be obsessive or inefficient in their verbal expression.

response is unclear, vague, or ambiguous, or if you feel that it is a 0.5- or 1.5-point response, you may use a neutral query to prompt a better response. Rapid Reference 2.6 lists telling behaviors to watch for and note during administration of Vocabulary.

Similarities

The first six WPPSI-R Similarities items require a pictorial stimulus book for administration in addition to the manual and record form. The last WPPSI-R Similarities items (7–20) and all the WISC-III Similarities items are administered only from the manuals and record forms. All children administered the WPPSI-R Similarities subtest begin with the picture items (1–6) and then, regardless of their performance (e.g., even if they obtain three consecutive failures on these items), are administered the Sentence Completion items. On Sentence Completion the child is required to provide a word that completes an orally presented sentence in a way that shows understanding of the similarity concepts. The last WPPSI-R items are in the same format as all the WISC-III Similarities items; the child is asked to tell how two different words are alike. It is important to note that the WPPSI-R Similarities subtest has separate discontinue rules for items 1–6 and 7–20 (e.g., three consecutive failures for items 1–6 and five consecutive failures for items 7–20).

On three of the WPPSI-R Similarities items and four of the WISC-III Similarities items, the examiner is to demonstrate a correct response if the child is unable to produce a correct response. Specifically, if the child gives an incorrect response for the first WPPSI-R Picture item (item 1), the examiner points to the correct answer and gives the reason why it is correct; if the child's response to WPPSI-R item 7 is incorrect, the examiner gives a correct answer; and if the child earns only a 1-point response on WPPSI-R item 13, the examiner gives a sample of a 2-point response. Similarly, if the child gives incorrect responses to either items 1 or 2 of the WISC-III Similarities subtest, the examiner says the correct answer; if the child gives only a 1-point response to WISC-III Similarities items 6 or 7, the examiner gives an example of a 2-point response. This guides children to the level of response the test is seeking. However, help on items beyond those listed in the manuals is prohibited. Neutral queries may be given throughout the subtest to clarify vague or ambiguous responses. Rapid Reference 2.7 lists telling behaviors to watch for and note during administration of Similarities.

≡ Rapid Reference

2.7 Behaviors to Note on Similarities

- Observe whether the child benefits from feedback on items that provide an example by the examiner (if feedback is given). Children who learn from the example given by the examiner may have flexibility, whereas those who cannot may be more rigid or concrete.

- Observe whether the quality of response decreases as the items become more difficult.

- On the WPPSI-R specifically, note whether the child has particular difficulty with the visual items in comparison to the auditory items. This could be indicative of processing difficulties.

- Be aware that length of verbal responses gives important behavioral clues. Overly elaborate responses may suggest obsessiveness.

- Be aware that quick responses or abstract responses to easy items may indicate overlearned associations rather than high-level abstract reasoning.

- Note how the child handles frustration on this test. For example, the child may respond by saying "They are not alike," indicating defensiveness or avoidance. Other children may give up when faced with frustration by repeatedly responding "I don't know."

WPPSI-R Verbal Subtests Only

Sentences

The only materials needed to administer the WPPSI-R Sentences subtest are the manual and record form. This subtest requires the examiner to read sentences aloud slowly and distinctly, but with natural intonation. The speed at which sentences are read should be consistent—at the rate of about two syllables per second. The sentences are to be read one time only. Demonstrations and second tries are given on certain items to ensure that the child understands the requirements of the task. These demonstrations are given for Sentences 1 and 2 for 3- to 4-year-olds and Sentence 6 for children age 5 and older, if a child doesn't repeat a sentence correctly on the first try. If a child asks you to repeat a sentence, say "If you're not sure, just guess at it." Do not repeat the sentence. Occasionally children begin repeating the sentence before you have completely read it. In such cases, make a nonverbal gesture to the child to wait until you are done. After the child is done it may be a good

≡ Rapid Reference

2.8 Behaviors to Note on Sentences (WPPSI-R Only)

- Note whether children add words that were not read in the stimulus sentence. These words may be idiosyncratic or peculiar.
- Note whether errors are made more often in the beginning, middle, or end of a sentence.
- Note signs of distractibility or inattention. Looking around the room, fidgeting, and other motor activities may increase as the test goes on.
- Be aware that auditory problems may exist if a child consistently misunderstands what is said or consistently does not hear what is said.
- Note articulation problems with certain speech sounds during the assessment. Children with speech difficulties may also avoid saying words that they know they have difficulty pronouncing.

idea to verbally remind him or her to wait until you have read the whole sentence before starting to respond. Recording responses verbatim is very important for scoring this subtest and for obtaining clinical information. You should try to phonetically spell words that a child misarticulates, as this may be informative if there is a pattern of articulation difficulties. Rapid Reference 2.8 lists telling behaviors to watch for and note during administration of Sentences.

WISC-III Verbal Subtest Only

Digit Span

The materials needed to administer the WISC-III Digit Span subtest include the manual and record form. All children begin the subtest with item 1 of Digits Forward. Each item has two trials. Once both trials of any item have been failed, the examiner proceeds to the sample item of Digits Backward. If the child can correctly complete the first Digits Backward sample, then the second sample is not administered and the child should immediately be administered trial 1 of the first Digits Backward item. However, if the child does not respond correctly to the first Digits Backward sample, then the examiner tells the child what the correct answer is and administers the second

≡ Rapid Reference

2.9 Behaviors to Note on Digit Span (WISC-III Only)

• Note whether children are attempting to use a problem-solving strategy such as "chunking." Some children use such a strategy from the beginning; others learn a strategy as they progress through the task.

• Note whether errors are due simply to transposing numbers or completely forgetting numbers.

• Be aware that attention, hearing impairment, and anxiety can impact this test; therefore such difficulties should be noted if present. If there is any interference with the quality of the testing conditions (e.g., noise outside the testing room), these should also be noted.

• Watch for rapid repetition of digits or beginning to repeat the digits before the examiner has completed the series. Such behavior may indicate impulsivity.

• Observe whether there is a pattern of failing the first trial and then correctly responding to the second trial. Such a pattern may indicate learning or may simply be a warm-up effect.

Digits Backward sample. Even if the child responds incorrectly to the second sample, no assistance is given and the child is to immediately begin trial 1 of the first Digits Backward item. The rate and intonation of the examiner's speech are important during this subtest. Each of the numbers is to be read at a rate of one per second, and at the end of the sequence of numbers the examiner's voice should drop slightly, indicating the end of a sequence. It is crucial not to inadvertently "chunk" the numbers into small groups while reading them, as this may provide extra help. Rapid Reference 2.9 lists telling behaviors to watch for and note during administration of Digit Span.

WPPSI-R and WISC-III Performance Subtests

Object Assembly

The Object Assembly subtests of the WPPSI-R and WISC-III both require the examiner to manipulate many materials at once: six puzzles, a layout shield, a stopwatch, a manual, and a record form. On the WPPSI-R Object Assembly subtest, assistance is given to a child if he or she does not place all the pieces of the first puzzle together correctly. On this item the examiner demonstrates the correct arrangement, and then the child is given a second trial (however, the second trial of item 1 is not scored). On both WPPSI-R Object Assembly items 1 and 2, the examiner is instructed to say "Now HURRY!" if the child dawdles or seems to be merely playing with the pieces. Young children often do not understand the concept of being timed and needing to work as quickly as they can. For the remaining four WPPSI-R items, no such prompts to hurry are given. On the WISC-III Object Assembly subtest the examiner demonstrates a sample task prior to administration of the actual items. During the directions for WISC-III items 1 and 2 the examiner tells the child what object he or she will be constructing, but for the remaining three items the examiner cannot tell the child what is to be constructed. Additionally, on the first WISC-III Object Assembly item the examiner demonstrates the correct arrangement of the puzzle pieces if the child's assembly is incomplete (however, no second trial is given to the child).

The handling of all materials needed for this subtest while keeping a child's attention can be tricky. The Object Assembly layout shield of both tests is to be utilized to prevent children from seeing the puzzle before the examiner arranges it. However, many children find this shield very tempting to grab or peek behind. In such situations you may want to turn your arranging of the puzzle into a game, such as asking the child to count to see how long it will take you to do your work behind the shield. Other tactics include telling them that they'll ruin the surprise if they peek ahead of time, or letting them know that when you are completely done with the test they can set up a puzzle for you behind the shield if they follow directions and don't peek during the test. Just chatting with children so they don't get bored while you are setting up each puzzle can also be effective for maintaining rapport.

Issues of timing discussed earlier in this chapter are especially important for this subtest because children can receive bonus points for speedy performance. For all Object Assembly items you should stop timing once it is clear that the child has completed a particular puzzle, and if you are uncertain you may ask the child if he or she is done. If a child continues to work even though he or she has said that he or she is done, you should restart the stopwatch and add the proper amount of time to the total completion time.

During the subtest itself, if a puzzle piece is turned over you should unob-

≡ *Rapid Reference*

2.10 Behaviors to Note on Object Assembly

• As on other performance subtests, observe how the child handles the puzzle pieces. Motor coordination and hand preference may be noted on this test.

• Note problem-solving approach (trial-and-error vs. systematic planned approach), which can be discerned by observing the child's approach to the task.

• Note the speed at which children proceed. Do they appear impulsive and careless but quick, or are they careful, slow, and methodical?

• Note whether children appear to be rigid and inflexible in their consideration of what the object is. For example, someone who is convinced that the ball is a turtle may continue to try to piece together the shell.

• Note whether children can piece together parts but cannot get the whole. For example, some children are able to assemble the front and back of the car separately but cannot figure out how to connect them.

• Note when children verbalize what the object is but are unable to construct it correctly. This may indicate integration difficulties or problems with motor output.

• Observe and note behaviors indicative of obsessiveness with details (as with Block Design). Some children may spend unnecessary time trying to get each of the pieces perfectly aligned.

• Observe how children handle frustration. Some may become angry and demand to know what the object is. Others may insist that you have not given them all the pieces. Still other children appear to give up well before the time limit has expired.

trusively turn it right side up. Careful behavioral observations should be taken during this subtest because much can be gleaned beyond the final score. Some children, for example, almost completely solve the puzzle but then become frustrated and mix up the pieces to start anew. Rapid Reference 2.10 lists telling behaviors to watch for and note during administration of Object Assembly.

Block Design

The stimulus materials for the Block Design subtest of the WPPSI-R are slightly different from those of the WISC-III. Both tests use red-and-white blocks, but the WPPSI-R uses six flat blocks that are red on one side and white on the other and eight flat blocks that are red on one side and half-red and half-white on the other. The WISC-III uses nine cubes that each have two red sides, two white sides, and two red-and-white sides. A stopwatch, the manual, and the record form are needed for both the WPPSI-R and WISC-III subtests. Timing is very important on both tests.

On the WPPSI-R Block Design subtest, two trials are permitted on every design. For WPPSI-R items 1–5 the solid-colored red-and-white blocks are used. The examiner sets up the model blocks behind a shield and then demonstrates how to put the blocks together with other blocks (using the exact wording in the manual) prior to allowing the child to attempt the first trial of items 1–7. If the child completes the design correctly within the time limit, you move on to the next item; otherwise you demonstrate a second time how to complete the design and give the child a second trial. For WPPSI-R Block Design items 6–14 eight new blocks are used (red on one side and half-red and half-white on the other). Again a shield is used while the examiner constructs the model, and on item 6 the examiner shows the child that the blocks are now different as part of the demonstration. WPPSI-R Block Design item 8 is the first one presented without a demonstration, but a demonstration can be given if a child cannot correctly assemble the puzzle during the first trial and the child is given a second trial. Beginning with item 9, a picture of a block design (rather than a three-dimensional model) is presented for the child to copy. The record form clearly denotes with an abbreviation which trials the examiner is required to demonstrate for the child (e.g., D = examiner demonstrates trial; ND = examiner does not demonstrate trial).

The WISC-III Block Design subtest provides two trials on items 1, 2, and 3. The child works directly from models that the examiner constructs on items 1 and 2, but for the remaining items the child constructs designs based on pictorial models presented in the stimulus booklet. Unlike on the WPPSI-R, no shield is used during construction of the models for the WISC-III Block Design subtest. Demonstrations are given by the examiner on both trials of WISC-III Block Design items 1–3. The second trial of each of these three items is only administered if the child is unable to correctly assemble the blocks within the time limit. Beginning with item 10, five additional blocks are provided for the child to use to construct the most complicated block designs.

≡ Rapid Reference

2.11 Behaviors to Note on Block Design

- Observe problem-solving styles during children's manipulation of the blocks. Some use a trial-and-error approach, whereas others appear to haphazardly continue to complete the design, seemingly without learning from earlier errors.

- Consider the level of planning involved. Does the child systematically examine the problem and appear to carefully plan before moving any of the blocks, or does the child appear to be implusive?

- Observe whether the child tends to pair up blocks and then integrate the smaller segments into the whole. On the designs requiring nine blocks, observe whether the child works from the outside in, or perhaps starts in one corner and works his or her way around the design.

- Be aware that motor coordination and hand preference may be apparent during this task. Note whether children seem clumsy in their manipulation of the blocks, have hands that are noticeably trembling, or move very quickly and steadily.

- Look to see whether children refer back to the model while they are working. This could indicate visual memory ability, cautiousness, or other factors.

- Examine whether children tend to be obsessively concerned with details (e.g., lining up the blocks perfectly). Such behaviors may negatively impact the child's speed.

- Observe how well children persist, especially when the task becomes more difficult and they may face frustration. Note how well they tolerate frustration. Do they persist and keep on working even past the time limit, or do they give up with time to spare?

- Look to see whether children lose the square shape for some designs, even if they have managed to re-create the overall pattern. This kind of response may indicate figure-ground problems.

- Note whether children are noticeably twisting their bodies to obtain a different perspective on the model or are rotating their own designs. Such behaviors may indicate visual-perceptual difficulties.

- Also note whether children fail to recognize that their designs look different from the models, as this may indicate visual-perceptual difficulties.

Several general directions should be remembered during administration of the WPPSI-R and WISC-III Block Design subtests. The child should be sitting squarely at the table because orientation of the child to the design is very important. The model or stimulus book should be placed approximately 7 inches away from the child's edge of the table and should be slightly to the left of the child's midline if the child is right-handed and slightly to the right if the child is left-handed. When laying out the blocks for the child, be sure that a variety of sides are facing upward.

The rules for rotation of designs that the child produces differ between the WPPSI-R and WISC-III. On the WPPSI-R a child is not penalized for rotation of a design. However, if the child rotates the design 30 degrees or more, the examiner is to correct the child the first two times such a rotation occurs. If the child completely reverses the design, it is considered a failure. On the WISC-III rotation of a design by 30 degrees or more is considered a failure, and the examiner is to show the child the correct design only one time during the test. Examiners should record responses, including those that are rotations, by sketching the design that the child has made in the space provided on the WISC-III record form or in a blank space on the WPPSI-R record form. This allows the analysis of any response patterns for interpretive purposes. Rapid Reference 2.11 lists telling behaviors to watch for and note during administration of Block Design.

Mazes

We recommend that the WISC-III Mazes subtest not be administered along with the rest of the battery. Its correlations with the Full Scale (.31) and the Performance Scale (.35) are weak. In addition, the WISC-III Mazes subtest is fairly unreliable (.78 for ages 6 to 8 years and .67 for ages 9 to 16 years) and is not stable (ranging from .54 for ages 14 to 15 years, to .60 for ages 6 to 7 years). As you may have noticed in the description of the WISC-III four factors, Mazes is not included as part of the factor structure. Thus there really is no reason to administer the Mazes subtest as part of the WISC-III battery (see Caution 2.4).

Although the WISC-III Mazes subtest is plagued with weak psychometric qualities, the WPPSI-R version of Mazes appears to be adequate and should be administered because it is utilized in calculation of the Performance IQ. For administration of the WPPSI-R Mazes subtest the following materials are

CAUTION

2.4 Don't Administer the WISC-III Mazes Subtest

Mazes is not recommended for the following reasons:
- low correlations with the WISC-III IQ scales
  - r with Full Scale IQ = .31
  - r with Performance IQ = .35
- low reliability coefficients
  - .78 for ages 6 to 8 years
  - .67 for ages 9 to 16 years
- poor test-retest reliability
  - .60 for ages 6 to 7 years
  - .56 for ages 10 to 11 years
  - .54 for ages 14 to 15 years
- not part of the WISC-III four-factor structure

needed: Mazes response booklet, two lead pencils without erasers, two red pencils (for the examiner), and a stopwatch. During Mazes the examiner demonstrates the task with a red pencil and the child works with a black lead pencil. As each maze is presented, only one page of the response booklet is exposed at a time.

The youngest children administered this test sometimes have difficulty understanding the directions; therefore the examiner is encouraged to supplement verbal communication with gesturing and pointing. Because of poor fine motor control, some of the youngest children may have difficulty holding the pencil. In this case the examiner is allowed to help the child hold the pencil during the first maze attempted.

Several prompts are identified in the manual (Wechsler, 1989, pp. 69–70) that may be given one time only during the subtest:

- "Don't stop. Keep going until you find your way out."
- "Don't start over. Keep going from here."
- "You should start here."
- "Go all the way to the tree. You must get all the way out."
- "You must start here."

For the first trial of Mazes 1 and 2 (and Maze 3 for children ages 5 to 7), the examiner demonstrates the task by actually drawing half of the correct path using the red pencil, and the child is then supposed to complete the path. It is important to read the directions verbatim, as specific wording is utilized to teach the child the nature of the task. Errors on the first trial of the maze are corrected by the examiner. Whether or not the child correctly completes the first trial of the maze, he or she is administered the second trial. Beginning with item 4 of Mazes, no further demonstrations are given except for the sample maze administered prior to item 5.

The point at which the child begins to work on the maze is when the timing begins. There are no bonus points for speedy performance, but there is a maximum allotted time for each item.

2.12 Behaviors to Note on Mazes

- Note whether the child appears to plan his or her route before moving the pencil or whether moves are made without forethought.
- Note if the children comment that they have experience with puzzles (e.g., "These are just like the puzzle books I have at home").
- Observe signs of fine motor control difficulties. Is there a tremor while holding the pencil? Is the grip on the pencil awkward or immature for the child's age?
- Note whether crossing the lines seems related to poor visual-motor coordination or to impulsivity.
- Observe whether children appear to learn how to implement planning as they move from maze to maze.

Recording behaviors and verbalizations are important for clinical interpretation of this subtest. Rapid Reference 2.12 provides a list of telling behaviors to watch for and note during the subtest.

Picture Completion

To administer the WPPSI-R and WISC-III Picture Completion subtests the pictorial stimulus book is needed, along with the manual, the record form, and a stopwatch. For each of the items there is a maximum amount of time allowed to solve the problem:

- WPPSI-R Picture Completion items 1 and 2: 15 seconds
- WPPSI-R Picture Completion items 3–28: 30 seconds
- WISC-III Picture Completion items 1–30: 20 seconds

On both the WPPSI-R and WISC-III Picture Completion subtests, sample items are given and demonstrations are provided on several items so that the child may have adequate opportunity to understand the task. On the WPPSI-R, for example, 3- to 4-year-old children are administered the sample item and then are told the correct response on items 1–4 if they respond incorrectly. On the WISC-III a sample item is administered to all children; if a child is administered items 1 and 2 but responds incorrectly, he or she is told the correct answer.

Most children find this subtest fun; thus it is generally fairly easy to administer. Examiners most frequently make errors on the queries that may be given during the subtest. If needed, the following queries are to be given a total of only two times during WPPSI-R administration and only once during WISC-III administration:

- "Yes, but what is *missing*?"
- "A part is missing *in* the picture. What is it that is missing?"
- "Yes, but what is the *most important* part that is missing?" (for use only during WISC-III administration)

The errors made by examiners using these queries include forgetting to say the queries altogether or using them more frequently than is allowed. Other errors may occur when a child produces a verbal response that is unclear. In such cases it may be necessary to query for further information or to prompt the child to point to the missing part. Either verbal or nonverbal responses are considered acceptable answers. However, if a child's nonverbal response is correct but his or her verbal response is incorrect, the answer is considered spoiled and no credit is given. The majority of children respond to the prompt "*Tell* me what is missing" by giving a verbal response, so it is noteworthy if a child consistently provides a nonverbal (e.g., pointing) response. Rapid Reference 2.13 lists other telling behaviors to watch for and note during administration of this subtest.

≡ Rapid Reference

2.13 Behaviors to Note on Picture Completion

- Note the speed at which a child or adolescent responds. A reflective individual may take more time in responding (but most likely can respond within the time limit), whereas an impulsive individual may respond very quickly but incorrectly.

- Note whether the child is persistent in stating that nothing is missing from the picture (rather than responding, "I don't know"), as it may reflect oppositionality or inflexibility.

- Note that consistently nonverbal responses (e.g., pointing) may be evidence of a word retrieval problem in children. Although it is acceptable to give a nonverbal response, it is far more common to give a verbal response.

- Be aware that verbal responses that are imprecise ("the thingy on the door") or overly elaborate ("the small piece of metal which forms a connection between the molding around the door frame and the door itself, allowing it to open easily") are also noteworthy.

- Note whether children give responses that consistently indicate a focus on details.

- Be aware that after individuals have been redirected (e.g., "Yes, but what is the *most important* part that is missing?"), it is important to note whether they still continue to respond with the same quality of response. This persistence in approach may indicate inability to understand the task or inflexibility in thinking.

WPPSI-R Performance Subtests Only

Animal Pegs

The WPPSI-R Animal Pegs board, a box of 28 colored pegs, a stopwatch, and the manual are needed for administration of this subtest. Prior to administering this subtest you must determine whether the child is left- or right-handed, as it will affect where the box of colored pegs is placed next to the child. Each animal on the pegboard corresponds with a certain color peg, and in giving directions the examiner shows the child which color goes with each animal. Then during administration of the first six animal figures the examiner may demonstrate for the child the correct color for each animal.

After the demonstration items are administered, the directions (which are somewhat lengthy for a young child) must be read carefully and slowly. The directions emphasize that no items should be skipped and all items should be completed quickly. If the child forgets the exact nature of the task or hesitates at the end of a row, the following prompts may be given:

• "Look at the top to get the right colors."
• "Go on to the next row."

Occasionally a child begins to fill in all the pegs under a certain kind of animal rather than working sequentially across a row. Although it may be a useful strategy, it is not allowed during this subtest and the child should be directed not to skip any (but may only be told so twice). Such a strategy should be noted and may be useful during interpretation of the subtest. Children sometimes also begin to remove the pegs that they have already inserted; if this occurs they should be directed not to take them out (but can only be cautioned twice). Some children (especially younger children) do not understand that they need to work as quickly as they can and may be prompted twice by saying "Now HURRY!" Each child should be allowed to work for a maximum of 5 minutes on the board; if the child completes the board prior to that time,

---

≡ Rapid Reference

2.14 Behaviors to Note on Animal Pegs (WPPSI-R Only)

• Note whether children are distracted by the stimuli in the task. Some children like to play with the pegs rather than inserting them in the board.

• Observe how children respond to being timed. Often very young children appear unconcerned that a watch is recording how quickly they work; however, some children become quite anxious about having their performance timed.

• Note whether children need to consistently look at the key row of animals and pegs or whether they can remember which color is paired with which animal without looking.

• Be aware that some children may begin to take the pegs out once they have completed a row. This may indicate that the child does not fully understand the directions or that the child is oppositional.

• Note whether children work with one hand or two. Some children pick up the pegs with one hand and insert them with the other. Working with both hands is a key behavior to note because this may be either an effective or ineffective strategy for the child.

the examiner should record the exact completion time on the record form. Telling behaviors to watch for and note during administration of Animal Pegs are listed in Rapid Reference 2.14.

Geometric Design

The Geometric Design subtest of the WPPSI-R has two parts: visual recognition and drawing. For the visual recognition portion, the small stimulus booklet with 16 pictures is needed for administration along with the manual and record form. For the drawing portion, additional materials include Geometric Design sheets, black lead pencils with erasers, and a stopwatch. All children are to be administered both the visual recognition items (up to three consecutive errors) and the drawing items (up to two consecutive errors). The scoring criteria for the drawing portion is provided in Appendix B of the WPPSI-R manual (Wechsler, 1989). A good rule to follow during administration is that if you are unsure whether a child should receive credit for a particular drawing, do not take the time to examine the details of the scoring criteria at that very moment; rather, continue to administer the drawing items until you are certain that two consecutive errors have been made. Although you should review the Geometric Design scoring criteria prior to administering the subtest, if you stop the pace of the testing to go back and check the details of the criteria in the middle of the subtest this will likely be distracting to the child.

During the visual recognition portion of Geometric Design, examiners are to demonstrate the correct answer to the first item if a child responds incorrectly. However, on no other items during this subtest is the examiner to provide help. Encouragement to "do the best you can" may be provided, but not answers. During the drawing portion of the subtest (items 8–16) some children may rotate the paper while drawing. If this occurs, it is important to note whether the child rotates the paper or whether the drawing is rotated in relation to the placement of the paper. Children also may spontaneously start over or erase figures that they have begun. These second attempts are permissible but should be noted in behavioral observations. There are no fixed time limits during this subtest; however, usually after about 30 seconds most children are able to complete their drawings. Using this amount of time as a general guideline, if a child is clearly unable to cope with the task or is producing an unrecognizable form, the examiner

≋ Rapid Reference

2.15 Behaviors to Note on Geometric Design (WPPSI-R Only)

- Observe for signs of fine motor control. Note the grip on the pencil—is it awkward?
- Note whether there is excessive pressure made with the pencil while drawing. Very dark or very light lines may be related to anxiety or poor motor control.
- Note how steadily lines are drawn. A shaky line may be related to a slight hand tremor.
- Observe whether children rotate their bodies or their papers in order to change the perspective on the drawings.
- Note any verbalizations that are made during the drawings. Some children have learned that verbal mediation is helpful.
- Observe whether children are impulsive in their drawings or whether they take time to systematically examine the model before drawing.
- Note whether the child consistently erases figures that were drawn. This may be related to impulsivity and poor planning or insecurity about one's abilities.

may use his or her judgment to remove the form after about 30 seconds and encourage the child to try the next figure. However, if a child is productively working on completing a design after about 30 seconds, the examiner should allow as much time as necessary to finish. These types of behaviors, as well as others that may be observed during administration of this subtest, are listed in Rapid Reference 2.15.

WISC-III Performance Subtests Only

Coding

The WISC-III has two different Coding forms: Form A for 6- to 7-year-olds and Form B for 8- to 16-year-olds. Along with the appropriate Coding form, examiners need two No. 2 pencils without erasers, a stopwatch, the manual, and the record form for administration of this subtest. During administration, the Coding forms should be separated from the WISC-III record form. If a child is left-handed, an extra Coding response key should be placed to the right of the child's response sheet so that he or she may have an unobstructed view of the Coding key (some left-handers' hand position obstructs the key on the record form).

The directions for Coding are very lengthy and contain a lot of important detail. Examiners must be prepared to look up from reading the directions to check that the child is following what is being said. Therefore the directions should be rehearsed and read carefully to each child. During administration of the sample items, if the child makes any mistake it should be corrected immediately. If the child does not appear to understand the task after the sample items have been completed, further instruction should be given until the child clearly understands the task.

Once the 120-second subtest has begun, examiners should be astute observers. Children are not to omit any item or complete all items of one type at a time, and if they are observed doing this they need to be told "Do them in order. Don't skip any." Some children appear to stop midway through the task and should be reminded to continue until you tell them to stop. Occasionally

≡ Rapid Reference

2.16 Behaviors to Note on Coding (WISC-III Only)

- Be aware that the eye movements of children taking the test can be very informative. Consistent glancing back and forth from the Coding key to the response sheet may indicate poor memory or insecurity. In contrast, a child who uses the key infrequently may have a good short-term memory and remember number-symbol pairs readily.
- Note impulsivity in responding when the child quickly but carelessly fills in symbols across the rows.
- Watch for shaking hands, a tight grip on the pencil, or pressure on the paper when writing. These behaviors may indicate anxiety.
- Observe signs of fatigue, boredom, or inattention as the Coding subtest progresses. Noting the number of symbols copied during 30-second intervals provides helpful behavioral information.
- Note obsessiveness or attention to detail if children spend a significant amount of time trying to perfect each of the symbols that are drawn.
- Note whether children have difficulty understanding that they are to work quickly. This behavior may be related to immaturity.

children appear frustrated at the end of the test because they are only able to complete a few lines; if this behavior is observed, you may want to reassure the child that most children are not able to complete the entire sheet. Any of the above-mentioned behaviors are worthy of noting. As discussed in Rapid Reference 2.16, clinical information about problem-solving style, planning, and memory, as well as other information, may be gleaned from behavioral observations made during this subtest.

Symbol Search

Like Coding, the WISC-III has two different Symbol Search response booklets: Response booklet A is for 6- to 7-year-olds, and response booklet B is for 8- to 16-year-olds. Along with the appropriate Symbol Search form, examiners need two No. 2 pencils without erasers, a stopwatch, the manual, and the record form for administration of this subtest. Prior to beginning the subtest itself, children must go through sample items and practice items that are not timed. It is important not to skip any of the demonstration, even if the child appears to readily understand the task. The directions to the sample, practice, and test items are lengthy and require multiple rehearsals in order to be able to complete them while maintaining rapport with the child. A minimum of paraphrasing is acceptable while reading the directions; every attempt should be made to state them verbatim from the manual. The task should not begin until it is clear that the child understands.

The timing of 120 seconds should be exact. Some children may purposefully or inadvertently skip items, and they should be reminded to go in order and not skip any. Other children may appear to stop the task before the 120-second time limit is up, and they should be reminded to keep going until they are told to stop. Rapid Reference 2.17 lists telling behaviors to watch for and note during administration of Symbol Search.

Picture Arrangement

The WISC-III Picture Arrangement subtest requires manipulation of many stimulus materials by the examiner: 15 sets of Picture Arrangement cards, manual, record form, and stopwatch. All children are administered the sample item prior to beginning the test. During administration of the sample item and items 1 and 2, the cards are to be placed in front of the child *before* the oral directions are said, but on items 3–14 the cards are to be laid out

≡ *Rapid Reference*

....

2.17 Behaviors to Note on Symbol Search (WISC-III Only)

- Note how the child handles the pencil. Is there pressure? Is the pencil dropped? Does the child seem coordinated?

- Observe attention and concentration. Is the child's focus consistent throughout the task, or does it wane as time goes on?

- Look to see whether children check each row of symbols only once, or whether they go back and recheck the row of symbols in an item more than once. Obsessive concern with detail may be noted.

- Make note of the child's response style. Impulsivity and reflectivity are usually observable in this task.

- Consider whether children are utilizing their visual memory well. Watch eye movements to determine whether the child is moving back and forth several times between the target and search groups before making a choice.

- Observe the child for signs of fatigue or boredom, as this subtest is one of the last administered.

- Observe whether the child's response rate is consistent throughout the subtest. Note the number of items answered during each of the four 30-second intervals within the 120-second time limit.

while the directions are being read. After the sample item has been shown, the child should be allowed to look at the completed arrangement for about 10 seconds. Two trials are given for items 1 and 2. On item 1, if the child does not correctly complete the arrangement within the time limit during the first trial, the examiner is to demonstrate how to do it before administering the second trial of the item. However, for item 2, the examiner does not demonstrate the entire arrangement before the second trial; rather, just the first card in the series is shown to the child and he or she must complete the arrangement from that point. Items 3–14 only have one trial, and beginning with item 4 the oral directions may be shortened if the child clearly understands the task.

Most children begin their arrangement of the cards on the left, but if it is unclear where the intended beginning of the story is, the examiner should ask the child to point to the beginning of the story. If a child makes arrangements such as this, or if she verbalizes a story as she works, these behaviors should

≋ Rapid Reference

2.18 Behaviors to Note on Picture Arrangement (WISC-III Only)

- Observe how children handle the cards so you can gain insight about their problem-solving approach. Trial and error versus insightful problem solving may be noted. Children who pair pictures seemingly at random until they make sense demonstrate one style. Another style involves selecting the picture that goes first in the story, then selecting the second card, and so on in sequence.

- Observe the child's learning ability if he or she is administered either of the items that demonstrates the correct response. Does the child seem to benefit from feedback?

- Note whether the child begins to move the cards before carefully examining the pictures in each. This behavior may indicate impulsivity. Such individuals are also unlikely to check their work before saying that they have completed it. Other children may jump in to start the task before the directions have been completely read.

- Note when a child studies the pictures for a few seconds prior to rearranging them. Such behavior may indicate a reflective style. Rechecking their work after they are done may also be noted in individuals with a reflective style.

- Observe whether there is verbalization during problem solving. Telling the story as the cards are rearranged is a helpful strategy for some children, whereas for others this vocalization may be disruptive.

- Note any behaviors that give clues to whether errors are owing to social or cultural misinterpretation, as opposed to visual-perceptual difficulties.

- Be aware that when the subtest is complete, it may be useful to return to arrangements that the child got wrong. Note the child's explanation of how the arrangement made sense to him or her, as it may provide useful clinical information. Some creative alternate arrangements may be reasonable (but not credited), whereas others may be totally nonsensical.

be noted. Other telling behaviors to watch for and note during administration of Picture Arrangement are listed in Rapid Reference 2.18.

Over many years of using the WISC-III and WPPSI-R, as well as supervising students that have used these instruments, we have found that there are some pitfalls that even the best examiners commonly run into. Although the test manuals are, of course, the final word on how to administer the tests, Caution

2.5 provides a list of pitfalls that examiners may encounter during administration. Reviewing this list prior to test administration may provide a quick
means by which the number of administration errors can be cut.

CAUTION

2.5 Common Pitfalls of WPPSI-R and WISC-III Subtest Administration

Verbal Subtests

Information

- defining words if asked by the child
- forgetting to give required prompts to an incomplete answer
- being unaware that neutral queries may be given to Information responses that are incomplete or ambiguous

Comprehension

- forgetting to query for a second response if necessary (WPPSI-R item 11, WISC-III items 2, 6, 7, 11, 12, 15, 17, and 18)
- neglecting to write down the exact verbal response
- explaining the meaning of a word if asked

Arithmetic

- forgetting to time the child
- stopping the stopwatch when a question is repeated
- repeating the questions more than one time
- allowing paper and pencil to be used

Vocabulary

- not recording exact verbal responses
- not querying vague or incomplete responses appropriately
- spelling the words if asked

Similarities

- forgetting to give an example of a 2-point response if the child's response to WISC-III items 6 or 7 or WPPSI-R item 13 is not perfect
- overquerying or underquerying vague responses

Sentences (WPPSI-R only)

- reading the sentences too quickly
- reading the sentences with an unnatural intonation

continued

- repeating a sentence if the child asks
- not recording exactly what the child has said on both attempts

Digit Span (WISC-III only)

- reading the sequence of digits too quickly
- inadvertently "chunking" the numbers as they are read
- repeating a digit sequence if asked
- giving extra help on Digits Backward
- forgetting to administer Digits Backward to children who receive 0 points on Digits Forward

Performance Subtests

Object Assembly

- administering fewer than five WISC-III Object Assembly puzzles or administering more puzzles than needed on WPPSI-R (discontinue after three consecutive failures)
- neglecting to turn over puzzle pieces if they are not face up
- forgetting to count the number of junctures correctly completed at the time limit when allowing the child to work beyond the time limit
- incorrectly counting the number of completed junctures

Block Design

- neglecting to make sure that the proper variety of block faces are showing before an item has been started
- neglecting to give the eight new blocks beginning on WPPSI item 6 or neglecting to give the five extra cubes on WISC-III item 10
- placing the model in an incorrect position
- correcting block rotations more than two times during the WPPSI-R or more than once during the WISC-III
- remembering to administer items 1 and 2 in normal order if the child fails *either* trial of WISC-III item 3
- remembering to administer items in reverse order until credit is obtained on two consecutive designs if the child fails *either* trial of WPPSI-R item 6
- remembering which trials of the WPPSI-R items require the examiner to provide a demonstration

Mazes

- choosing to administer WISC-III Mazes subtest to children
- exposing more than one page of the WPPSI-R Mazes booklet at a time
- forgetting to administer the second trial of WPPSI-R Mazes 1 and 2, even if the child correctly completed the first trial of the maze

Picture Completion

- forgetting to time the WISC-III Picture Completion items (20-second limit) or WPPSI-R items (15-second limit for items 1–11 and 30-second limit for items 12 23)
- giving allowed queries too often
- forgetting to give the correct response to WISC-III items 1 and 2 or WPPSI-R items 1–4 if the child doesn't give the correct response

Animal Pegs (WPPSI-R only)

- placing the box of pegs on the wrong side of the child (right-handers have box on right, left-handers on left)
- allowing the child to skip an item
- burying your head in the manual while reading the lengthy directions

Geometric Design (WPPSI-R only)

- forgetting to administer the drawing items to children who cannot correctly complete all the recognition items
- not allowing the child to erase
- not keeping track of how long the child has been working on any particular item

Coding (WISC-III only)

- losing rapport with the child by burying your head in the administration manual while reading long directions
- proceeding with the task before the child clearly understands what is required
- not paying attention to the child and allowing him or her to skip over items

Symbol Search (WISC-III only)

- proceeding with the task before the child clearly understands what is required
- burying your head in the manual while reading directions
- not paying attention to the child and allowing him or her to skip over items

Picture Arrangement (WISC-III only)

- placing cards in front of the child in the wrong order
- neglecting to ask where the story begins if the child lays out the picture from right to left
- asking the child to explain what is happening in the story *during* the administration of the subtest (such verbal explanations can only be requested after the entire subtest has been completed)

🐟 TEST YOURSELF 🐟

1. **You have to test a girl age 6 years 6 months, believed to have average intelligence, who is suspected of having a learning disability. Which Wechsler scale should be administered?**

   (a) the WISC-III because it has more recent norms and yields four factor indexes

   (b) the WPPSI-R because it has a larger normative sample

   (c) the WISC-III because it is developed from a more sound theoretical base than the WPPSI-R

   (d) the WPPSI-R because it yields more stable IQs at age 6 years 6 months than the WISC-III

2. **It is never appropriate to have the parent of a 3-year-old child accompany you to the testing room because the parent may be distracting to the child.** True or False?

3. **You are explaining to a parent how to describe the testing to her 7-old-child; the following is a good example of what the parent may say to the child:**

   (a) "You will be tested by the doctor for about 2 or 3 hours."

   (b) "If you finish all of the tests, even the hard tests, you will get a treat."

   (c) "You just have to play with the nice doctor for a little bit. She'll let you pick the games you want to play."

   (d) "You are going to look at some puzzles, play with some blocks, be asked some questions, and do other activities like that."

4. **You are scheduled to test a 10-year-old girl with cerebral palsy. What are some ways that you may need to adapt the testing to accommodate her?**

5. **While administering the Similarities subtest, you realize that if the child obtains a 0 score on the next item he will have reached the discontinue rule. The response the child gives to this question, even after a query, seems to fall right between a 0-point and 1-point response. You should**

   (a) take an extra few minutes to reread all the responses in the 0-point and 1-point category while the child waits patiently.

   (b) continue administering further items until you are sure that the discontinue criterion has been met.

   (c) count it as a 0-point response because the child was so close to meeting the discontinue rule.

   (d) give the child the benefit of the doubt and score it as a 1-point response.

6. **If a child stops during the middle of a timed test to ask you a question, it is important to immediately stop timing and resume the timing only when the child's question has been answered.** True or False?

7. **You can query virtually any response that the child gives if you feel that it is vague, incomplete, or ambiguous.** True or False?

8. **Jake is being administered a subtest and asks for an item to be repeated. On which of the following subtests would that procedure be allowed?**

(a) Digit Span

(b) Sentences

(c) Vocabulary

(d) Block Design

Answers: 1. a; 2. False; 3. d; 4. Extend or eliminate time limits, administer only the Verbal Scale if she has severe motor difficulties, allow a nonverbal or written response if she has severe expressive difficulties; 5. b; 6. False; 7. True; 8. c

Three

HOW TO SCORE THE WISC-III AND WPPSI-R

TYPES OF SCORES

Administration of both the WPPSI-R and WISC-III results in three types of scores: raw scores, scaled scores, and IQs. The WISC-III also yields factor indexes. The first score that an examiner encounters is the raw score, which is simply a total of points earned on a single subtest. The raw score by itself is meaningless because it is not norm referenced. To interpret a child's raw score, one must convert it into a standard score (a scaled score, IQ, or index). The various metrics for each type of Wechsler standard score are listed in Rapid Reference 3.1. Individual subtests produce scaled scores with a mean of 10 and a standard deviation of 3 (ranging from 1 to 19 for most subtests). The IQs and factor indexes have a mean of 100 and a standard deviation of 15 (ranging from about 45 to 160 for most WPPSI-R scales and from about 46 to 155 for most WISC-III scales).

Because intellectual ability in the general population is distributed on a

≡ Rapid Reference

3.1 Metrics for Standard Scores

Type of Standard Score	Mean	Standard Deviation	General Range of Values	
Scaled score	10	3	1–19	
IQ	100	15	46–155 on WISC-III	45–160 on WPPSI-R
Index (WISC-III only)	100	15	50–150	

normal curve, most children earn scores on these tests that are within 1 standard deviation from the mean. About 66 of every 100 children tested earn IQs or indexes between 85 and 115. A greater number of children (about 95%) earn scores that are from 70 to 130 (2 standard deviations from the mean). The number of children earning extremely high scores (above 130) is only about 2.2%, and the number earning very low scores (less than 70) is also about 2.2%.

STEP-BY-STEP: HOW THE WISC-III AND WPPSI-R ARE SCORED

Raw Scores

Each of the items of a subtest contributes directly to the raw score. The scoring for most of the WPPSI-R and WISC-III subtests is not complex and can be readily done, but there are a few subtests (mainly on the Verbal scales) in which

---

CAUTION

3.1 Common Errors in Raw Score Calculation

- neglecting to add points earned from the first few items that weren't administered to the total raw score
- neglecting to add the points recorded on one page of the record form to the points recorded on the next (e.g., WISC-III Vocabulary lists the first 6 questions on one page and the last 24 on the next, WISC-III Comprehension lists the first 7 questions on one page and the last 11 on the next, and WPPSI-R lists the first 6 Block Design questions on one page and the last 9 items on the next)
- forgetting to subtract the number of incorrect responses from the number of correct responses on Symbol Search
- neglecting to multiply the number of correct junctures by the designated number on Object Assembly
- transferring total raw scores incorrectly from inside the record form to the front page of the record form
- miscalculating the raw score sum via an addition mistake
- including points earned on items that were presented after the discontinue criterion was met

subjectivity presents constant challenges to the examiner during the scoring process. Pointers for proper scoring of "tricky" subjective responses are discussed later in this chapter. Most examiners who can do simple addition (with or without counting on fingers and toes) can calculate the subtests' raw scores. Caution 3.1 notes errors that examiners make in the calculation of raw scores.

Scaled Scores

Converting the raw scores obtained from the WPPSI-R or WISC-III to scaled scores is a simple process. The data and materials needed are as follows: (a) the child's chronological age, (b) the child's raw scores on all subtests, and (c) Tables 24 and 25 from the WPPSI-R manual (Wechsler, 1989) or Table A.1 from the WISC-III manual (Wechsler, 1991). Once the raw scores have been transferred from the inside of the record form to the front cover, the conversion to scaled scores can begin. In the appropriate table, determined by the child's chronological age, look up the child's raw score and its corresponding scaled score equivalent. Write the scaled score equivalents in the appropriate boxes on the front of the record form. On the WPPSI-R all scaled scores are recorded in one column. However, on the WISC-III each of the scaled scores is recorded in two places: in the appropriate IQ column (either Verbal or Performance) and in the appropriate factor index column (either Verbal Comprehension, Perceptual Organization, Freedom from Distractibility, or Processing Speed). Caution 3.2 lists common errors in obtaining scaled scores.

CAUTION

3.2 Common Errors in Obtaining Scaled Scores

- miscalculating a sum when adding scores to obtain the raw score or the sum of scaled scores
- writing illegibly, which leads to errors
- using a score conversion table that references the wrong age group
- misreading across the rows of the score conversion tables
- forgetting to write the WISC-III scaled scores in both an IQ column and a factor index column

IQs and Factor Indexes

Obtaining the IQs and factor indexes is next in the process of score conversion. The following steps showing how to convert scaled scores to IQs should be carefully followed to obtain accurate scores. (Don't Forgets 3.1 and 3.2 list subtests that make up WISC-III IQs and factor indexes, as well as WPPSI-R IQs.)

1. Whether you have administered the WPPSI-R or the WISC-III, calculate the sum of the appropriate subtests' scaled scores for the Verbal and Performance IQs. Be sure to note that on the WPPSI-R the Animal Pegs and Sentences subtests are not used in the sums of scaled scores *unless* they are replacing another subtest, and on the WISC-III the Symbol Search, Digit Span, and Mazes subtests are not used in the sums of scaled scores *unless* they are replacing another subtest.

1a. For the WISC-III only, calculate the sum of the appropriate subtests' scaled scores for the four factor indexes.

2. Add the sum of the Verbal and Performance scales' sums of scores to obtain the Full Scale score. Then record this number in the appropriate box beside the Full Scale score.

DON'T FORGET

3.1 Subtests Making Up WISC-III IQs and Factor Indexes

V-IQ	P-IQ	VCI	POI	FDI	PSI
Information	Picture Completion	Information	Picture Completion	Arithmetic	Coding
Similarities	Coding	Similarities	Picture Arrangement	Digit Span	Symbol Search
Arithmetic	Picture Arrangement	Vocabulary	Block Design		
Vocabulary	Block Design	Comprehension	Object Assembly		
Comprehension	Object Assembly				

Note. V-IQ = Verbal IQ; P-IQ = Performance IQ; VCI = Verbal Comprehension Index; POI = Perceptual Organization Index; FDI = Freedom from Distractibility Index; PSI = Processing Speed Index.

DON'T FORGET

....

3.2 Subtests Making Up WPPSI-R IQs

Verbal IQ

Information

Comprehension

Arithmetic

Vocabulary

Similarities

Performance IQ

Object Assembly

Geometric Design

Block Design

Mazes

Picture Completion

Note. Sentences is a supplementary test that can substitute for other Verbal subtests under certain circumstances. Animal Pegs is a supplementary subtest that can substitute for other Performance subtests under certain circumstances.

3. The scores for the three scales (plus the four factor index scores if you have administered the WISC-III) should be transferred to the table that holds one column for scaled scores and one for IQs.

4. For each scale, determine the appropriate IQ (and Index) based on the sum of scaled scores. For the WPPSI-R see Table 27 of the WPPSI-R manual (Wechsler, 1989), and for the WISC-III see Tables A.2 to A.7 of the WISC-III manual (Wechsler, 1991). Note that we make a special recommendation for determining the WISC-III Performance IQ and Full Scale IQ (see the Special Considerations section that follows).

5. On the WISC-III examiners should also record the percentile ranks and confidence intervals for each of the scales. These are found in Tables A.2 to A.7 of the WISC-III manual (Wechsler, 1991).

Special Considerations for Calculating WISC-III Performance IQ and Full Scale IQ

There are multiple reasons that the WISC-III Symbol Search subtest should routinely replace the Coding subtest as a part of the IQ calculations. The psychometric qualities of Symbol Search are undoubtedly better: Symbol Search correlates .58 with the Performance Scale whereas Coding correlates only .32;

Symbol Search correlates .56 with the Full Scale IQ but Coding correlates only .33; the loading for Symbol Search on the Perceptual Organization factor in a two-factor solution is .54, whereas Coding's is only .39, and the *g* loading of Symbol Search is .56 whereas Coding's *g* loading is .41 (Kaufman, 1994a).

Following the recommendation made by Kaufman (1994a), we encourage examiners to administer both Symbol Search and Coding but to routinely substitute Symbol Search for Coding in computation of the Performance IQ and Full Scale IQ. The manual does not provide norms for Performance IQ and Full Scale IQ when using Symbol Search rather than Coding, but another group of researchers has done the necessary calculations to provide new norms. Appendix A presents normative tables for calculating the WISC-III Performance IQ and Full Scale IQ when Symbol Search is substituted for Coding based on the work of Reynolds, Sanchez, and Willson (1996). Making this substitution does not lower the reliability of the Performance IQ or Full Scale IQ because the subtests have similar stability coefficients.

It is crucial to decide whether to substitute Symbol Search for Coding *prior to* administering the battery (Kaufman, 1994a). Even though a child may earn a higher score on Coding than on Symbol Search or vice versa, it is never acceptable to make such a decision on the basis of the child's obtained scores. Although we do recommend administering both subtests (so you can obtain all four factor index scores), the decision to substitute one subtest for the other must be made a priori.

Special Considerations for IQs With Subtest Raw Scores of Zero

Subtest raw scores of zero deserve special consideration when being converted to scaled scores and IQs. The problem with a raw score of zero is that you cannot determine the child's true ability to perform on the test. A zero raw score does not indicate that a child lacks a certain ability, but it does mean that the particular subtests did not have enough low-level easy items (floor items) to adequately assess the child's skills. On both the WPPSI-R and WISC-III, unless the child obtains raw scores greater than zero on at least three Verbal subtests, no Verbal IQ should be derived. Likewise, if three or more zero raw scores on Performance subtests are obtained, then the Performance IQ should not be derived. In either case, a Full Scale IQ should not be computed.

Prorating and Scoring Options

The WPPSI-R and the WISC-III provide options for scoring if the regular five subtests that make up the Verbal IQ or the five that make up the Performance IQ cannot be used. This situation may occur if a subtest is spoiled during administration or if a special handicap makes the administration of a particular subtest inadvisable. On the WPPSI-R, if one of the five regular Verbal subtests is unusable, then Sentences may be used in the calculation of the IQ; and if a Performance subtest needs to be replaced, then Animal Pegs may be used as an alternate. On the WISC-III, the Digit Span subtest may replace one of the Verbal subtests in the calculation of the Verbal IQ if necessary. And, as mentioned earlier, we recommend that Symbol Search be routinely substituted for Coding on the Performance IQ. (Don't Forget 3.3 summarizes the options for replacing certain subtests with others.)

The decision to substitute one subtest for another cannot be made arbitrarily. There must be substantial reason supporting the choice to make the substitution. We have already discussed reasons for substituting Symbol Search for Coding on the WISC-III. The decision to substitute Sentences for Arithmetic on the WPPSI-R may be made, for example, if Arithmetic is spoiled because of distracting noises during administration. A valid reason to substitute Animal Pegs for Picture Completion on the WPPSI-R may be, for example, if the child is not able to produce verbal responses on Picture Completion because of poor language ability. If the examiner is aware of this ex-

---

DON'T FORGET

3.3 Replacing Certain Subtests

Original WPPSI-R Subtest		Replacement WPPSI-R Subtest
Any Verbal Scale subtest	⇔	Sentences
Any Performance Scale subtest	⇔	Animal Pegs
Original WISC-III Subtest	⇔	**Replacement WISC-III Subtest**
Any Verbal Scale subtest	⇔	Digit Span
Coding[a]	⇔	Symbol Search[a]

[a]We recommend that Symbol Search routinely replace Coding on the WISC-III.

pressive language difficulty, the decision may be made ahead of time to utilize Animal Pegs in the Performance IQ because it minimizes the effect of expression of English language. The bottom line is that you should not substitute one subtest for another simply because a child has performed better or worse on one or the other.

If only four Verbal subtests or four Performance subtests are available, the process of prorating becomes necessary to calculate an IQ. Both the WPPSI-R and the WISC-III provide a way to estimate the sum of the Verbal or Performance scales so that an IQ can be derived. Full Scale IQs and factor indexes cannot be prorated themselves, but the Full Scale IQ can be computed *after* the Verbal or Performance Scale has been prorated. To prorate the Verbal or Performance Scale on the WPPSI-R, Table 26 of the WPPSI-R manual (Wechsler, 1989) may be used; to prorate either scale on the WISC-III, Table A.8 of the WISC-III manual (Wechsler, 1991) may be used. Whenever a score is prorated, this should be indicated on the record form by writing the abbreviation *PRO* next to the prorated score.

Scoring Subtests Requiring Judgment

While administering the WPPSI-R and WISC-III you will likely find (or may have discovered if you are an experienced tester) that the Verbal subtests elicit many more responses than are listed in the manuals. The multitude of responses can be interesting but also frustrating during the process of scoring that involves subjective judgment. Although Wechsler (1989, 1991) has sought to objectify as much as possible the responses on Vocabulary, Similarities, Comprehension, and Information, the information in the manuals is not all-inclusive and can only be used as a general guide.

Many times we have administered a test to a child who blurts out a beautiful 1.5-point answer, seeming to fit in neither the 2-point nor 1-point category listed in the manual. This type of borderline response may be frustrating, but by having a clear understanding of the general scoring criteria provided in the manual examiners can make a good judgment of how to score any response. The general scoring criteria for WPPSI-R Verbal subtests may be found in the WPPSI-R manual on pages 79–80 and 94 (Wechsler, 1989). For the WISC-III, general scoring criteria may be found on pages 84, 121–122, and 143 of the WISC-III manual (Wechsler, 1991).

There are some basic rules to consider while scoring Verbal subtests. First, a child cannot be penalized for poor grammar or improper pronunciation. Although grammar and pronunciation are important to note for clinical reasons, it is the *content* of what a child says that is most important for scoring a response. Second, long and elaborate answers are not necessarily worth more points than short, concise ones. Some children have a tendency to respond in paragraph form, which leads to two or three answers rolled into one. If this occurs, either spontaneously or after a query, it is the examiner's job to determine (a) whether the response has been spoiled, (b) which part of the response was intended as the final response, and (c) which part of the response is worth the highest number of points. If a child reveals a fundamental misconception in his or her long and elaborate response, then the entire response may be spoiled and the response scored a zero. If a child's response contains many answers but none that spoils the response, further querying may be necessary. Sometimes it is clear that in a series of responses, the last answer is the final response. In that case, the final response should be the one scored. At other times it is unclear whether the second or third response is intended as the actual response. In such a case, ask the child to clarify his or her response. For clarification purposes you may ask, "You said, _____, _____, and _____. Which one was your answer?" In some instances children say that their *entire* long response was what they intended the answer to be, and embedded in that long response are 0-, 1-, and 2-point answers. In such a case, if no answer spoils part of the long response, then simply score the *best* response.

Subtest-by-Subtest Scoring Keys

The following section lists important points to remember when scoring each of the WPPSI-R and WISC-III subtests. We do not review all the nuances of scoring each part of the tests here, but we do cover areas that commonly cause difficulty for examiners.

WPPSI-R AND WISC-III VERBAL SUBTESTS

Information

- On the first six WPPSI-R items, if the child points to the correct picture but says an incorrect verbal response, the item is scored 0.
- On both WPPSI-R and WISC-III, responses listed in the manual are

not all-inclusive. Give credit for responses that are of the same caliber as those in the manual.

- For the WISC-III, add 1 point to the raw score for each of the unadministered reversal items.

Comprehension

- Use the specific scoring examples and the general 0-, 1-, and 2-point scoring criteria.
- For items that require responses from two different general categories, if a child gives two responses from one general category, only 1 point is earned.
- If a child spontaneously improves his or her answer or improves the answer after a query, the child is given credit for that improvement.

Arithmetic

- For all WISC-III Arithmetic items and items 12–23 of WPPSI-R Arithmetic, children producing correct responses after the time limit do not earn credit for their response (although a note should be made of the belated correct response).
- On the WPPSI-R, if a child responds by holding up a number of fingers to indicate a response, he or she earns credit for that response unless it is accompanied by an incorrect verbal response.
- If a child gives the correct numeric value for a response but gives the wrong scale (e.g., dollars instead of cents), the answer is scored 0.
- Add 1 point to the raw score for each of the unadministered reversal items.

Vocabulary

- Items 1–3 of WPPSI-R Vocabulary are worth 0 to 1 point each, but the remaining WPPSI-R items and all the WISC-III Vocabulary items are worth 0, 1, or 2 points.
- Slang and regionalisms not in the dictionary are scored 0.
- Poor grammar is not penalized in scoring.
- Any meaning found in a standard dictionary is given credit.
- Utilize the general 0- to 2-point scoring criteria and the specific examples.
- On WISC-III Vocabulary, add 1 point to the raw score for each of the unadministered reversal items.

Similarities
- WPPSI-R Similarities items 1–12 and WISC-III Similarities items 1–5 are worth either 0 or 1 point each, and the remaining WPPSI-R and WISC-III Similarities items are worth 0, 1, or 2 points each.
- For the Verbal Analogies section of WPPSI-R Similarities and for all WISC-III Similarities items, use the general 0- to 2-point scoring criteria and specific examples.
- Key to scoring is the degree of abstraction.

WPPSI-R VERBAL SUBTESTS ONLY

Sentences
- Children should not be penalized for faulty pronunciation.
- Give full credit for each of the unadministered reversal items if no errors are made on Sentence 6 (if the child is age 5 or older).
- Errors are given for mistakes in four different categories: Omissions, Transpositions, Additions, and Substitutions.
- More than one error for each of the four categories may be scored in each sentence.
- On the Sentences score sheet, the values in columns at the end of each sentence are not the number of errors themselves, but the points earned on that item. Thus you must look at the top of the score sheet to reference the number of errors made in each sentence, and then in the appropriate row below you must circle the corresponding number of points.

WISC-III VERBAL SUBTESTS ONLY

Digit Span
- One point per trial is given for exact correct repetition (there are two trials per item).
- Self-corrections are given credit.
- The Digit Span raw score is equivalent to the sum of the raw score for Digits Forward and the raw score for Digits Backward.

WPPSI-R AND WISC-III PERFORMANCE SUBTESTS

Object Assembly
- The number of correct junctures (where two pieces join) at the precise moment that the time limit expires must be counted first.

- A juncture is given credit even if it is between two pieces that are separate from the rest of the puzzle.
- Bonus points for speedy performance are only awarded if the child has assembled the object perfectly. No bonus points are awarded for partial assemblies.
- To obtain a raw score for objects that are partially assembled on WISC-III Object Assembly, multiply the number of correct junctures by 1 for items 1, 3, and 4 and by ½ for items 2 and 5.
- On item 1 of WPPSI-R Object Assembly, no points may be given if a child earns a score of 0 on trial 1, even if trial 2 is completed correctly.

Block Design

- For items 1–7 of WPPSI-R Block Design and items 1–3 of WISC-III Block Design, successful completion on the first trial earns 2 points.
- For Items 7–14 of WPPSI-R Block Design and items 4–12 of WISC-III Block Design, bonus points are awarded on the basis of completion time.
- On both the WPPSI-R and WISC-III, 2 points per item are awarded for reversal items that are not administered.
- On both the WPPSI-R and WISC-III, if a child correctly completes a design after the time limit has expired, no points are awarded (although a note should be made of the child's performance).
- Partially completed designs receive 0 points.
- Rotations of designs of 30 degrees or more are scored 0 on the WISC-III; however, on the WPPSI-R rotations of designs are not penalized unless the child's design is a complete reversal of the model.

Mazes

- No points are awarded on an item if it is completed after the time limit has expired.
- If a child fails to reach an exit, the item is scored 0 points.
- If a child eliminates a significant portion of the maze while completing an item, no points are awarded.
- If a child begins a maze at the wrong point, no points are earned on that item.

- One point per item is awarded for reversal items that are not administered.
- An infinite number of errors may be scored on each item.
- Errors may occur in any of three categories (see description on pp. 223–225 of the WPPSI-R manual; Wechsler, 1989).
- If a child crosses a wall due to an obvious overshoot, do not score it as an error.
- Cutting corners and lifting the pencil are not counted as errors.
- If it is not easily discernible whether the child has actually entered an alley (e.g., the tracing has grazed the entrance), then no error is scored.

Picture Completion
- Add 1 point to the raw score for each of the unadministered reversal items.
- If the child responds with a correct description using a synonym or his or her own words, score 1 point.
- Score 1 point for items on which the child correctly points to the missing place.
- If the child's verbal response is incorrect but the pointing response is correct, score 0.
- On the WISC-III, if the child doesn't respond within the 20-second time limit, score 0. However, on the WPPSI-R there is no time limit for each item (although there are recommended minimum working times).

WPPSI-R PERFORMANCE SUBTESTS ONLY

Animal Pegs
- If a child has incorrectly placed a colored peg, this is considered an error.
- Leaving a peg hole empty is recorded as an omission, not an error. Omissions are also counted for items that are not completed by the end of the time limit.
- The number of pegs placed, both those that are correct and those that are incorrect, should be recorded in the "pegs placed" blank (the maximum number of pegs is 20).
- The raw score is calculated from a transformation of number of

errors and omissions and the completion time. Using these three pieces of data, you can look up the raw score in Table 24 of the WPPSI-R manual (Wechsler, 1989).

Geometric Design

- Each of the first seven items may be scored 0 or 1 point.
- The value of each of the drawing items (items 8–16) is variable and ranges from 4 to 12 points, with a total possible of 57 points.
- Each of the listed drawing criteria for the items is worth 1 point.
- The specific scoring criteria on pp. 201–221 of the WPPSI-R manual (Wechsler, 1989), along with the scoring templates, must be utilized to properly score the drawing items.

WISC-III PERFORMANCE SUBTESTS ONLY

Coding

- One point is given for each correctly drawn symbol (drawn within 120 seconds).
- Sample items do not count toward the final score.
- The Coding template should be used to score the items.
- Symbols do not have to be drawn perfectly to obtain credit, they just must be recognizable.
- If a child has spontaneously corrected his or her drawing, give credit to the corrected drawing.
- On Coding A, if a child completes all items correctly and has completed the items within the time limit, he or she receives bonus points based on the completion time.
- On Coding B, points are awarded for the number of correctly drawn items (no bonus points are awarded).

Symbol Search

- Careful placement of the Symbol Search template is necessary for accurate scoring.
- If a child has marked both "Yes" and "No" for the response to one item, it is scored 0.
- The number of correct items and the number of incorrect items are summed separately.
- The raw score is calculated by subtracting the number of incorrect items from the number correct.

- Only items completed before the 120-second time limit expires are counted toward the score.
- Skipped items are not counted toward the score.

Picture Arrangement
- Items 1 and 2 are worth 2 points each if the cards are correctly assembled within the time limit on the first trial.
- Add 2 points to a child's score for each of the unadministered reversal items.
- On items 3–14, children may earn bonus points for correct completion depending on the completion time.
- Cards correctly arranged after the time limit has expired are scored 0.
- Item 12 has two possible correct solutions.
- Item 14 has one alternate acceptable solution that is scored 1 point.

COMPUTER SCORING PROCEDURES

Computer software is available for scoring and interpreting the WPPSI-R and WISC-III.

- *The WPPSI-R Writer* (The Psychological Corporation, 1991) is an interpretive software system available from The Psychological Corporation. Users of *The WPPSI-R Writer* can enter either raw scores or scaled scores to obtain percentiles, age equivalents, and IQ scores. The program also generates a profile analysis.
- *Report Writer: WISC-III/WISC-R/WPPSI-R* (Dougherty, 1992) is an interpretive software package available from Psychological Assessment Resources. It requires users to enter scaled scores and IQ data, and it generates sections on the statistical analysis of scaled and IQ scores, factor scores, subtest combinations, and educational recommendations.
- *Scoring Assistant for the Wechsler Scales* (SAWS; The Psychological Corporation, 1994a), published by The Psychological Corporation, is a scoring program for the WISC-III and Wechsler Individual Achievement Test (WIAT). After users enter raw scores, the program completes all norms table conversions, calculates IQ and index scores, and per-

forms other statistical tests on the profile. In addition, SAWS generates discrepancy scores between the WISC-III and WIAT.

- *WISC-III Writer* (The Psychological Corporation, 1994b), published by The Psychological Corporation, is a scoring and interpretive program. It converts raw scores, entered by the examiner, into scaled scores, IQs, and index scores. It provides an analysis of children's profiles and generates a report based on composite shared abilities. Data from the WIAT and the *Guide to the Assessment of Test Session Behavior* (Glutting & Oakland, 1992) may also be combined in the program's interpretive report.
- The *Kaufman WISC-III Integrated Interpretive System* (K-WIIS; Kaufman, Kaufman, Dougherty, & Tuttle, 1996), published by Psychological Assessment Resources, is an interpretive program. After the examiner enters scaled scores, IQ scores, and index scores, as well as behavioral observations, the program produces interpretive hypotheses. It can also produce graphs of a child's strengths and weaknesses from the WISC-III profile.

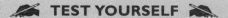

TEST YOURSELF

1. **While administering the WPPSI-R Arithmetic subtest to Annie, several interruptions cause a recurring loss of her attention that, in your clinical judgment, has spoiled the subtest. Which subtest may you replace Arithmetic with in calculation of the Verbal IQ?**

    (a) Information

    (b) Animal Pegs

    (c) Sentences

    (d) Vocabulary

2. **Because each of the WPPSI-R and WISC-III subtests begin at points that are calibrated for the individual child's chronological age, the raw scores are meaningful and interpretable without being converted to a standard score metric.** True or False?

continued

3. **The best method of deciding when to utilize the Symbol Search subtest rather than the Coding subtest in calculation of the Performance IQ and Full Scale IQ is to**

(a) wait to see on which test the child performs the best.

(b) make an a priori decision to use one rather than the other, even before the subtests are administered.

(c) flip a coin.

(d) ask the child which one he or she liked better.

4. **Lewis, age 9, is administered the WISC-III and obtains a raw score of 0 on Picture Completion, Block Design, Object Assembly, and Information. You should**

(a) not calculate the Performance IQ.

(b) not calculate the Verbal IQ.

(c) calculate neither the Verbal IQ nor the Performance IQ.

(d) consider the entire test invalid.

5. **If a child gives a long, elaborate response to the Vocabulary subtest, and you are unsure of the intended response, it is appropriate to ask the child to specify his or her intended answer.** True or False?

Answers: 1. c; 2. False; 3. b; 4. a; 5. True

Four

This chapter is designed to simplify the daunting task of interpreting the volume of scores and clinical data obtained from administering the WISC-III or the WPPSI-R. The system of interpretation outlined here will help you organize the test data in systematic ways, facilitating insightful interpretation. First we analyze each subtest, then we present a step-by-step method of interpreting the WISC-III and WPPSI-R from IQs all the way through the profile of subtest scores. We emphasize not only interpretation of the numerical values obtained from each test, but also how these scores can (and indeed must) be integrated with background and behavioral information.

The key to accurately characterizing a child's strong and weak areas of functioning is to examine his or her performance across several subtests, not individual subtest scores in isolation. This chapter offers general information about each subtest along with clinical and empirical data to clarify how each task contributes to the WPPSI-R or the WISC-III profile. The step-by-step process of interpretation provides a mechanism by which hypotheses about a child's performance can be tested when multiple subtests are examined together. The shared or overlapping abilities in performance across several subtests are crucial in creating a meaningful understanding of a child's cognitive abilities. Thus although one should be aware of the unique skills tapped by a single subtest, it is important to examine the abilities measured by many WISC-III or WPPSI-R subtests to glean the most information.

ANALYSIS OF EACH SUBTEST

Empirical, cognitive, and clinical data are provided for each of the WPPSI-R and WISC-III subtests. The following section on empirical analysis describes subtest specificity and general intelligence (*g* loadings). The cognitive analysis section presents a summary of cognitive abilities that each subtest is believed to measure. The final section provides an analysis of clinical considerations.

Empirical Analysis

Empirical analysis of the WPPSI-R and WISC-III subtests is based on data from each of the tests' standardization samples.

Loadings on the General Factor

How well each of the subtests measures general intelligence, or *g*, is determined for our purposes by the loadings on the unrotated first factor in the principal component analysis. Factor loadings of .70 or greater are considered good measures of *g*, loadings of .50 to .69 are deemed fair, and loadings below .50 are usually considered poor. Rapid Reference 4.1 reports data on the *g* loadings for both the WPPSI-R and WISC-III.

Some slight differences in *g* loadings, not shown in Rapid Reference 4.1, have been noted at different ages on the WPPSI-R (Sattler, 1992). At ages 3 to 5 average *g* loadings accounted for 45 to 50% of the variance, at ages 5 to 7 average *g* loadings accounted for 34 to 44% of the variance, and at age 7 the average proportion of variance attributed to *g* was only 34%. Thus the highest *g* loadings were found in the youngest age ranges. On the WISC-III, age trends were relatively minor. The occasional differences that appeared between age groups on the WISC-III appeared to be arbitrary fluctuations rather than systematic ones (Kaufman, 1994a).

The strongest *g* loadings on both the WPPSI-R and the WISC-III were found in the Verbal subtests. All five of the regularly administered WPPSI-R Verbal subtests were good measures of *g*, and four of the five regularly administered WISC-III subtests were in that category as well. The one WISC-III Verbal subtest that fell in the fair rather than good category was Comprehension. On the Performance Scale, the highest *g* loadings were found on the WISC-III's Block Design and on the WPPSI-R's Picture Completion. Only the WISC-III had subtests that fell in the category of poor measures of *g*; these included Digit Span and Coding (and on the WPPSI-R, Animal Pegs came close).

The meaningfulness of *g* loadings, or the general intelligence concept, has

≡ Rapid Reference

4.1 WPPSI-R and WISC-III Subtests as Measures of General Ability (g)

WPPSI-R Subtests

Good Measures of g		Fair Measures of g		Poor Measures of g	
Information	(.79)	Picture Completion	(.69)	none	
Arithmetic	(.76)	Block Design	(.68)		
Comprehension	(.72)	Sentences	(.68)		
Similarities	(.72)	Geometric Design	(.61)		
Vocabulary	(.71)	Object Assembly	(.57)		
		Mazes	(.56)		
		Animal Pegs	(.52)		

WISC-III Subtests

Good Measures of g		Fair Measures of g		Poor Measures of g	
Vocabulary	(.80)	Comprehension	(.68)	Digit Span	(.47)
Information	(.78)	Object Assembly	(.61)	Coding	(.41)
Similarities	(.77)	Picture Completion	(.60)		
Arithmetic	(.76)	Symbol Search	(.56)		
Block Design	(.71)	Picture Arrangement	(.53)		

Note. g loading in parentheses. WPPSI-R values are from Assessment of children: WISC-III and WPPSI-R supplement (Table G-6, p. 985), by J. M. Sattler, 1992, San Diego, CA: Author. Copyright 1992 by Jerome Sattler. Used with permission. WISC-III values are from Intelligent testing with the WISC-III by A. S. Kaufman, 1994, New York: Wiley.

been debated (Jensen, 1998; Neisser, 1998). We do know that this value represents how well the subtests "hang together" psychometrically. However, what is debatable is the theoretical construct that underlies the g value. Thus a subtest with a strong g loading should not be interpreted as the ultimate representation of a child's level of cognitive ability.

Specificity of Subtests

The unique proportion of variance of each subtest is referred to as subtest specificity. This is the proportion of variance that is not shared with other subtests. When deciding whether it is feasible to interpret the unique abilities or traits measured by a subtest, you should take into account the subtest specificity. In addition, you must take into account the error variance when deciding whether to interpret a subtest's unique characteristics. Generally, if about 25% or more of the total variance is specific and the specific variance exceeds the error variance, then interpretation of "specific" measured abilities may be made. Rapid Reference 4.2 shows the amount of subtest specificity for each WPPSI-R and WISC-III subtest.

Although relatively few WPPSI-R or WISC-III subtests have "inadequate" specificity, this doesn't mean that all examiners should simply interpret each of the subtest's unique measured abilities. As mentioned earlier, the first plan of attack when examining a child's subtest profile is to create hypotheses on the basis of the shared abilities measured by many subtests.

Abilities Shared With Other Subtests

Numerous measured abilities are hypothesized to underlie each of the WPPSI-R and WISC-III subtests. In this chapter we present these hypothesized abilities according to the organized structure of the Information Processing Model (Silver, 1993). Within this framework each measured ability of a subtest is categorized into one of three groups: (a) input, which involves abilities relating to the type of information that is to be handled (e.g., visual or auditory stimuli); (b) integration/storage, which involves abilities that relate to processing and memory components; and (c) output, which represents how individuals express their response (e.g., motor coordination or verbal expression). See Figure 4.1 for a schematic representation of the Information Processing Model.

The two-category organization (Verbal and Performance) of subtests is the same across all Wechsler tests. However, many new organizational models have been proposed for interpretation of the subtests. In the Subtest-by-Subtest Analysis section of this chapter several hypothesized measured abilities are listed under each subtest; many of these come from theoretical

≋ Rapid Reference

4.2 WPPSI-R and WISC-III Subtests Categorized by Specificity

WPPSI-R Subtests

Ample Specificity		Adequate Specificity		Inadequate Specificity	
Animal Pegs	(.43/.34)	Block Design	(.29/.15)	Object Assembly	(.23/.37)
Picture Completion	(.42/.15)	Vocabulary	(.26/.16)	Information	(.18/.16)
Mazes	(.39/.23)	Arithmetic	(.28/.20)		
Geometric Design	(.34/.21)	Comprehension	(.23/.17)		
Sentences	(.34/.18)				
Similarities	(.36/.14)				

WISC-III Subtests

Ample Specificity		Adequate Specificity		Inadequate Specificity	
Digit Span	(.63/.15)	Symbol Search	(.34/.26)	Object Assembly	(.26/.31)
Coding	(.49/.23)	Arithmetic	(.30/.22)		
Picture Arrangement	(.48/.24)	Comprehension	(.30/.23)		
Picture Completion	(.39/.23)	Information	(.25/.16)		
Block Design	(.34/.13)	Vocabulary	(.24/.13)		
		Similarities	(.23/.19)		

Note. Subtest specificity is followed by error variance in parentheses. WPPSI-R values are from "General-factor and specific variance in the WPPSI-R," by G. H. Roid and J. Gyurke, 1991, *Journal of Psychoeducational Assessment, 9*, Table 2, p. 217. Copyright 1991 by G. H. Roid and J. Gyurke. Used with permission. WISC-III values are from *Intelligent testing with the WISC-III* by A. S. Kaufman, 1994, New York: Wiley.

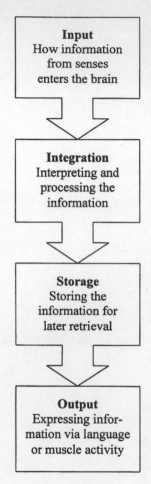

Figure 4.1 Information Processing Model

reorganizations of the Wechsler subtests. We do not provide an in-depth discussion of theoretical and research-based recategorization of the WPPSI-R and WISC-III because this information is available in other sources (see Kaufman, 1994a; Sattler, 1992). Instead we outline different methods of recategorizing the Wechsler subtests. Guilford (1967), Horn (1989), Horn and Cattell (1966, 1967) and Bannatyne (1974) are the authors emphasized in this section (see Rapid References 4.3 through 4.8).

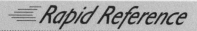 *Rapid Reference*

4.3 WPPSI-R Subtests in the Horn Model

Fluid Intelligence (Gf)	Crystallized Intelligence (Gc)	Short-Term Acquisition and Retrieval (SAR)	Broad Visualization (Gv)
Similarities	Vocabulary	Arithmetic	Picture Completion
Object Assembly	Information	Animal Pegs	Block Design
Block Design	Similiarities	Sentences	Object Assembly
Mazes	Arithmetic		Geometric Design
Arithmetic			Mazes

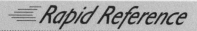 *Rapid Reference*

4.4 WISC-III Subtests in the Horn Model

Fluid Intelligence (Gf)	Crystallized Intelligence (Gc)	Short-Term Acquisition and Retrieval (SAR)	Broad Visualization (Gv)	Broad Speediness (Gs)
Picture Arrangement	Information	Arithmetic	Picture Completion	Coding
	Similarities	Digit Span	Block Design	Symbol Search
Block Design	Vocabulary		Object Assembly	Object Assembly
Object Assembly	Comprehension			
Similarities	Picture Arrangement			
Arithmetic				

≡ *Rapid Reference*

4.5 WISC-III Factors Corresponding to Horn's Theory

WISC-III Factor		Horn's Construct
VCI	⇔	Gc
POI	⇔	Gv and Gf
FDI	⇔	SAR (or Gsm)
PSI	⇔	Gs

Note. VCI = Verbal Comprehension Index; POI = Perceptual Organization Index; FDI = Freedom from Distractibility Index; PSI = Processing Speed Index; Gc = Crystallized Intelligence; Gf = Fluid Intelligence; SAR (or Gsm) = Short-Term Acquisition and Retrieval; Gs = Broad Speediness.

≡ *Rapid Reference*

4.6 Guilford's Operations and Contents

Operations (Intellectual Processes)	Description
Cognition (C)	Immediate awareness, recognition, or comprehension of stimuli
Memory (M)	Retention of information in the same form in which it was stored
Evaluation (E)	Making judgments about information in terms of a known standard
Convergent Production (N)	Responding to stimuli with the unique or "best" answer
Divergent Production (D)	Responding to stimuli where the emphasis is on a variety or quality of response (associated with creativity)

Contents (Nature of the Stimuli)	Description
Figural (F)	Shapes or concrete objects
Symbolic (S)	Numerals, single letters, or any coded symbol
Semantic (M)	Words and ideas that convey meaning
Behavioral (B)	Primarily nonverbal, involving human interactions with a stress on attitudes, needs, thoughts, and so on

4.7 Classification of WISC-III Subtests in Guilford's Model

WISC-III Subtest	Cognition	Memory	Evaluation	Convergent Production
Verbal Comprehension				
Information		Semantic		
Similarities	Semantic			
Vocabulary	Semantic			
Comprehension			Semantic	
Perceptual Organization				
Picture Completion	Figural		Figural	
Picture Arrangement			Semantic	Semantic
Block Design	Figural		Figural	
Object Assembly	Figural		Figural	
Freedom from Distractibility				
Arithmetic	Semantic	Symbolic		
Digit Span		Symbolic		
Processing Speed				
Coding A			Figural	Figural
Coding B			Symbolic	Symbolic
Symbol Search			Figural	Figural

Note. Subtests are listed according to Guilford's (1967) Original Structure of Intellect Model.

≡ Rapid Reference

4.8 Classification of WPPSI-R and WISC-III Subtests According to Bannatyne's Model

Verbal Conceptualization Ability	Spatial Ability	Sequential Ability	Acquired Knowledge
WISC-III Subtests			
Similarities	Picture Completion	Arithmetic	Information
Vocabulary	Block Design	Digit Span	Arithmetic
Comprehension	Object Assembly	Coding	Vocabulary
WPPSI-R Subtests			
Similarities	Picture Completion	Arithmetic	Information
Vocabulary	Block Design	Sentences	Arithmetic
Comprehension	Object Assembly	Animal Pegs	Vocabulary
	Geometric Design		
	Mazes		

Clinical Considerations

In addition to understanding the psychometric aspects of the subtests and the shared abilities underlying the subtests, one must consider clinical factors when interpreting the subtests. The analysis that follows presents clinical considerations for each subtest that are based on clinical experience and the literature, including the following sources: Kamphaus (1993), Kaufman (1990a, 1994a), Reitan and Wolfson (1992), Sattler (1988, 1992), and Zimmerman and Woo-Sam (1973). Although a wide variety of clinical considerations are provided, these suggestions are merely hypotheses. To best interpret any particular piece of clinical evidence, each psychologist must use his or her own theoretical framework.

It is important to note that there is little empirical validation for the diverse clinical hypotheses suggested by many clinicians. Instead, clinical interpretation is a complex process, not one in which individual pieces of data can be considered in isolation. Because each clinician goes through a somewhat idiosyncratic process in making inferences about data, even the best clinicians may disagree on hypotheses generated from any particular piece of clinical data (Lipsitz, Dworkin, & Erlenmeyer-Kimling, 1993).

SUBTEST-BY-SUBTEST ANALYSIS

Abilities with an asterisk (*) denote those that are unique to the particular subtest being discussed.

WPPSI-R AND WISC-III VERBAL SUBTESTS

Information: Abilities Shared With Other Subtests

Input

auditory perception of complex verbal stimuli (understanding questions)
simple verbal directions (WPPSI-R Information items 1–6)
visual-motor channel (WPPSI-R Information items 1–6)
visual perception of complete meaningful stimuli (WPPSI-R Information items 1–6)

Integration/Storage

Acquired Knowledge (Bannatyne)
Crystallized Intelligence—Gc (Horn)
culture-loaded knowledge
fund of information
long-term memory
memory (primarily), mostly of semantic stimuli (Guilford)
Verbal Comprehension (factor index)
*range of general factual knowledge

Output

simple vocal response
visual-motor coordination (WPPSI-R Information items 1–6)

Information: Influences Affecting Subtest Scores

- alertness to the environment
- cultural opportunities at home

- foreign language background
- intellectual curiosity and striving
- interests
- outside reading
- richness of early environment
- school learning

Information: Clinical Considerations

- Items are generally nonthreatening and emotionally neutral.
- Rationalizations and excuses may be produced in response to this test (e.g., "That isn't important.").
- Effortless, automatic responding facilitates good performance. Children with chronic anxiety may suffer early failures and depressed , scores in general.
- Retrieval difficulties may be revealed on this test when success on harder items is preceded by failure on easy items.
- Alertness to the environment, in addition to formal schooling, constitute the source of most of the factual knowledge needed for success.
- Unnecessary detail and trivial responses may suggest obsessiveness.
- Intellectual ambitiousness may be reflected in high scores on this subtest, which are often coupled with high scores on Vocabulary.
- A perfectionistic approach may be evident when no response is preferred to an imperfect answer.
- A child's pattern of responses may be indicative of cultural background. For example, questions pertaining to the president of the United States or other famous leaders in America may pose more difficulty than those pertaining to general geography or science for individuals who are not originally from the United States.
- Bizarre or odd responses can shed light on an individual's mental state. For example, responses such as "There are 1,000 days in a week," or "George Washington is the guy I saw at the supermarket" may indicate a need to further explore mental functioning or to ask whether the child is taking the test seriously.
- Problems with numbers may cause substantially lower scores for younger and lower functioning children. On the WISC-III, numbers or number concepts are measured by items 2, 3, 8, 9, 10, 11, 21, and 29.

On the WPPSI-R, numbers or number concepts are measured by items 8, 15, 23, and 24.

Comprehension: Abilities Shared With Other Subtests

Input
   auditory perception of simple verbal stimuli (understanding questions)
Integration/Storage
   cognition of semantic stimuli (Guilford)
   common sense (cause-effect relationships)
   Crystallized Intelligence—Gc (Horn)
   culture-loaded knowledge
   language development
   reasoning (verbal)
   social judgment (social intelligence)
   Verbal Comprehension (WISC-III factor index)
   Verbal Conceptualization (Bannatyne)
   *demonstration of practical information
   *evaluation and use of past experiences
   *knowledge of conventional standards of behavior
Output
   verbal expression

Comprehension: Influences Affecting Subtest Scores

- cultural opportunities at home
- development of conscience or moral sense
- flexibility (ability to shift from social reasoning to proverb items, and ability to give a "second reason")
- negativism ("We shouldn't have to pay taxes.")
- overly concrete thinking

Comprehension: Clinical Considerations

- A stable and emotionally balanced attitude and orientation are necessary for success on this subtest. Any type of maladjustment may lower scores.
- A high score on Comprehension alone is not enough evidence to interpret strong social adjustment. Corroborating evidence must be obtained from clinical observations, background information, or adaptive behavior inventories.

- Responses offer clues about a disturbed individual's social-adaptive functioning in practical, social situations, but examiners should be cautious about generalizing from single-issue questions to the complexities of the real world.
- The items on the WPPSI-R and many of those on the WISC-III do not have moral implications or call on social judgment; rather, they are objective and detached from emotion (e.g., wearing shoes, keeping milk in the refrigerator, turning off lights, knowing the advantages of paperback books). However, some WISC-III items do call on some type of social judgment (e.g., items 1, 2, 4, 5, 8, 16, and 18). These WISC-III Comprehension questions involve such issues as finding a wallet or keeping a promise. Because these items occur mostly during the beginning of the test and are among the easiest, they are of more clinical value for younger and lower functioning children. Children above approximately age 9 typically give automatic, socially appropriate responses to these items. Thus for many children the WISC-III is not an emotional, morally challenging task but rather a "can you explain this" task.
- When responses appear overlearned, stereotypical, or "parroted," test the limits to determine level of real understanding and reasoning ability.
- Like responses to Similarities and Vocabulary, responses to Comprehension may vary in their degree of abstractness. Ability to think in abstract terms (*seatbelts* are "for safety") is distinct from more concrete types of responses (*seatbelts* keep you "from breaking your neck").
- Some Comprehension items require further questioning if only one response is given and all questions allow querying for clarification of responses. Analyze how individuals respond to follow-up questioning. Do they become defensive? Are they inflexible and unable to move beyond their original response? Clinically relevant bits of information can be gleaned from observing the difference between someone who is spontaneously able to produce two concise responses and someone who needs constant structure and prodding.

Arithmetic: Abilities Shared With Other Subtests

Input

> auditory perception of complex verbal stimuli (understanding questions)
> mental alertness

simple verbal directions (WPPSI-R Arithmetic items 1–7)

visual-motor channel (WPPSI-R Arithmetic items 1–7; WISC-III items 1–5)

visual perception of complete meaningful stimuli (WPPSI-R Arithmetic items 1–7; WISC-III items 1–5)

Integration/Storage

Acquired Knowledge (Bannatyne)

cognition of semantic stimuli (Guilford)

facility with numbers

figural evaluation (Guilford) (WPPSI-R Arithmetic items 1–7)

Fluid Intelligence—Gf (Horn)

Freedom from Distractibility (WISC-III factor index)

long-term memory

memory of symbolic stimuli (Guilford)

reasoning (numerical)

Sequential (Bannatyne)

sequential processing

Short-Term Acquisition and Retrieval—SAR (Horn)

speed of mental processing

Verbal Comprehension

*computational skill

*quantitative reasoning

Output

simple vocal

visual-motor coordination (WPPSI-R Arithmetic items 1–7; WISC-III items 1–4)

Arithmetic: Influences Affecting Subtest Scores

- anxiety
- attention span
- attention-deficit hyperactivity disorder
- concentration
- distractibility
- hearing difficulties
- learning disabilities
- school learning
- working under time pressure

Arithmetic: Clinical Considerations

- Inferring the cause of the error is useful: whether it was computational, reasoning, failure to attend, or misunderstanding the meaning of a question. For example, in response to a question about the number of hours it takes to walk 5 miles at the rate of ½ mile per hour, the answer "7" reflects a computational error, whereas "30" reflects a reasoning error and "5,000" is bizarre. A bizarre response may suggest inattention, lack of comprehension, or a thought disorder. Such an unusual response on Arithmetic should be explored further.

- Testing the limits by removing the time limit and allowing paper and pencil is often helpful in assessing the effects of anxiety and concentration on test performance.

- For older retarded children the subtest measures a portion of adaptive functioning, as items involve money, counting, and real-life situations.

- Children who have struggled with mathematics in school may become anxious when asked to respond to school-like Arithmetic questions. Their response to the anxiety and frustration may be clinically interesting: Can they compose themselves? Do they respond with hostility? Do they reject the test?

- It is important to consider when individuals are able to correctly respond to the questions but fail to do so within the time limits. Those who tend to be reflective, compulsive, obsessive, or neurologically impaired may exhibit this pattern of responding.

- Watch for signs of trying to compensate for the auditory nature or memory requirements of the task (e.g., finger writing on the table, or asking for a pencil and paper or a calculator).

- What is required for success on the WPPSI-R and WISC-III Arithmetic subtests varies across items. For example, the first seven WPPSI-R items require knowledge of quantitative concepts such as *tallest*, *most*, or *biggest*. Numeric knowledge demonstrated via counting is required for WPPSI-R items 8–11 and WISC-III items 1–2. The remaining WPPSI-R items require simple mathematical computations (that are closely aligned to counting), as do items 3–11 of the WISC-III. Most of the remaining WISC-III items require good computational skills and arithmetic reasoning ability.

Vocabulary: Abilities Shared With Other Subtests

Input

    auditory perception of simple verbal stimuli (understanding single words)

    visual perception of complete meaningful stimuli (WPPSI-R Vocabulary items 1–3)

Integration/Storage

    Acquired Knowledge (Bannatyne)

    cognition of semantic stimuli (Guilford)

    Crystallized Intelligence—Gc (Horn)

    degree of abstract thinking

    fund of information

    language development

    learning ability

    long-term memory

    Verbal Comprehension (WISC-III factor index)

    verbal concept formation

    Verbal Conceptualization (Bannatyne)

    *word (lexical) knowledge

Output

    simple vocal expression (WPPSI-R Vocabulary items 1–3)

    verbal expression

Vocabulary: Influences Affecting Subtest Scores

- cultural opportunities at home
- foreign language experience
- intellectual curiosity and striving
- interests
- outside reading
- richness of early environment
- school learning *Poor?*

Vocabulary: Clinical Considerations

- Repression may lead to poor performance by pushing out of consciousness any word meanings that are even mildly conflict-laden. Repression may also impair the acquisition of new word meanings as well as the recall of specific words on the Vocabulary subtest.
- As in the Information subtest, high scores relative to other Verbal

subtests may reflect intellectual ambitiousness or stress for achievement in the child's life.

- The content presented in children's responses lends itself to analysis regarding the child's fears, guilt, preoccupations, feelings, interests, background, cultural milieu, bizarre thought processes, perseveration, and "clang" associations (*hat-cat, thief-leaf*). Themes in response content may occur also in conjunction with Comprehension or Similarities, as well as in spontaneous conversation during the assessment.
- Perseveration is sometimes evidenced when individuals give the same opening line for each response ("*Confide,* that's a hard one to define . . .").
- Responses that are overlearned, almost booklike definitions should be distinguished from those that appear to be driven by intellectual vigor and personalization of the responses with current experiences.
- The open-ended nature of the Vocabulary responses makes it possible to glean information about an individual's verbal fluency, not just word knowledge. Some words are easily defined by one-word synonyms, but certain individuals may give excessive verbiage in their response or may respond in a roundabout manner.
- Hearing difficulties may become apparent for those individuals who are illiterate (cannot read the visually presented word list) or for those who only focus on the auditory stimuli. Because the words are presented in isolation, there is no context by which to help understand the word.
- Level of abstract thinking can also be evaluated in Vocabulary items. Some responses may be abstract (*affliction* is "a handicap") or more concrete (*seclude* is "locking yourself in the closet").

SIMILARITIES: Abilities Shared With Other Subtests

Input

auditory perception of simple verbal stimuli (understanding simple words)

visual perception of complete meaningful stimuli (WPPSI-R Similarities items 1–6)

Integration/Storage

cognition of semantic stimuli (Guilford)

Crystallized Intelligence—Gc (Horn)

degree of abstract thinking

distinguishing essential from nonessential details
figural evaluation (Guilford) (WPPSI-R Similarities items 1–6)
Fluid Intelligence—Gf (Horn)
language development
reasoning (verbal)
Verbal Comprehension (WISC-III factor index)
verbal concept formation
Verbal Conceptualization (Bannatyne)
*logical abstractive (categorical) thinking
Output
verbal expression
visual-motor coordination (WPPSI-R Similarities items 1–6)

Similarities: Influences Affecting Subtest Scores

- flexibility
- interests
- negativism ("They're not alike.")
- outside reading
- overly concrete thinking

Similarities: Clinical Considerations

- Degree of abstractness should be evaluated; responses may be *abstract* (*table* and *chair* are "furniture"), *concrete* (*cat* and *dog* "have paws"), or *functional* (*statue* and *painting* "provide decoration").
- Clinically rich information can be gleaned from the nature of the verbal response: Overelaboration, overly general responses, overly inclusive responses, or self-references should be noted. Overelaboration may suggest obsessiveness. Overly inclusive responses may suggest a thought disorder. Self-references are unusual during Similarities and may be indicative of personal preoccupation.
- Obsessive children may provide responses that vary in quality by embedding a 2-point response among 1- or 0-point responses. This may lead to unusually high scores, as long as no response spoils the answer.
- The pattern of responses should be examined. A child who earns a raw score by accumulating several 1-point responses may differ substantially in potential from a child who earns the same raw score

with some 2-point and 0-point responses. The individual who mixes the 2s and 0s probably has a greater capacity for excellent performance.

- Creativity may be exhibited in trying to come up with the relationship between two concepts. Sometimes visual imagery may be used. The creativity doesn't invariably mean a wrong response (as in Comprehension).
- Correct responses on the easier items may simply reflect overlearned, everyday associations rather than true abstract thought.
- Children who miss the first item administered provide the opportunity to see how they benefit from feedback. The examiner gives an example of a correct answer if the child doesn't provide a perfect answer to the first item administered. Children who catch on quickly to these prompts demonstrate flexibility and adaptability. On the other hand, rigidity may be evident if the child continues to insist that certain pairs are "not alike."
- Formal learning is less emphasized than "new problem solving" (Horn's fluid classification). The child's task is to relate to verbal concepts, but the individual concepts tend to be simple and well known (*table-chair*).

WPPSI-R VERBAL SUBTESTS ONLY

Sentences: Abilities Shared With Other Subtests
Input
    auditory perception of complex stimuli (understanding sentences)
    auditory-vocal channel
    encode information for processing
    understanding words
Integration/Storage
    language development
    memory of semantic stimuli (Guilford)
    semantic content
    Sequential (Bannatyne)
    sequential processing
    Short-Term Acquisition and Retrieval (Horn)
    short-term memory (auditory)
    Verbal Conceptualization

verbal knowledge
*immediate rote recall of meaningful stimuli
Output
simple vocal response

Sentences: Influences Affecting Subtest Scores

- anxiety
- attention-deficit hyperactivity disorder
- attention span
- concentration
- distractibility
- hearing difficulties
- learning disabilities

Sentences: Clinical Considerations

- The quality of a child's response may be informative.
- Note whether any words are added and whether there is a pattern in the words added. Some children perseverate and add the same words to multiple sentences (e.g., having the subject of each sentence be "mommy").
- Analyze where in the sentence errors are made. Missing words at the beginning, versus middle or end, may indicate primacy or recency effects.
- Note whether sentences are completely missed (e.g., "I don't know.") or whether part of the sentence is missing. Missing an entire sentence may be more indicative of serious attention or memory problems.
- Impulsivity may be evident if a child is unable to wait until the examiner has completely read the sentence before beginning to repeat it.
- Tangential thoughts may be elicited by some of the sentences. For example, a child may respond by saying "I have a blue coat" when the sentence to repeat was "Mary had a red coat." This could indicate that the child has become distracted or lost track of what the task was, or he may be "testing the limits" of the examiner.

WISC-III VERBAL SUBTESTS ONLY

Digit Span: Abilities Shared With Other Subtests
Input
auditory perception of simple stimuli (understanding single words)
understanding words

Integration/Storage
   encoding information for further cognitive processing (Digits Backward)
   facility with numbers
   Freedom from Distractibility (WISC-III factor index)
   memory of symbolic stimuli (Guilford)
   Sequential (Bannatyne)
   sequential processing
   Short-Term Acquisition and Retrieval (Horn)
   short-term memory (auditory)
   *immediate rote recall
Output
   simple vocal

Digit Span: Influences Affecting Subtest Scores
- ability to receive stimuli passively
- anxiety
- attention-deficit hyperactivity disorder (ADHD)
- attention span
- distractibility
- flexibility (when stitching from forward to backward span)
- hearing difficulties
- learning disabilities
- negativism (refusal to try to reverse digits, to exert effort until the more challenging Digits Backward series, or to take a "meaningless" task)

Digit Span: Clinical Considerations
- Recording responses will help to discern whether failure is due to poor sequential ability (putting right numbers in wrong order) or due to poor rote memory (forgetting digits but otherwise correctly repeating the series). Problems with inattention, distractibility, or anxiety may be evident in responses that bear little relationship to the actual stimuli.
- After the task, testing the limits and questioning whether any strategy was employed can help to differentiate among poor strategy generation (e.g., "chunking"), low motivation, anxiety, distractibility, sequencing problems, and memory problems.
- Digits Backward, which requires mental manipulation or visualization of the numbers, is more impacted by number ability than is Digits For-

ward. Thus children who have better number ability may perform better on Digits Backward.

- The average forward span stays consistent across the age span. From ages 6 to 8 the typical span length is five digits, and for ages 9 to 16 the typical span length is six digits. A more prominent developmental trend is evident on Digits Backward: Children ages 6 to 8 have an average three-digit span, ages 9 to 12 have an average four-digit span, and ages 13 to 16 have an average five-digit span.
- Typically children produce forward spans that are two digits longer than backward spans. Longer backward than forward spans occur relatively rarely within the normal population of children and are therefore noteworthy. One explanation for a longer backward span is that children may find it to be more challenging and worthy of sustaining effort; another is that children may have better skill at representational (high level) tasks than at automatic (overlearned) tasks such as Digits Forward.
- Less than ideal testing conditions (visual or auditory distractions) may adversely affect performance on this subtest, and hearing impairment may make a child vulnerable to failure.
- Repeating digits seems to be more impaired by state anxiety (or test anxiety) than by chronic (trait) anxiety.
- Impulsivity may be evident when children begin to respond before the examiner has completed the series of digits or when the child repeats the digits very rapidly.
- Learning ability may be evident when children make errors on the first trial but then pass the second trial. Look for this pattern in other subtests as well (Block Design, Coding, Symbol Search).

WPPSI-R AND WISC-III PERFORMANCE SUBTESTS

Object Assembly: Abilities Shared With Other Subtests

Input
    simple verbal directions
    visual-motor channel
    visual perception of meaningful stimuli (people-things)

Integration/Storage
    ability to benefit from sensory-motor feedback
    anticipation of relationships among parts

cognition and evaluation of figural stimuli (Guilford)

Fluid Intelligence—Gf (Horn)

holistic (right-brain) processing

Perceptual Organization (WISC-III factor index)

planning ability

reasoning (nonverbal)

simultaneous processing

Spatial (Bannatyne)

speed of mental processing

synthesis (part-whole relationships)

trial-and-error learning

Visual Processing—Gv (Horn)

*ability to benefit from sensory-motor feedback

*anticipation of relationships among the parts

Output

Broad Speediness—Gs (Horn)

visual-motor coordination

Object Assembly: Influences Affecting Subtest Scores

- ability to respond when uncertain
- cognitive style (field dependence–field independence)
- experience with puzzles
- flexibility
- persistence
- visual-perceptual problems
- working under time pressure

Object Assembly: Clinical Considerations

- For preschool-age children, this test typically serves as a good icebreaker as it is the first one administered on the WPPSI-R. Usually children find it nonthreatening and enjoyable.
- Because of the bonus points awarded for quick performance, reflectivity or obsessive concern with detail can lower scores substantially. On the WISC-III, perfect performance that earns no bonus points yields a scaled score of 11 for a 10-year-old, a scaled score of 9 for a 12-year-old, and a scaled score of 7 for a 16-year-old. On the WPPSI-R, the bonus points have the greatest impact on the oldest age groups. Perfect

performance with no bonus points earned on the WPPSI-R is equivalent to a scaled score of 6 for a 7-year-old, a scaled score of 7 for a 6-year-old, and a scaled score of 9 for a 5½-year-old.

- How children manipulate the puzzle pieces is informative. Problem-solving approach may be noted: trial-and-error versus a systematic and insightful attack, impulsive versus reflective cognitive style, and carelessness versus cautiousness. Rigidity or perseveration (trying repeatedly to put the same puzzle piece in the same wrong place) may be evident. Motor coordination, concentration, persistence, and speed of processing may all be inferred from behaviors and performance on this subtest.
- Also of interest is *when* during the problem-solving process the child realizes what the object is that he or she is trying to assemble on the last three items. Some children know what it is immediately after being shown the disassembled object; others are not sure until the figure has been put together.
- Visual-perceptual problems may be indicated if children cannot determine what they are assembling. Similarly, input problems may be present if objects are constructed upside down or at an angle.
- Integration problems are demonstrated when separate groups of pieces are assembled but the individual cannot get the "whole." At times individuals insist that a piece is missing from the puzzle when they cannot completely integrate the given pieces.
- Output or coordination problems are evident when the child aligns the puzzle pieces correctly but too far apart or inadvertently misaligns a piece or two while adding pieces to complete the puzzle.
- Children who try to peek behind the screen while the examiner is arranging the puzzle pieces may be revealing impulsivity, insecurity, or low moral development, or they may be "testing the limits" of the examiner.
- The concrete approaches of some brain-damaged patients may not affect Object Assembly performance (because of the construction of meaningful pictures), although the approaches are likely to impair Block Design performance. However, patients with right posterior cortex damage may have difficulty due to the visual-spatial concepts in the Object Assembly task.

Block Design: Abilities Shared With Other Subtests

Input

   auditory perception of complex verbal stimuli (following directions)

   visual-motor channel

   visual perception of abstract stimuli (designs-symbols)

Integration/Storage

   cognition and evaluation of figural stimuli (Guilford)

   Fluid Intelligence—Gf (Horn)

   integrated brain functioning (analytic and synthetic)

   Perceptual Organization (WISC-III factor index)

   planning

   reproduction of models

   simultaneous processing

   Spatial (Bannatyne)

   spatial visualization

   speed of mental processing

   synthesis (part-whole relationships)

   trial-and-error learning

   Visual Processing—Gv (Horn)

   *analysis of whole into component parts (analytic strategies)

   *nonverbal concept formation

Output

   visual-motor coordination

Block Design: Influences Affecting Subtest Scores

- cognitive style (field dependence–field independence)
- flexibility
- visual-perceptual problems
- working under time pressure

Block Design: Clinical Considerations

- Scores may be substantially lowered by obsessive concern with detail or reflectivity. Bonus points can be earned for quick, perfect performance (a total of 27 raw score bonus points may be earned). On average, perfect performance with no bonus points is only equivalent to a scaled score of 11.

- Visual-perceptual problems are often apparent on this subtest. If a low score occurs, the input of the visual material may be related to inaccurate perception rather than to problem-solving ability or motor output. Testing the limits can help to determine whether the child is having perceptual difficulties or other problems.
- Scores should be interpreted in light of problem-solving approaches that were observed. Some children use a trial-and-error approach, some a systematic and planned approach. Factors such as rigidity, perseveration, speed of mental processing, carelessness, self-concept, cautiousness, and ability to benefit from feedback impact the test performance.
- Some individuals may have little motivation to try and therefore give up easily; others learn as they take the test and sometimes "catch on" just when they discontinue. In such cases, testing the limits by administering further items can be of great clinical value (although any extra items administered beyond the discontinue rule cannot be counted in the score).
- Performance on this test is impacted by any kind of cerebral brain damage (especially right hemisphere). Lesions to the posterior region of the right hemisphere, especially the parietal lobes, can strongly impact performance on Block Design.

Picture Completion: Abilities Shared With Other Subtests

Input
    simple verbal directions
    visual-motor channel
    visual perception of meaningful stimuli (people-things)

Integration/Storage
    cognition and evaluation of figural stimuli (Guilford)
    distinguishing essential from nonessential details
    holistic (right-brain) processing
    Perceptual Organization (WISC-III factor index)
    simultaneous processing
    Spatial (Bannatyne)
    Visual Intelligence—Gv (Horn)
    visual organization without essential motor activity
    *visual recognition without essential motor activity

Output
simple motor or vocal (pointing or one-word response)

Picture Completion: Influences Affecting Subtest Scores
- ability to respond when uncertain
- alertness to the environment
- cognitive style (field dependence–field independence)
- concentration
- negativism ("Nothing is missing.")
- working under time pressure

Picture Completion: Clinical Considerations
- This test typically serves as a good icebreaker, as it is the first one administered on the WISC-III. Usually children find it nonthreatening and enjoyable.
- Although this subtest is timed, usually the WISC-III 20-second limit and the WPPSI-R 30-second limit provide ample time for children who are neither mentally retarded nor neurologically impaired. Implusivity may be indicated by extremely quick, incorrect responses. Failure to respond within the limit is of potential diagnostic value, as even reflective children typically respond within the limit.
- Verbal responses are far more common than nonverbal responses on this Performance task, especially because the directions explicitly say "TELL me what is missing." Although nonverbal responses are also considered correct, the frequency of such responses should be evaluated and may indicate word retrieval problems. Verbal responses that are imprecise or vague may also indicate word retrieval problems. In preschool-age children, nonverbal or vague verbal responses may occur frequently.
- Negativity or hostility may be noted in persistent "Nothing is missing" responses.
- Obsessiveness or concentration problems may be evident in responses that are focused on trivial details of a picture (i.e., the "No. 2" on the pencil). Similarly, confabulatory responses or responses indicating that something not in the picture is missing (e.g., the legs of the man who is missing the watchband) are of clinical interest. Giving trivial or

confabulatory responses several times during the subtest is of potential diagnostic interest, especially because examiners are instructed to redirect individuals the first time they give a trivial or confabulatory response.

- This task appears to be relatively resilient to the impact of brain damage. It is not able to consistently or reliably indicate right cerebral damage, which may be related to the nature of verbal responding by most children, and "it is entirely possible that the nature of the task is not as heavily demanding of adequate brain functions as are some of the other subtests" (Reitan & Wolfson, 1992, p. 107).

WPPSI-R Performance Subtests Only

Animal Pegs: Abilities Shared With Other Subtests

Input
   complex verbal directions
   encode information for processing
   visual perception of complete meaningful stimuli
   visual-motor channel

Integration/Storage
   convergent production (Guilford)
   figural evaluation (Guilford)
   learning ability
   memory of figural stimuli (Guilford)
   planning ability
   Sequential (Bannatyne)
   sequential processing
   Short-Term Acquisition and Retrieval (Horn)
   short-term memory (visual)
   visual sequencing
   *immediate rote recall
   *Processing Speed—Gs (Horn)

Output
   visual-motor coordination

Animal Pegs: Influences Affecting Subtest Scores

- anxiety
- attention-deficit hyperactivity disorder

- attention span
- concentration
- distractibility
- learning disabilities
- persistence
- visual-perceptual problems
- working under time pressure

Animal Pegs: Clinical Considerations

- Watch how the child manipulates the colored pegs. Level of finger and manual dexterity may impact performance.
- Speed of responding is rewarded during this task (e.g., a perfect score obtained in 9 seconds obtains 70 raw score points, but a perfect score obtained in 5 minutes earns only 12 raw score points).
- Changes in rate of responding during the subtest may be related to motivation, distraction, fatigue, boredom, and so forth. Thus it is a good idea to note the number of pegs placed during each of the 30-second intervals during the child's performance.
- You must rule out visual or motor impairment before interpreting a low score.
- Astute observation is key to interpreting scores on this subtest. Include the following in your interpretation of the score: coordination (manipulation of pegs), attention/concentration, distractibility, motivation level, visual-perceptual problems, perseveration (placing the same color peg for a whole line), or anxiety.
- Some children appear to have to search for each animal in the row of stimulus pairs, seemingly unaware that the order of animals in the top stimulus row is not changing; this behavior could be indicative of sequencing problems.
- Short-term visual memory deficits may be evident if children keep referring back to the "key" before deciding which peg goes with which animal (or these children may be insecure). Children who have memorized several animal-color pairs are likely to have a good visual memory (if they aren't making errors in their response).
- You can use testing-the-limits procedures to figure out why a child earned a particular score, whether it be due to memory ability or pure psychomotor speed. After the subtest is completely over you can

remove all the pegs from the peg board and ask the child to fill in the top row of pegs from memory. Then, to see how quickly a child is able to fill in the peg board, ask the child to work as quickly as he or she can to fill up each of the holes in the board, disregarding the colors (time how long it takes the child to fill as many holes as were completed during the task itself).

Geometric Design: Abilities Shared With Other Subtests
Input
  simple verbal directions
  visual-motor channel
  visual perception of abstract stimuli
Integration / Storage
  cognition (Guilford) (Geometric Design items 1–7)
  convergent production (Guilford)
  figural cognition (Guilford) (Geometric Design items 1–7)
  figural evaluation (Guilford) (Geometric Design items 1–7)
  holistic (right-brain) processing
  planning ability
  reproduction of models
  simultaneous processing
  Spatial (Bannatyne)
  spatial visualization
  synthesis
  Visual Processing—Gv (Horn)
  *reproduction of abstract geometric figures
Output
  *finger dexterity
  visual-motor coordination (Geometric Design items 8–16)
  visual organization (Geometric Design items 1–7)

Geometric Design: Influences Affecting Subtest Scores
  • cognitive style (field dependence–field independence)
  • flexibility
  • learning disabilities
  • motivation level
  • negativism

- obsessive concern with accuracy and detail
- persistence
- visual-perceptual problems

Geometric Design: Clinical Considerations

- The first seven WPPSI-R Geometric Design items require visual recognition and discrimination, whereas the last nine items require visual-motor coordination. Observe any marked differences in level of anxiety, attention, or other behavioral changes between these two halves of the subtest.
- Impulsivity may be noted on the perceptual recognition items if a child has not carefully examined all four possible choices. On the visual-motor part of the task, impulsivity may be noted if a child dives into drawing without carefully examining the model and carelessly makes errors.
- Level of development of fine-motor ability may be apparent during the visual-motor portion of this task. Note how the child grasps the pencil, whether there is a tremor, the quality of lines drawn, and so on.
- Note whether the child has more difficulties with certain types of figures (e.g., those that require integration of shapes, those with multiple angles, those with curves, those that may be rotely learned like a circle or square, or those that are more novel like the hexagonal figure).
- Some children may attempt to utilize verbal mediation (e.g., they may talk their way through the task). For some it may be a helpful strategy; for others it may be disruptive.

Mazes: Abilities Shared With Other Subtests

(*Note.* Although Mazes is also included in the WISC-III battery, we recommend not to give or integrate it. See the discussion under Mazes on pages 47–49 of Chapter 2.)

Input
　complex verbal directions
　visual-motor channel
　visual perception of abstract stimuli

Integration/Storage
　figural cognition (Guilford)
　figural evaluation (Guilford)

holistic (right-brain) processing
planning ability
simultaneous processing
Spatial (Bannatyne)
spatial visualization
trial-and-error learning
Visual Processing—Gv (Horn)
*spatial scanning
Output
visual-motor coordination

Mazes: Influences Affecting Subtest Scores
- cognitive style (field dependence–field independence)
- concentration
- distractibility
- flexibility
- motivation level
- obsessive concern with accuracy and detail
- persistence
- visual-perceptual problems
- working under time pressure

Mazes: Clinical Considerations
- Note the speed at which the child approaches the mazes. Young children may not appear to understand or care that they are being timed. Impulsive children may work very quickly without spending time on planning before they move.
- Signs of poor visual-motor coordination may be apparent in how the child holds and manipulates the pencil. Look for a tremor or an awkward grip on the pencil.
- Note whether the child appears to realize that he or she has made mistakes.
- You can test the limits after the subtest has been administered by going back and asking a child about his or her errors (e.g., "Why did you go that way?"). This may give you insight into the child's planning ability or lack thereof.
- Watch to see if a child learns from maze to maze about how to avoid

blind alleys or other mistakes. Or does the child approach every maze as if it were a new maze, not learning from previous experience?
- Level of persistence and way of dealing with frustration may be noted on this task. Some children may give up midway through a maze, whereas others keep trying even after making multiple errors.

WISC-III PERFORMANCE SUBTESTS ONLY

CODING: Abilities Shared With Other Subtests
Input
    auditory perception of complex verbal stimuli (following directions)
    visual-motor channel
    visual perception of abstract stimuli (designs-symbols)
Integration/Storage
    convergent production and evaluation of figural stimuli (Coding A) (Guilford)
    convergent production and evaluation of symbolic stimuli (Coding B) (Guilford)
    encoding information for further cognitive processing
    facility with numbers (Coding B only)
    integrated brain functioning (verbal-sequential and visual-spatial)
    learning ability
    perceptual organization
    planning
    reproduction of models
    Sequential (Bannatyne)
    sequential processing
    short-term memory (visual)
    visual sequencing
Output
    clerical speed and accuracy
    paper-and-pencil skill
    Processing Speed (WISC-III factor index)
    processing speed (Horn)
    visual-motor coordination
    *psychomotor speed

Coding: Influences Affecting Subtest Scores

- anxiety
- attention-deficit hyperactivity disorder
- distractibility
- learning disabilities
- motivation level
- obsessive concern with accuracy and detail
- persistence
- visual-perceptual problems
- working under time pressure

Coding: Clinical Considerations

- Visual or motor impairment must be ruled out before interpreting a low score.
- Children who have demonstrated perfectionistic or compulsive tendencies prior to Coding should be told *during the sample items* that they need to copy the symbols legibly but not perfectly.
- Changes in rate of responding during the subtest may be related to motivation, distraction, fatigue, boredom, and so forth. Thus it is a good idea to note the number of symbols copied during each of the four 30-second periods within the 120-second limit.
- Astute observation is key to interpreting scores on this subtest. Include the following in your interpretation of the score: coordination (grip on the pencil), attention/concentration, distractibility, motivation level, visual-perceptual problems (rotating or distorting symbols), perfectionistic tendencies, perseveration (copying the same symbol for a whole line), or anxiety.
- Some individuals appear to have to search for each number in the row of stimulus pairs, seemingly unaware that the "5" is always right before the "6." This behavior could be indicative of sequencing problems.
- Short-term visual memory deficits may be evident if children keep referring back to the "key" before copying symbols (or these individuals may be insecure). Those who have memorized several pairs of symbols are likely to have good visual memory (if they aren't making errors in their response).

- Testing-the-limits procedures can be used to help to determine what caused a low Coding score. After the entire WISC-III has been administered, the following suggestions may be employed. To see how well a child can attend to, process, and remember the symbols and which numbers they are paired with, give the child a list of numbers and ask her to write down as many of the symbols as she can remember that correspond with the numbers. Additionally you can attempt to measure how many symbols can be recalled, regardless of the numbers, by asking the child to write as many of the different symbols as she can recall. Errors in rotation, distortion, or inversion may occur. A final procedure is to ask the child how she remembered which symbol went with which number. Sometimes children are able to articulate that they verbally encoded the symbols or used another sort of strategy. Thus performance on each of these testing-the-limits procedures will help decipher why a subject earned a particular score and whether it is due to memory ability or lack of an efficient problem-solving strategy.

SYMBOL SEARCH: Abilities Shared With Other Subtests
Input
    auditory perception of complex verbal stimuli (following directions)
    distinguishing essential from nonessential details
    visual-motor channel
    visual perception of abstract stimuli (designs-symbols)
Integration/Storage
    convergent production and evaluation of symbolic stimuli (Guilford)
    encoding information for further cognitive processing
    figural evaluation (Guilford)
    integrated brain functioning (verbal-sequential and visual-spatial)
    learning ability
    perceptual organization
    planning
    short-term memory (visual)
    spatial visualization
    speed of mental processing
    visual memory
    *speed of visual search

Output

Broad Speediness — Gs (Horn)

clerical speed and accuracy

paper-and-pencil skill

Processing Speed (WISC-III factor index)

visual-motor coordination

Symbol Search: Influences Affecting Subtest Scores

- anxiety
- attention-deficit hyperactivity disorder
- distractibility
- learning disabilities
- motivation level
- obsessive concern with accuracy and detail
- persistence
- visual-perceptual problems
- working under time pressure

Symbol Search: Clinical Considerations

- As on many of the Performance subtests, visual impairment should be ruled out before interpreting a low Symbol Search score.
- As noted in Chapter 2 of this book, it is important to be an astute observer during administration, as many observed behaviors can help in interpreting the Symbol Search score. Concentration, distractibility, obsessive concern with detail, impulsiveness, reflectivity, motivation level, visual-perceptual problems, or anxiety are just some of the factors that may be related to performance on Symbol Search.
- A learning curve may be present on this test. Children who begin to answer later items more quickly than earlier items may have developed a plan or strategy after completing the earlier items. To note whether speed of responding is in fact increasing, track how many items were answered during each of the four 30-second intervals during the subtest.
- As this is one of the last subtests administered, fatigue and boredom should be ruled out as possible explanations for a low score.
- Visual-memory ability can sometimes be inferred from observations on

this task. Some children may look at the target symbols only once and then find the response in the search group; others may look back and forth several times between the target and search groups before marking "yes" or "no." The repeated referring back and forth between the symbols may indicate poor visual memory (or insecurity).

- After the entire test has been administered, you may test the limits to help discern why certain responses were made. Point to some items answered correctly and some that were wrong, and ask the child to explain why he or she chose "yes" or "no."

Picture Arrangement: Abilities Shared With Other Subtests

Input
  auditory perception of complex verbal stimuli (following directions)
  distinguishing essential from nonessential details
  visual-motor channel
  visual perception of meaningful stimuli (people-things)

Integration/Storage
  common sense (cause-effect relationship)
  convergent production and evaluation of semantic stimuli (Guilford)
  Crystallized Intelligence—Gc (Horn)
  Fluid Intelligence—Gf (Horn)
  integrated brain functioning (verbal-sequential and visual spatial/synthetic)
  Perceptual Organization (WISC-III factor index)
  planning
  reasoning (nonverbal)
  simultaneous processing
  social judgment (social intelligence)
  speed of mental processing
  synthesis (part-whole relationships)
  visual organization without essential motor activity
  Visual Processing—Gv (Horn)
  visual sequencing
  *anticipation of consequences
  *temporal sequencing and time concepts

Ouput
  simple motor

Picture Arrangement: Influences Affecting Subtest Scores

- creativity
- cultural opportunities at home
- exposure to comic strips
- flexibility
- working under time pressure

Picture Arrangement: Clinical Considerations

- Clinical information about social adjustment may be gleaned from Picture Arrangement, but only with other corroborating evidence from a similar level of performance on Comprehension and from clinical observations, background information, or data from adaptive behavior scales.
- An impulsive or reflective cognitive style may be evident during this task. Impulsive children are likely to jump right in and begin moving the cards before examining the detail in the pictures. Reflective individuals, on the other hand, may carefully study the pictures before moving any of them. After the cards have been moved, impulsive individuals may begin to pick them up for you to begin the next item, whereas reflective children are more likely to continue to check their arrangements even after they appear to be done. These styles in solving the problems may also provide information about a trial-and-error versus insightful approach.
- Clinical information may be gathered about a child's thought processes by testing the limits. After the subtest has been completed the cards may be laid out in the order that they were arranged by the child, and then you may ask the child to verbalize the story. It is important *not* to ask for a story explanation during the subtest because it violates the norms and may inadvertently give the child a strategy for solving harder items.
- The drawings on the Picture Arrangement cards are detailed, requiring good visual perception. Therefore visual acuity and visual perception should be ruled out as possible reasons for a low score.
- Poor performance on some items may be related to cultural background, which may teach different interpretations of pictures that depict social situations.
- Children with thought disorders may struggle on this task because of its logical, time-dependent, and sequential nature.

- Children may attempt to test the limits of the examiner by looking at the letters and numbers on the back of the cards. This type of behavior may be interpreted as manipulative or antisocial if there is other supportive information.
- Feedback is provided for children on the first and second items. These provide an opportunity to observe children's learning ability and the degree to which they benefit from feedback. This information is especially valuable when assessing low-functioning children or those in the youngest age groups (6 to 7 years).
- Speed is very important in determining a child's Picture Arrangement score. Children age 12 who complete every item correctly but earn no bonus points for speed earn a scaled score of 8. At age 16 the maximum score with no bonus points is 6. In fact, when a factor analysis was done of the WISC-III subtests on a sample of 78 special education children, Picture Arrangement loaded with Coding and Symbol Search on the Processing Speed factor (Hishinuma & Yamakawa, 1993).

STEP-BY-STEP: HOW TO INTERPRET THE WPPSI-R PROFILE

The following section provides a systematic way to approach and interpret the WPPSI-R profile. Rather than suggesting a random look at scores that appear interesting, we provide a useful approach that leads you from the most global score to the most specific. This process enables you to make the most meaningful hypotheses about the child's abilities.

This section presents six steps for interpreting WPPSI-R profiles. Step 1 considers the most global scores. Steps 2 and 3 deal with the Verbal and Performance IQs and their discrepancy. Step 4 examines the subtest scatter. Steps 5 and 6 address strengths and weaknesses in the subtest profile. The practical meaningfulness of the IQs is examined throughout the steps. This method provides a recipe that can be followed like a cookbook, but you also have to know when to deviate from the recipe and use clinical information to reject empirical rules in favor of alternative interpretations of the data. To gain an in-depth understanding of each child's peaks and valleys of abilities, you must apply a combination of theory, clinical skill, and knowledge of the instrument.

Each step of interpretation of the WPPSI-R profile is explained in the following pages. We have developed a summary of these steps in a worksheet

Table 4.1   Emma K.'s WPPSI-R Profile

Scale	IQ	90% Confidence Interval	Percentile Rank
Verbal Scale	124	119–129	95
Performance Scale	105	98–111	63
Full Scale	116	111–121	86

Verbal Subtest	Scaled Score	Percentile Rank	Performance Subtest	Scaled Score	Percentile Rank
Information	12	75	Object Assembly	6	9
Comprehension	16	98	Geometric Design	12	75
Arithmetic	14	91	Block Design	9	37
Vocabulary	14	91	Mazes	11	63
Similarities	12	75	Picture Completion	16	98
Sentences	11	63	Animal Pegs	14	91

form (see the WPPSI-R Interpretive Worksheet in Appendix B). The illustrative samples of how to use the steps in the interpretive process utilize data from Emma K.'s profile (see Table 4.1). Emma is a 3-year, 3-month-old girl who was referred for assessment due to her parents' concern about how to best help her develop her cognitive strengths. All the illustrative cases presented in this book have had the identifying information changed to protect the confidentiality of the clients. This child's profile is also presented in the last chapter of this book to demonstrate how the empirical framework is translated into understanding actual clinical cases.

Step 1: Interpret WPPSI-R Full Scale IQ

The WPPSI-R Full Scale IQ is the most reliable score obtained on the test. It has a mean split-half coefficient of .96 and a stability coefficient of .91. The standard error of measurement at each of the nine age levels is about 3 points. Due to these strong psychometric qualities, the Full Scale IQ should be considered first in interpretation of the profile. Also important are the confidence interval (Table 4.2), percentile ranks (Wechsler, 1989, p. 124), and descriptive

Table 4.2   Confidence Intervals for WPPSI-R Scales

Age Level	Performance Scale IQ		Verbal Scale IQ		Full Scale IQ	
	90% confidence level	95% confidence level	90% confidence level	95% confidence level	90% confidence level	95% confidence level
2y, 11m, 16d through 3y, 5m, 15d	±7	±8	±5	±6	±5	±6
3y, 5m, 16d through 3y, 11m, 15d	±7	±8	±5	±6	±5	±6
3y, 11m, 16d through 4y, 5m, 15d	±7	±8	±5	±6	±5	±6
4y, 5m, 16d through 4y, 11m, 15d	±7	±8	±5	±6	±5	±6
4y, 11m, 16d through 5y, 5m, 15d	±7	±9	±5	±7	±5	±6
5y, 5m, 16d through 5y, 11m, 15d	±8	±9	±6	±7	±5	±6
5y, 11m, 16d through 6y, 5m, 15d	±7	±9	±6	±7	±5	±6
6y, 5m, 16d through 6y, 11m, 16d	±8	±9	±7	±8	±7	±7
6y, 11m, 16d through 7y, 3m, 15d	±8	±10	±8	±10	±6	±8

≡ Rapid Reference

4.9 WPPSI-R Interpretive Worksheet, Step 1: Interpret the Full Scale IQ

Scale	IQ	Confidence Interval (90%) or 95% (circle one)	Percentile Rank	Descriptive Category
Full Scale	116	111—121	86	High Average–Superior
Performance	105	99—111	63	Average–High Average
Verbal	124	119—129	95	High Average–Superior

⇩

category (Wechsler, 1989, p. 125). As with the confidence interval, we encourage examiners to identify the descriptive category range in which a child is functioning. For example, if a child's Full Scale IQ is 108 and the confidence interval is 104 to 112, then the child is functioning in the Average to High Average level of intelligence. Using the range of ability helps facilitate accurate communication between professionals and laypeople, and it avoids pigeonholing the child as well. This signals that there is error obtained with the score, which puts the score in perspective. Rapid Reference 4.9 shows a completed example of Step 1 of the WPPSI-R Interpretive Worksheet.

We encourage examiners to look at the Full Scale IQ first, but the interpretive process certainly does not stop there. In fact, in progressing through the rest of the steps examiners may find that the Full Scale IQ score is meaningless and is therefore rendered uninterpretable. If there are large differences between the Verbal and Performance IQs or too much scatter among the subtests, then the importance of the Full Scale IQ is diminished. Additional factors such as the child's fatigue, anxiety, or cultural background may also affect the interpretability of the Full Scale IQ.

A child's abilities can rarely be captured accurately via one number (or even three IQ values). Thus it is inappropriate to attribute too much weight to the Full Scale IQ alone. To understand the complex nature of cognitive functioning you must consider many different abilities rather than just looking at a summary of those abilities, as is done with the Full Scale IQ.

Step 2: Is the WPPSI-R Verbal IQ Versus Performance IQ Discrepancy Significant?

One level below the Full Scale IQ is the Performance and Verbal IQs. In this step of WPPSI-R interpretation, the size of the difference between the Performance IQ and Verbal IQ should be computed. For the purposes of this calculation, the size rather than the direction of the difference is important.

The WPPSI-R manual (Wechsler, 1989) only gives values for statistical significance between the Verbal IQ and Performance IQ at the .05 and .15 levels. However, we feel that the .15 level is too liberal for most testing purposes, as it contains too much built-in error. The WPPSI-R Interpretive Worksheet (Appendix B) presents difference values at the .01 and .05 levels, using the average of all ages. At the .01 level, a 15-point discrepancy between the Verbal and Performance IQs is necessary for significance; at the .05 level, an 11-point discrepancy is necessary for significance. Rapid Reference 4.10 shows a completed example of Step 2 of the WPPSI-R Interpretive Worksheet.

It is up to each examiner to determine the level of confidence (and error) that he or she is willing to accept. When considering difference scores, the level of confidence should at least be 95%. The purpose of calculating the difference scores in the profile is to generate useful hypotheses. To allow flexible interpretation, the 95% level of confidence may provide more information than the conservative 99% level.

If no significant difference is found between the WPPSI-R Verbal IQ and Performance IQ, you can assume that overall the child's verbal and nonverbal skills are fairly evenly developed. The Step 2 Decision Box in the WPPSI-R Interpretive Worksheet tells you that you may now skip to Step 4, as the third step considers whether the discrepancy is abnormally large. Obviously if the difference is not large enough to be statistically significant, it is not abnormally large.

4.10 WPPSI-R Interpretive Worksheet, Step 2: Is the Verbal IQ Versus Performance IQ Discrepancy Significant?

V-IQ	P-IQ	Difference	Significant ($p < .01$) 15 or more	Significant ($p < .05$) 14–11	Not Significant 0–10	Is there a significant difference? YES NO
124	105	19				(YES) NO

Step 2 Decision Box

If the answer to Step 2 is **NO**, there is not a significant difference between the V-IQ and P-IQ. ⇨ First explain the meaning of the scales not being significantly different. Then **Skip to STEP 4.**

If the answer to Step 2 is **YES**, there is a significant difference between the V-IQ and P-IQ. ⇨ Continue on to **STEP 3.**

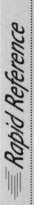

Step 3: Is the WPPSI-R Verbal IQ Versus Performance IQ Discrepancy Abnormally Large?

In this step we ask whether the size of the difference found in Step 2 is abnormally large (i.e., so large that it is rare among the normal population). By so doing we attempt to find out how frequently a discrepancy of a given magnitude occurs in the normal population.

Most children have some degree of discrepancy between their Verbal and Performance IQs. On average, 50% of the children administered the WPPSI-R have discrepancies of 9 points and 25% of the normal population have discrepancies of 15 points (Wechsler, 1989), which is considered a significant discrepancy at the $p < .01$ level. Only an 11-point difference is necessary to be considered statistically significant at the $p < .05$ level (Step 2). Thus it is not uncommon for a typical child to display differences between IQs. Rapid Reference 4.11 shows a completed example of Step 3 of the WPPSI-R Interpretive Worksheet.

Because statistically significant differences are not necessarily "abnormal," we should investigate how large a discrepancy must be to be abnormally large. How frequently a discrepancy occurs in the normal population is presented in Table 16 of the WPPSI-R manual (Wechsler, 1989). The data provided in Step 3 of the WPPSI-R Interpretive Worksheet show that for a V-IQ versus P-IQ discrepancy on the WPPSI-R to be considered abnormal (e.g., occurring in 15% or less of the normal population), a 20-point difference between the IQs must be present (Gyurke, Prifitera, & Sharp, 1991). In addition to the extreme 15%, we present the extreme 1%, 2%, 5%, and 10% in the WPPSI-R Interpretation Worksheet (Appendix B) so that examiners can determine more exactly how rare a given discrepancy is. Gyurke, Prifitera, and Sharp (1991) report discrepancy data for groups in the WPPSI-R standardization sample with differing Full Scale IQ ranges. These data are presented in Table 4.3. It is also interesting to note that Gyurke et al. found that when the discrepancy was due to a larger Performance than Verbal IQ (P-IQ > V-IQ), the difference on average was greater than those discrepancies that were due to a larger Verbal than Performance IQ (V-IQ > P-IQ). However, the direction of the discrepancy (e.g., V-IQ > P-IQ or P-IQ > V-IQ) did not vary according to ability level.

If an abnormally large difference is found between a child's verbal and nonverbal abilities, the discrepancy should be addressed and interpreted. An abnormally large discrepancy should be interpreted even in the face of scatter

4.11 WPPSI-R Interpretive Worksheet, Step 3:
Is the V-IQ Versus P-IQ Discrepancy Abnormally Large?

V-IQ vs. P-IQ Discrepancy	Percentage of Normal Children Showing Discrepancy	Size of V-IQ vs. P-IQ Discrepancy Needed to Be Considered Abnormally Large	Is there an abnormally large V-IQ vs. P-IQ discrepancy? (at least 20 pts)
19	Extreme 15%	20	
	Extreme 10%	22	YES (NO)
	Extreme 5%	26	
	Extreme 2%	32	
	Extreme 1%	36	

⇨

Step 3 Decision Box

If **ANY abnormal** differences are found	⇨ then this **abnormally** large discrepancy should be interpreted, even if significant subtest scatter exists (Step 4).	⇨ Explain the **abnormally** large Vertal & Performance differences. Then **go to STEP 5**
If **NO abnormal** difference are found	⇨ then you must determine if the noted significant differences between V-IQ and P-IQ are interpretable.	⇨ Review subtest scatter examined in **Step 4,** prior to making global interpretations.

⇨

Table 4.3   Percentage of Sample at or Above Each Level of Performance IQ–Verbal IQ Discrepancy in the WPPSI-R Standardization Sample

V-IQ vs. P-IQ Discrepancy	Full Scale IQ					
	≤ 79	80–89	90–109	110–119	120+	All
40	.0%	.4%	.5%	1.0%	1.3%	.6%
39	.0	.4	.6	1.0	1.3	.6
38	.0	.7	1.0	1.4	1.3	.9
37	.0	1.1	1.0	1.4	1.3	1.0
36	.0	1.1	1.3	1.7	1.3	1.2
35	.5	1.1	1.7	1.7	3.2	1.6
34	.0	1.5	1.8	1.7	3.2	1.7
33	.0	1.9	2.5	2.4	3.8	2.3
32	.0	2.2	3.0	3.1	3.8	2.7
31	.0	3.0	3.1	3.4	3.8	2.9
30	.7	3.0	3.7	3.7	4.5	3.4
29	1.4	3.4	4.3	4.7	5.8	4.1
28	1.4	3.7	5.6	5.4	6.4	5.0
27	1.4	3.7	6.2	6.1	8.3	5.6
26	2.8	4.1	6.9	7.5	9.0	6.4
25	2.8	4.1	8.1	8.5	9.0	7.2
24	3.5	5.2	8.8	10.5	12.2	8.4
23	3.5	6.0	10.1	11.5	13.5	9.5
22	4.2	7.5	11.7	12.5	14.7	10.8
21	4.9	9.7	13.9	15.6	15.4	12.9
20	5.6	10.8	15.6	19.7	17.3	14.9
19	7.0	13.8	18.2	20.3	17.9	16.9
18	9.9	16.0	21.5	22.7	20.5	19.8
17	16.2	18.7	23.8	24.7	23.1	22.5

Table 4.3   continued

	Full Scale IQ					
V-IQ vs. P-IQ Discrepancy	≤ 79	80–89	90–109	110–119	120+	All
16	18.3	20.9	7.2	26.4	25.0	25.1
15	21.1	23.9	29.4	29.8	31.4	28.1
14	24.6	26.9	32.2	33.6	33.3	31.3
13	28.9	28.4	36.2	39.0	36.5	34.9
12	31.0	31.3	39.2	43.1	39.7	38.0
11	36.6	37.3	43.5	46.4	42.9	42.4
10	41.5	40.7	47.9	52.9	44.9	46.8
9	45.8	46.6	52.8	58.6	52.6	52.2
8	50.7	51.9	56.7	64.7	57.7	56.9
7	54.9	57.1	62.5	69.8	61.5	62.2
6	62.0	63.4	67.3	74.9	67.3	67.6
5	67.6	71.3	72.8	81.4	71.8	73.5
4	73.2	75.7	78.4	85.1	79.5	78.8
3	83.8	82.8	84.6	90.8	87.2	85.6
2	90.8	89.9	91.9	93.9	96.2	91.8
1	95.8	97.8	97.3	98.0	98.1	97.4
0	100.0	100.0	100.0	100.0	100.0	100.0
N	142	268	839	295	156	1700
M	8.92	9.76	10.98	11.89	11.42	10.81
SD	6.61	8.17	8.68	8.67	9.56	8.57
Median	8.00	8.00	9.00	10.00	9.00	9.00

Note. From "Frequency of Verbal and Performance IQ Discrepancies on the WPPSI-R at Various Levels of Ability," by J. S. Gyurke, A. Prifitera, and S. A. Sharp, 1991, *Journal of Psychoeducational Assessment, 9,* pp. 230–239. Adapted and reproduced by permission. All rights reserved.

within the IQs. The Step 3 Decision Box (Rapid Reference 4.11) explains that if the size of the discrepancy is not abnormal, then the scatter in the IQs should be examined in Step 4. However, if there is an abnormally large discrepancy, then examiners should proceed right to Step 5.

Step 4: Is the WPPSI-R V-IQ Versus P-IQ Discrepancy Interpretable?

Before any significant discrepancies found in Step 2 can be interpreted, further investigation must occur. Sometimes one or both of the IQs are found not to be interpretable because they do not represent unitary abilities. Step 4 provides a process by which to examine whether the Verbal IQ versus Performance IQ discrepancy is interpretable in a practical and clinical sense. However, if Step 3 has revealed an abnormally large discrepancy between the Verbal and Performance IQs, then Step 4 should be skipped and the abnormally large discrepancy should be interpreted.

The amount of scatter among the five Verbal subtests that constitute the Verbal IQ indicates how variable or diverse a child's abilities are within the verbal domain. If an abnormal amount of scatter is present across subtest scores, it can be assumed that a global verbal ability is not responsible for the individual's scaled scores. Similarly, if an unusually large amount of scatter is present among the Performance subtests, then the Performance IQ is not very meaningful or interpretable.

The amount of scatter among the five subtests that are used in the calculation of the Verbal IQ is determined by taking the difference between the highest and lowest of the five scaled scores. Scatter on the Verbal Scale is considered abnormal if the difference is 7 points or more. To calculate the scatter among the five subtests of the Performance IQ, a similar process is undertaken. If the difference between the highest and lowest of the five Performance IQ subtests is 8 points or greater, then the Performance Scale is considered to have abnormally large scatter. Scatter of this size on either Verbal or Performance occurs in 15% or fewer of the cases tested on the WPPSI-R (Gyurke, Prifitera, & Sharp, 1991). Rapid Reference 4.12 shows a completed example of Step 4 of the WPPSI-R Interpretive Worksheet.

If an abnormal amount of scatter is found on the Verbal Scale, then this variability indicates that the Verbal IQ probably does not reflect a unitary construct for the child and should probably not be interpreted. Similarly, if abnormally large scatter is found on the Performance IQ, then the Perfor-

4.12 WPPSI-R Interpretive Worksheet, Step 4:
Is Verbal Versus Performance IQ Discrepancy Interpretable? ⇨

A. Is there abnormal verbal scatter?

High Scaled Score of 5 V-IQ Subtests	Low Scaled Score of 5 V-IQ Subtests	High-Low Difference	Abnormal Scatter	Not Abnormal	Is there abnormal scatter?
16	12	4 ⇨	7 or more	0–6	YES (NO)

B. Is there abnormal performance scatter?

High Scaled Score of 5 P-IQ Subtests	Low Scaled Score of 5 P-IQ Subtests	High-Low Difference	Abnormal Scatter	Not Abnormal	Is there abnormal scatter?
6	16	10 ⇨	8 or more	0–7	(YES) NO

Step 4 Decision Box

If the answers to both STEP 4 questions (A and B) are **NO** ⇨ then V-IQ **versus** P-IQ discrepancy is interpretable. ⇨ Explain the meaningful difference between V-IQ & P-IQ. **Then go to STEP 5.**

If the answers to either STEP 4 question (A or B) are **YES** ⇨ then the V-IQ **versus** P-IQ difference should probably **not** be interpreted. ⇨ Examine the strengths and weaknesses in **STEP 5.**

Note. If there is a significant difference between the component parts of the Full Scale IQ (i.e., the Verbal IQ and the Performance IQ or significant subtest scatter), the Full Scale IQ should not be interpreted as a meaningful representation of the individual's overall performance.

mance IQ does not represent a unitary construct and the Performance IQ should not be interpreted. For a more detailed breakdown of subtest scatter see Table 4.4, which presents the frequency of scatter at different levels of Verbal and Performance IQ.

If either the Verbal or Performance IQ is deemed uninterpretable because of the variability within the scale, this renders the difference between the scales also uninterpretable. The discrepancy between the Verbal IQ and Performance IQ does not meaningfully represent a difference in global verbal versus nonverbal intelligence, if either of the global IQs do not represent unitary factors. If abnormally large scatter is not present, then the scales are considered unitary and the difference between them should be interpreted. However, if the discrepancy between Verbal and Performance is not interpretable, then the most meaningful representation of a child's abilities may be in his or her individual relative strengths and weaknesses on the WPPSI-R (discussed in Steps 5 and 6).

Interpreting the Global Verbal and Nonverbal Dimensions
If you are able to interpret the Verbal and Performance IQs, you must explore a variety of interpretive hypotheses. These may be derived from clinical, theoretical, and research-based information. In this section we outline of some of the possible interpretations; more thorough discussion of these hypotheses is available in Kaufman (1994a), Prifitera and Saklofske (1998), and Flanagan, McGrew, and Ortiz (in press). Chapter 6 of this book also reviews some research on Verbal-Performance patterns that are typically found in populations such as children with learning disabilities, attention-deficit hyperactivity disorder, and mental retardation, and those who are gifted.

Horn and Cattell's Fluid Crystallized Theory Horn and Cattell distinguished two broad concepts: Crystallized Intelligence (Gc) and Fluid Intelligence (Gf) (1966, 1967). Learning that is dependent on a child's school-acquired knowledge and acculturation is categorized as Gc, whereas one's ability to solve novel problems that do not depend on formal schooling or acculturation is categorized as Gf (Cattell & Horn, 1978). The original Gc-Gf theory put forth by Horn has been expanded to include roughly eight abilities. Additional factors include Short-Term Acquisition and Retrieval (SAR or Gsm), Broad Speediness (Gs), Broad Visualization (Gv), Quantitative Thinking (Gq), Auditory Processing (Ga), and Long-Term Retrieval (TSR or Gln). The

Table 4.4   Verbal Scale (Five Subtests) and Performance Scale (Five Subtests) Percentage of Sample at or Above Each Level of Scatter in the WPPSI-R Standardization Sample

	Verbal IQ					
Scatter (Range)	≤ 79	80–89	90–109	110–119	120+	All
13	.0%	.0%	.0%	.0%	.0%	.0%
12	.7	.0	.2	.0	.0	.2
11	.7	.4	.6	.3	.0	.5
10	1.4	.8	1.8	.6	.6	1.3
9	1.4	1.8	4.0	1.9	2.5	3.1
8	2.1	5.6	8.3	6.8	7.0	7.0
7	5.7	10.5	16.0	45.7	20.0	14.6
6	12.8	20.7	26.5	31.8	36.9	26.4
5	32.1	37.8	46.0	53.1	53.8	45.6
4	53.5	65.0	68.9	73.4	78.5	68.7
3	84.9	82.5	87.7	89.8	92.1	87.5
2	95.6	95.9	97.8	97.7	98.6	97.4
1	99.2	99.6	100.0	99.7	100.0	99.8
0	100.0	100.0	100.0	100.0	100.0	100.0
N	140	246	855	305	154	1700
M	3.91	4.22	4.58	4.71	4.91	4.53
SD	1.68	1.84	1.94	1.81	1.78	1.88
Median	4.00	4.0	4.00	5.0	5.0	4.00

continued

Table 4.4   continued

	Performance IQ					
Scatter (Range)	≤ 79	80–89	90–109	110–119	120+	All
14	.0%	.0%	.0%	.0%	.0%	.0%
13	.0	.0	.1	.0	.0	.1
12	.0	.4	.8	.0	.0	.5
11	.0	1.2	1.5	.4	.6	1.1
10	.0	2.7	2.5	1.8	1.8	2.2
9	.8	5.3	7.0	6.4	5.3	6.2
8	6.3	10.6	13.8	15.5	10.6	12.7
7	17.6	22.3	26.0	27.1	25.2	24.9
6	33.1	38.9	42.4	43.6	41.6	41.3
5	52.1	59.3	60.3	65.0	60.3	60.4
4	71.8	75.1	77.3	82.2	78.4	77.6
3	88.7	91.7	91.0	95.5	93.6	92.1
2	97.2	98.1	98.5	99.4	99.4	98.7
1	100.0	96.6	100.0	100.0	100.0	99.9
0	100.0	100.0	100.0	100.0	100.0	100.0
N	142	265	837	285	171	1700
M	4.70	5.05	5.22	5.36	5.16	5.17
SD	1.84	2.03	2.12	1.92	1.92	2.04
Median	5.00	5.00	5.00	5.00	5.00	5.00

Note. From "Frequency of Verbal and Performance IQ Discrepancies on the WPPSI-R at Various Levels of Ability," by J. S. Gyurke, A. Prifitera, and S. A. Sharp, 1991, *Journal of Psychoeducational Assessment, 9*, pp. 230–239. Adapted and reproduced by permission. All rights reserved.

expansion of the Horn constructs was intended to provide more "pure" measures of intelligence. The "pure" tests of fluid ability (Gf) do not include variables such as processing speed, visualization, or memory but do focus on reasoning (Horn, 1989, 1991; Kaufman & Horn, 1996). The "pure" tests of crystallized ability (Gc) minimize the effects of short-term memory and fluid reasoning and focus on knowledge and comprehension.

Tasks that call for "fluent visual scanning, Gestalt Closure, mind's eye rotations of figures and ability to see reversals" are those that are categorized as Gv (Horn, 1989, p. 80). Tasks that require basic immediate recall of stimuli are categorized as SAR (Horn & Hofer, 1992). Tasks that relate to "carefulness, strategies (or metacognition), mood (such as depression), and persistence" are Gs tasks (Horn, 1989, p. 84).

The theories of Horn and Cattell have been applied to the Wechsler scales many times (Flanagan, McGrew, & Ortiz, in press; Kaufman, 1994a; Matarazzo, 1972). The works of Horn (1989, 1991), Kaufman (1994a), Woodcock (1990), and Flanagan, McGrew, and Ortiz (in press) were considered in determining the categorizations of each of the WISC-III and WPPSI-R subtests. Rapid References 4.3 and 4.4 categorize WPPSI-R and WISC-III subtests according to their Gc and Gf components and some of Horn's other expanded factors.

Although the WPPSI-R and WISC-III Verbal and Performance IQs cannot be cleanly broken apart into the pure Gc and Gf factors (see Kaufman, 1994a), there are many Verbal subtests that are related to Gc or SAR and many Performance subtests that are related to Gf or Gs (see Rapid References 4.3 and 4.4). The four WISC-III factors can be interpreted within the Horn framework: The Verbal Comprehension Index is primarily a measure of Gc; the Perceptual Organization Index is a blend of Gv and Gf; the Freedom from Distractibility Index is SAR; and the Processing Speed Index is Gs (Rapid Reference 4.5). Object Assembly also may have a Gs interpretation along with the Processing Speed subtests, and Picture Arrangement has associations with both Gc and Gf (Kaufman, 1994a).

Some authors firmly espouse that each of the WPPSI-R and WISC-III subtests can be categorized into only one of Horn's expanded theory categories (Flanagan, McGrew, & Ortiz, in press). However, it is our belief that some of the Wechsler subtests assess more than one aspect of Horn's theory. For example, Similarities has a Gc component (word knowledge) and a Gf component (using reasoning to figure out the similarity); Arithmetic has components of Gc, Gq, and Gf; Block Design and Object Assembly have Gv as well as Gf components. Thus clearly the WISC-III and WPPSI-R subtests are complex in terms of what underlies them (e.g., Gc, Gf, Gv, Gs). For any particular child, it is possible that one factor is a stronger driving force in his or her performance than another. Therefore before automatically interpreting a subtest as a measure of any theoretical construct, you should consider background information, behavioral observations, and supplementary test scores as supportive data.

Step 5: Interpret Significant Strengths and Weaknesses of WPPSI-R Subtest Profile

The first steps of WPPSI-R interpretation involve examination of the global scores, but Step 5 addresses the fine details of the subtest profile. Each child is truly unique, and at this level of profile analysis the child's special characteristics come to light as hypotheses are made about his or her strong and weak areas of cognitive functioning. Before delving into how to generate hypotheses, we first review some empirical guidelines.

An ipsative comparison is one that examines how well a child is performing on each subtest relative to his or her own average score. The ipsative comparison is quite different from the comparison between an individual's subtest scores and those of the normative group. When we compare each of an individual's subtest scores to the mean of all of his subtest scores, we discover what relative strengths and weaknesses he has regardless of how he looks when compared to the normative group. For example, a developmentally delayed child may earn a scaled score of 10 on one subtest, which is in the Average range compared to the normative group, but when comparing this score of 10 to the child's mean subtest score of 7, that scaled score is considered a personal relative strength.

In Step 5 you are instructed to use either the mean of all subtests administered or the mean of the Verbal subtests plus the mean of the Performance subtests. How do you decide which is the correct mean(s) to use? If a child's WPPSI-R Verbal versus Performance IQ discrepancy is 20 points or more, then you should use two separate means (the mean of all Verbal subtests administered and the mean of all Performance subtests administered). However, if the Verbal IQ versus Performance IQ discrepancy is between 0 and 19 points, then you should use the mean of all the WPPSI-R subtests administered. In other words, when the discrepancy between the Verbal and Performance IQ is abnormally large, you should compare the mean of each of the subtests to the scale on which they fall. If the discrepancy between these two global IQs is not abnormally large, then you should use the mean of all the WPPSI-R subtests administered as the basis of comparison for every subtest.

≡ Rapid Reference

4.13 WPPSI-R Interpretive Worksheet, Step 5:
Interpret Significant Strengths and Weaknesses of Profile

V-IQ–P-IQ discrepancy

			Overall Mean	Rounded Mean
0–19	Then use	⇨ mean of all subtests administered[a]	⇨	$^{147}/_{12} = 12.25$	12

			Verbal Subtests' Mean	Rounded Mean
20 or more	Then use	⇨ mean of all Verbal subtests administered[a] and also use	⇨	___	___

			Performance Subtests' Mean	Rounded Mean
		⇨ mean of all Performance subtests administered[a]	⇨	___	___

[a]After calculating means, round to the nearest whole number.

4.14 WPPSI-R Interpretive Worksheet, Step 5 (continued): Interpret Significant Strengths and Weaknesses of Profile

Verbal Subtest	Scaled Score	Rounded Mean	Difference[b]	Size of Difference Needed for Significance	Strength or Weakness (S or W)	Percentile Rank (see Table 4.5)
Information	12	12	0	±3	—	75
Comprehension	16	12	+4	±3	S	98
Arithmetic	14	12	+2	±3	—	91
Vocabulary	14	12	+2	±3	—	91
Similarities	12	12	0	±3	—	75
Sentences	11	12	-1	±3	—	63
Performance Subtest						
Object Assembly	6	12	-6	±4	W	9
Geometric Design	12	12	0	±3	—	75
Block Design	9	12	-3	±3	W	37
Mazes	11	12	-1	±4	—	63
Picture Completion	16	12	+4	±3	S	98
Animal Pegs	14	12	+2	±4	—	91

[b]Difference = subtest scaled score minus appropriate rounded mean.

Rapid References 4.13 shows how to calculate the mean or means used in Step 5 of the WPPSI-R Interpretive Worksheet.

To prevent errors in calculation, we suggest that after the correct mean(s) have been calculated you round the mean(s) to the nearest whole number (see Rapid Reference 4.13 and 4.14). Kaufman (1994a, pp. 125–128) reviews some controversial issues surrounding various methods of calculating subtest strengths and weaknesses.

After the scaled scores have been recorded in the WPPSI-R Interpretive Worksheet, then the difference between each of the 12 subtests (or however many were administered) and the rounded mean(s) should be calculated. It is important to note with a plus sign (+) or minus sign (–) whether each subtest falls above or below the subtest mean (see Rapid Reference 4.14). Subtests that fall above the mean should have a positive valence, and those falling below should have a negative valence.

The next part of Step 5 determines whether the size of the difference between each subtest and the rounded mean of all subtests is large enough to be significantly different. We provide the sizes needed in the WPPSI-R Interpretive Worksheet (Appendix B). The values presented in the WPPSI-R manual (Wechsler, 1989) are exact values; however, we present an overview with rounded values. If you wish you may refer to the manual for exact values, although the rounded values are sufficient to calculate the strengths and weaknesses, and they minimize the risk of clerical error and reduce dependency on tables.

If the difference between each scaled score and the individual's mean is large enough to be statistically significant, then it may be considered a strength (if significantly above the mean) or weakness (if significantly below the mean). On the WPPSI-R Interpretive Worksheet, the strengths and weaknesses may be denoted by the letters S and W, respectively. However, if scaled scores do not differ significantly from the appropriate mean, they should be considered chance fluctuations. Nonsignificant differences should not be interpreted as strengths or weaknesses per se, but they may be utilized to support hypotheses (see Step 6).

One of the additional components of Step 5 involves converting the scaled scores to percentile ranks (see Rapid Reference 4.14). Most people are not familiar with the scaled score's mean of 10 and standard deviation of 3 but are likely to understand the commonly used percentile rank. In the "Interpretation of Test Results" section of a report, the metric of per-

Table 4.5   National Percentile Ranks Corresponding to Scaled Scores

Percentile Rank	Scaled Score	Corresponding IQ
99.9	19	145
99.6	18	140
99	17	135
98	16	130
95	15	125
91	14	120
84	13	115
75	12	110
63	11	105
50	10	100
37	9	95
25	8	90
16	7	85
9	6	80
5	5	75
2	4	70
1	3	65
0.4	2	60
0.1	1	55

centile rank can be very useful in communicating to parents and professionals alike. Percentile ranks for the scaled score values are shown in Table 4.5.

Step 6: Generate Hypotheses About Strengths and Weaknesses in the WPPSI-R Profile

This step is one of the most important in the process of WPPSI-R interpretation. It requires integration of data obtained from the subtest strengths and weaknesses with that obtained from behavioral observations, background information, and supplemental testing in order to confirm or disconfirm hypotheses. When interpretations are validated by multiple types as data such as these, then strong and sensible recommendations can be made for intervention.

Step 6 is designed to help derive meaning from the relative strengths and weaknesses noted in Step 5. One of the challenges in creating hypotheses is to find abilities that are shared by two or more subtests, rather than simply stating what the textbook definition of each subtest purportedly measures. The potential problem with using definitions of single subtests is this: When hypotheses are considered in isolation, there is risk of missing contradictory information that may be present. For example, when children earn high scores on WPPSI-R Geometric Design, some examiners automatically state that children have strong "visual-motor" skills. However, such a statement made in isolation might neglect the relative trouble that was evidenced on Object Assembly and Mazes, in addition to parents' comments about their child's difficulty writing the letters of the alphabet.

Finding information that is consistent across the entire profile is a goal that each examiner should have. Each strength and weakness should be supported by two or more subtests and whenever feasible, by clinical observations, background information, and supplementary cognitive or achievement measures. Occasionally a profile may be entirely flat, evidencing no relative strengths or weaknesses. Examination of this type of profile will not likely provide a great deal of information. It may be necessary to administer supplemental subtests that measure abilities not well tapped by the WPPSI-R.

INTRODUCTION TO WPPSI-R SUBTEST INTERPRETIVE TABLES

Rapid Reference 4.15 lists the abilities that are believed to underlie each WPPSI-R subtest and as such is useful in facilitating the process of hypothesis generation. The information summarizes material included in the subtest-by-subtest analysis at the beginning of this chapter. Abilities and influences that are shared by at least two WPPSI-R subtests are presented in an organized manner in this Rapid Reference.

Because some of the WPPSI-R subtests involve different abilities in earlier items than in later items, there are certain times when closer examination of specific items must occur before you can accept a shared ability as a hypothesis.

4.15 Abilities Shared by Two or More WPPSI-R Verbal and Performance Subtests

Ability	Verbal Subtests						Performance Subtests						Reliability[a]	
	I	C	A	V	S	Sen	OA	GD	BD	Mz	PC	AP	r_{xx}	r_{12}
Input														
Attention-concentration			A			Sen					PC	AP	.90	.88
Auditory-vocal channel		C	A	V		Sen						AP	.95	.93
Complex verbal directions									BD	Mz		AP	.86	.80
Distinguishing essential from nonessential detail					S						PC		.90	.83
Encode information for processing			A			Sen						AP	.86	.84
Simple verbal directions	I (1–6)		A (1–7)				OA	GD			PC		.87	.83
Understanding long questions	I	C	A										.92	.89
Understanding words				V	S	Sen	OA						.92	.88
Visual-motor channel	I (1–6)		A (1–7)				OA	GD	BD	Mz	PC	AP	.92	.89
Visual perception of abstract stimuli	I (1–6)		A (1–7)					GD	BD	Mz			.90	.82

Ability	Verbal Subtests						Performance Subtests						Reliability[a]	
	I	C	A	V	S	Sen	OA	GD	BD	Mz	PC	AP	r_{xx}	r_{12}
Input (cont.)														
Visual perception of complete meaningful stimuli	I (1–6)		A (1–7)	V (1–3)	S (1–6)						PC	AP	.82	.80
Visual perception of stimuli							OA				PC		.81	.79
Integration/Storage														
Achievement (Horn)	I	C	A	V	S								.95	.92
Acquired knowledge (Bannatyne)	I		A	V									.92	.88
Cognition (Guilford)			A	V	S		OA	GD (1–7)	BD		PC		.94	.91
Concept formation				V	S				BD				.92	.86
Convergent production (Guilford)								GD				AP	.79	.75
Crystallized ability (Horn)	I	C		V	S								.94	.91
Culture-loaded knowledge	I	C											.90	.88
Evaluation (Guilford)		C					OA	GD (1–7)	BD		PC		.90	.88
Figural cognition (Guilford)							OA	GD (1–7)	BD	Mz	PC		.90	.86
Figural evaluation (Guilford)			A (1–7)		S (1–6)		OA	GD (1–7)	BD	Mz	PC	AP	.90	.87
Fluid ability (Horn)			A		S		OA		BD	Mz			.90	.87

continued

Ability	Verbal Subtests						Performance Subtests						Reliability[a]	
	I	C	A	V	S	Sen	OA	GD	BD	Mz	PC	AP	r_{xx}	r_{12}
Integration/Storage (cont.)														
Fund of information	I			V									.90	.86
General ability	I	C	A	V	S				BD				.95	.93
Handling abstract verbal concepts				V	S								.90	.82
Holistic (right-brain) processing							OA	GD		Mz	PC		.89	.84
Language development		C		V	S	Sen						AP	.94	.91
Learning ability				V								AP	.80	.77
Long-term memory	I		A	V									.92	.88
Memory (Guilford)	I		A			Sen							.91	.89
Planning ability							OA	GD	BD	Mz		AP	.90	.86
Reasoning		C	A		S		OA						.90	.86
Reproduction of models								GD	BD			AP	.87	.84
Semantic cognition (Guilford)			A	V	S								.92	.86
Semantic content (Guilford)	I	C	A	V	S	Sen							.95	.93
Sequential (Bannatyne)			A			Sen						AP	.86	.84
Short-term memory (auditory or visual)						Sen						AP	.80	.78
Simultaneous processing							OA	GD	BD	Mz	PC		.92	.88

Ability	Verbal Subtests						Performance Subtests						Reliability[a]	
	I	C	A	V	S	Sen	OA	GD	BD	Mz	PC	AP	r_{xx}	r_{12}
Integration/Storage (cont.)														
Spatial (Bannatyne)							OA	GD	BD	Mz	PC		.92	.88
Spatial visualization								GD	BD	Mz			.90	.82
Synthesis							OA	GD	BD				.88	.84
Trial-and-error learning							OA		BD	Mz			.87	.81
Verbal concept formation				V	S								.90	.82
Verbal conceptualization (Bannatyne)		C		V	S	Sen							.94	.91
Verbal reasoning		C			S								.90	.83
Visual memory											PC	AP	.82	.80
Visual processing (Horn)							OA	GD	BD	Mz	PC		.92	.88
Output														
Much verbal expression		C		V	S								.93	.88
Simple vocal expression	I		A V (1–3)			Sen					PC		.93	.91
Visual organization								GD		Mz	PC		.89	.82
Visual-motor coordination	I (1–6)	C	A (1–7)		S (1–6)		OA	GD	BD	Mz		AP	.90	.86
Influences Affecting Scores														
Ability to respond when uncertain							OA				PC		.81	.77

continued

Ability	Verbal Subtests						Performance Subtests						Reliability[a]	
	I	C	A	V	S	Sen	OA	GD	BD	Mz	PC	AP	r_{xx}	r_{12}
Influences Affecting Scores (cont.)														
Alertness to environment	I										PC		.89	.87
Anxiety			A			Sen						AP	.86	.84
Attention span			A			Sen						AP	.87	.83
Cognitive style (field dependence)							OA	GD	BD	Mz	PC		.92	.88
Concentration			A			Sen				Mz	PC	AP	.91	.88
Cultural opportunities	I	C		V									.93	.90
Distractibility			A			Sen				Mz		AP	.88	.83
Flexibility					S	Sen	OA	GD	BD	Mz			.92	.87
Foreign language background	I			V									.90	.86
Hearing difficulties			A			Sen							.87	.83
Intellectual curiosity and striving	I			V									.90	.86
Interests	I			V	S								.93	.88
Learning disabilities			A			Sen		GD				AP	.89	.86
Motivation level								GD		Mz		AP	.85	.77
Negativism		C			S			GD			PC		.92	.88
Obsessive concern with detail and accuracy								GD		Mz		AP	.85	.77

Ability	Verbal Subtests						Performance Subtests						Reliability[a]	
	I	C	A	V	S	Sen	OA	GD	BD	Mz	PC	AP	r_{xx}	r_{12}
Influences Affecting Scores (cont.)														
Outside reading	I			V	S								.93	.88
Overly concrete thinking		C			S								.90	.83
Persistence							OA	GD		Mz		AP	.86	.81
Richness of early environment	I			V									.90	.86
School learning	I		A	V									.92	.88
Visual-perceptual problems							OA	GD	BD	Mz		A?	.90	.86
Work under time pressure							OA	GD	BD	Mz	PC	AP	.90	.87

Note. I = Information; I (1–6) = first six Information items only; C = Comprehension; A = Arithmetic; A (1–7) = first seven Arithmetic items only; V = Vocabulary; V (1–3) = first three Vocabulary items only; S = Similarities; S (1–6) = first six Similarities items only; Sen = Sentences; OA = Object Assembly; GD = Geometric Design; GD (1–7) = first seven Geometric Design items only; BD = Block Design; Mz = Mazes; PC = Picture Completion; AP = Animal Pegs.

[a]r_{xx} = split-half reliability; r_{12} = test-retest reliability.

In addition to the abilities measured by the subtest in its entirety, the following subtests have specific abilities listed that pertain to just the first few items: Information, Geometric Design, Arithmetic, Vocabulary, and Similarities (see Rapid Reference 4.15). Each of the first few items of these five subtests have stimuli that are pictorial in nature and require a child to point to the correct response (Information, Arithmetic, Similarities, and Geometric Design) or give a one-word response (Vocabulary). In contrast, the remaining higher level items on these five tasks have auditory stimuli and require a vocal response (Information, Arithmetic, Vocabulary, and Similarities) or have visual stimuli and require a motor response (Geometric Design). We discuss how to use these listings in the How to Use Information About Shared Abilities section that follows.

The WPPSI-R shared abilities tables are organized according to the Information Processing Model: Input-Integration/Storage-Output. This model considers the following:

• To what type of stimuli does the individual have to respond?
• How is the information processed and remembered?
• How is the person required to respond?

Apart from the content of the task, it is important to consider aspects of the stimulus or response that may affect a child's performance on certain subtests. Rapid Reference 4.15 provides a number of hypothesized abilities, but these are intended only as a guideline. The lists are not exhaustive and should be used as a reference that is open to expansion. The examiner must consider the individuality of each child and each testing situation during profile analysis.

Reliability Coefficients of Shared Abilities

For each group of subtests listed in Rapid Reference 4.15, the split-half and test-retest reliabilities are provided. These values are based on the average reliability values presented in the WPPSI-R manual (Wechsler, 1989) and on the intercorrelations among the subtests in each cluster. The formula for calculating the composite was applied (Tellegen & Briggs, 1967).

How to Use Information About Shared Abilities

This section provides sequential guidelines of how to best utilize the information in Rapid Reference 4.15 to generate hypotheses. We use Emma K.'s profile to demonstrate how to identify potentially strong and weak abilities to investigate.

Guideline 1

Choose one of the strengths (S) or weaknesses (W) determined in Step 5. Write down all the shared abilities and influences that involve this subtest. For example, we would choose the first relative strength found in Emma K.'s profile: Comprehension. Table 4.6 (pp. 150–151) shows all the possible shared abilities for Comprehension (this information was pulled from Rapid Reference 4.15). Next to this list are all other subtests that may also measure this ability.

Special consideration should be made when including shared abilities that tap the earliest items of the Information, Geometric Design, Arithmetic, Vocabulary, and Similarities subtests. As mentioned earlier, for each of these subtests Rapid Reference 4.15 lists abilities measured by all items and also lists those abilities only measured by the first items that are pictorial (e.g., these are listed as "I (1−6)"). Rapid Reference 4.16 lists the pictorial items in each of the five subtests. These items should be pulled from Rapid Reference 4.15 and written down (see Emma's case in Table 4.6).

≡ Rapid Reference

4.16 Pictorial Items That Require Special Consideration in Interpretation

WPPSI-R Subtest	Pictorial Items
Geometric Design	1−7
Information	1−6
Vocabulary	1−3
Arithmetic	1−7
Similarities	1−6

Guideline 2

Evaluate each ability listed for the first strength or weakness (examined in Guideline 1) to determine how the child performed on the other subtest(s) that also measure the identified abilities. In deciding which abilities explain

Table 4.6   Example List of Shared Abilities for WPPSI-R Comprehension

Ability	Verbal Subtests						Performance Subtests					
	I	C	A	V	S	Sen	OA	GD	BD	Mz	PC	AP
Input												
Auditory-vocal channel	I	C	A	V	S	Sen						
Understanding long questions	I	C	A									
Integration/Storage												
Achievement (Horn)	I	C	A	V	S							
Crystallized ability (Horn)	I	C		V	S							
Culture-loaded knowledge	I	C										
Evaluation (Guilford)		C					OA	GD (1–7)	BD		PC	
General ability	I	C	A	V	S				BD			
Language development		C	A	V	S	Sen						
Reasoning		C	A	V	S		OA					
Semantic content (Guilford)	I	C	A	V	S	Sen						
Verbal conceptualization (Bannatyne)		C	A	V	S	Sen						
Verbal reasoning		C			S							

Table 4.6 continued

Ability	Verbal Subtests							Performance Subtests				
	I	C	A	V	S	Sen	OA	GD	BD	Mz	PC	AP
Output												
Much verbal expression		C		V	S							
Influences Affecting Scores												
Cultural opportunities	I	C		V								
Negativism		C			S			GD			PC	
Overly concrete thinking		C			S							

Note. I = Information; C = Comprehension; A = Arithmetic; V = Vocabulary; S = Similarities; Sen = Sentences; OA = Object Assembly; GD = Geometric Design; GD (1–7) = first seven Geometric Design items only; BD = Block Design; Mz = Mazes; PC = Picture Completion; AP = Animal Pegs.

the strength or weakness, apply less stringent criteria than in determining significant strengths and weaknesses (in Step 5). You simply want to consider whether the child has scored above, below, or equal to his or her own mean score on all pertinent subtests for an ability. (This information has already been calculated in Step 5 and is recorded in the "difference" column on Step 5 of the WPPSI-R Interpretive Worksheet). Record this information on your list of shared abilities by writing the following notations next to each subtest (except the *first* items of Information, Arithmetic, Vocabulary, Similarities, and Geometric Design):

- − (indicating performance below the child's mean subtest scaled score)
- + (indicating performance above the child's mean subtest scaled score)
- 0 (indicating performance exactly at the child's mean subtest scaled score).

When items 1−6 of Information, 1−7 of Arithmetic, 1−3 of Vocabulary, 1−6 of Similarities, or 1−7 of Geometric Design are listed as shared abilities for special consideration, do not write a +, −, or 0 next to these "part subtests" (see Caution 4.1). This is because a scaled score is not obtained for the initial items of a subtest. Therefore you cannot determine whether these items are above, below, or equivalent to the overall subtest mean. In Guideline 3 that follows, we discuss how to examine and integrate a child's performance on these items of a subtest if necessary.

Again using the example of Emma K.'s relative strength in Comprehension, Table 4.7 demonstrates how to fill in the +, −, or 0 next to the pertinent subtests. For exam-

> # CAUTION
>
> ### 4.1 Exception to Guideline 2 of How to Use Information About WPPSI-R Shared Abilities
>
> When determining whether a subtest is above, below, or equivalent to the mean subtest scaled score, do not write +, −, or 0 next to pictorial items in the following subtests:
>
> - Information (items 1−6)
> - Geometric Design (items 1−7)
> - Arithmetic (items 1−7)
> - Vocabulary (items 1−3)
> - Similarities (items 1−6)
>
> This should not be done because these are only select items; they do not represent entire subtest scaled scores.

Table 4.7 Example List of Shared Abilities for WPPSI-R Comprehension With +, −, 0 Completed From Emma K.'s Profile

Ability	Verbal Subtests						Performance Subtests					
	I	C	A	V	S	Sen	OA	GD	BD	Mz	PC	AP
Input												
Auditory-vocal channel	I0	C+	A+	V+	S0	Sen−						
Understanding long questions	I0	C+	A+									
Integration/Storage												
Achievement (Horn)	I0	C+	A+	V+	S0							
Crystallized ability (Horn)	I0	C+		V+	S0							
Culture-loaded knowledge	I0	C+										
Evaluation (Guilford)		C+					OA−	GD (1–7)	BD−		PC+	
General ability	I0	C+	A+	V+	S0				BD−			
Language development		C+		V+	S0	Sen−						
Reasoning		C+	A+		S0		OA−					
Semantic content (Guilford)	I0	C+	A+	V+	S0	Sen−						
Verbal conceptualization (Bannatyne)		C+		V+	S0	Sen−						
Verbal reasoning		C+			S0							

continued

Table 4.7 continued

Ability	Verbal Subtests						Performance Subtests					
	I	C	A	V	S	Sen	OA	GD	BD	Mz	PC	AP
Output												
Much verbal expression		C+		V+	S0							
Influences Affecting Scores												
Cultural opportunities	I0	C+		V+								
Negativism		C+			S0			GD0			PC+	
Overly concrete thinking		C+			S0							

Note. I = Information; C = Comprehension; A = Arithmetic; V = Vocabulary; S = Similarities; Sen = Sentences; OA = Object Assembly; GD = Geometric Design; GD (1–7) = first seven Geometric Design items only; BD = Block Design; Mz = Mazes; PC = Picture Completion; AP = Animal Pegs.

0 = subtest scaled score is equal to mean subtest scaled score.

+ = subtest scaled score is above mean subtest scaled score.

– = subtest scaled score is below mean subtest scaled score.

ple, in the first row "auditory-vocal channel" is listed as a hypothesized shared ability. The first subtest listed with this ability is Information, and because Emma's Information scaled score was exactly equivalent to her overall mean subtest scaled score (see Rapid Reference 4.14), a 0 is placed next to the Information subtest abbreviation. Also listed with the auditory-vocal channel are Comprehension, Arithmetic, Vocabulary, Similarities, and Sentences. The appropriate symbols are placed next to each of these subtest abbreviations, according to whether Emma scored above, below, or equivalent to her own scaled score mean. Table 4.7 shows a partially completed example of this process.

Guideline 3

Examine each ability written on the list (in Guideline 1) to determine whether it should be considered strong or weak. In general, shared strengths are those in which a person has scored above his or her own mean score on all pertinent subtests, with at least one discrepancy reaching statistical significance. However, exceptions to this general rule are described in Don't Forget 4.1. The rules of whether to accept or reject abilities as strengths or weaknesses should be treated as rules of thumb rather than as rigid principles. At times an overabundance of other clinical data from the background information, behavioral observations, or supplemental testing may support a shared ability as a strength or weakness (even if the guidelines in Don't Forget 4.1 are not met). If multiple sources of information support a particular ability as worthy of interpretation, it is best to accept it as a relative strength or weakness.

When WPPSI-R items 1–6 of Information, 1–7 of Arithmetic, 1–3 of Vocabulary, 1–6 of Similarities, or 1–7 of Geometric Design are listed as shared abilities for special consideration, examine these prior to making a judgment about whether an ability is a relative strength or weakness. If a child has made two or more errors on items 1–6 of Information, 1–7 of Arithmetic, 1–6 of Similarities, or 1–7 of Geometric Design or one error on items 1–3 of Vocabulary, these first items may be considered as supportive evidence for a relative weakness (after applying the "Rules for Accepting and Rejecting Potential Hypotheses" in Don't Forget 4.1 to the other subtests listed with the hypothesized ability). If a child has no errors on items 1–6 of Information, 1–7 of Arithmetic, 1–6 of Similarities, 1–7 of Geo-

4.1 Rules for Accepting and Rejecting Potential Hypotheses

Number of Subtests Constituting a Shared Ability	Rule for Interpreting Ability as a Strength (*at least one subtest is a significant strength*)	Rule for Interpreting Ability as a Weakness (*at least one subtest is a significant weakness*)
2	• *All subtests must be above the mean.*	• *All subtests must be below the mean.*
3 or 4	• *At least two or three subtests must be above the mean, and only one subtest may be equivalent to the mean.*	• *At least two or three subtests must be below the mean, and only one subtest may be equivalent to the mean.*
5 or more	• *At least four subtests must be above the mean, and only one subtest may be equal to the mean or less than the mean.*	• *At least four subtests must be below the mean, and only one subtest may be equal to the mean or greater than the mean.*

CAUTION

4.2 How to Evaluate Abilities Associated with Pictorial Items in Information, Geometric Design, Arithmetic, Vocabulary, and Similarities Subtests

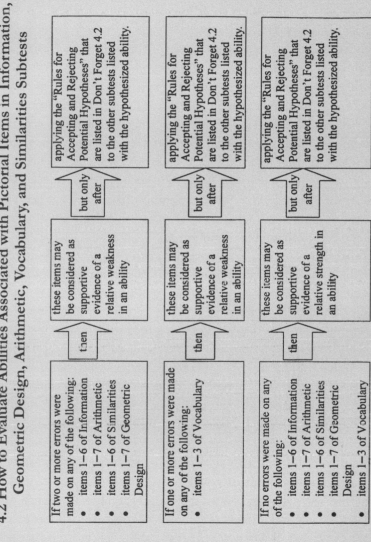

If two or more errors were made on any of the following:
- items 1–6 of Information
- items 1–7 of Arithmetic
- items 1–6 of Similarities
- items 1–7 of Geometric Design

then these items may be considered as supportive evidence of a relative weakness in an ability

but only after applying the "Rules for Accepting and Rejecting Potential Hypotheses" that are listed in Don't Forget 4.2 to the other subtests listed with the hypothesized ability.

If one or more errors were made on any of the following:
- items 1–3 of Vocabulary

then these items may be considered as supportive evidence of a relative weakness in an ability

but only after applying the "Rules for Accepting and Rejecting Potential Hypotheses" that are listed in Don't Forget 4.2 to the other subtests listed with the hypothesized ability.

If no errors were made on any of the following:
- items 1–6 of Information
- items 1–7 of Arithmetic
- items 1–6 of Similarities
- items 1–7 of Geometric Design
- items 1–3 of Vocabulary

then these items may be considered as supportive evidence of a relative strength in an ability

but only after applying the "Rules for Accepting and Rejecting Potential Hypotheses" that are listed in Don't Forget 4.2 to the other subtests listed with the hypothesized ability.

metric Design, or 1–3 of Vocabulary, these first items may be considered as supportive evidence for a relative strength (after applying the rules in Don't Forget 4.1 to the other subtests listed with the hypothesized ability). See Caution 4.2 for an explanation of how to evaluate abilities associated with pictorial items in WPPSI-R subtests.

Emma did not make errors on items 1–7 of Geometric Design, items 1–6 of Information, items 1–3 of Vocabulary, or items 1–7 of Arithmetic. Thus any abilities associated with perfect performance on the first few items of these four subtests may demonstrate a relative strength. However, she did make two errors on the first six items of Similarities and then went on to obtain points for four of the higher level, nonpictorial items. Thus when examining any of the hypothesized weak abilities associated with items 1–6 of Similarities, her errors may provide supportive evidence of a relative weakness.

Table 4.8 shows how the rules of thumb have been applied to Emma's Comprehension example that we have been following any (see the strengths and weaknesses column on the far right). We consider each of the hypothesized abilities one by one to determine whether any may be deemed a relative strength. For example, the auditory-vocal channel is an ability that is hypothesized to underlie six subtests (Information, Comprehension, Arithmetic, Vocabulary, Similarities, and Sentences). The symbols next to these subtest abbreviations show that three subtests are above the mean, one is below the mean, and two are equivalent to the mean. The rules for accepting and rejecting potential hypotheses tell us that for an ability to be considered a strength when there are five or more subtests, at least four subtests must be above the mean (only one subtest may be equal to or below the mean). The six subtests do not meet these criteria, so we cross it off the list and do not consider it as a possible strong ability.

The next ability to consider with Emma's profile is "understanding long questions." Three subtests are noted to have this underlying ability. On two of them Emma earned scaled scores above the average subtest mean, and on the third her score was equivalent to the mean. Thus because three subtests constituted this shared ability, two were above the mean, and only one was equivalent to the mean, "understanding long questions" may be considered a relative strength in Emma's profile. On Table 4.8, this ability is noted as a strength by writing an *S* at the end of the row.

Table 4.8 Example List of Shared Abilities for WPPSI-R Comprehension With Abilities Ruled in or out as Strengths Underlying Emma K.'s Profile

Ability	Verbal Subtests						Performance Subtests						Strength or Weakness (S or W)
	I	C	A	V	S	Sen	OA	GD	BD	Mz	PC	AF	
Input													
Auditory-vocal channel	I0	C+	A+	V+	S0	Sen–							None
Understanding long questions	I0	C+	A+										S
Integration/Storage													
Achievement (Horn)	I0	C+	A+	V+	S0								None
Crystallized ability (Horn)	I0	C+		V+	S0								None
Culture-loaded knowledge	I0	C+											None
Evaluation (Guilford)		C+					OA–	GD (1–7)	BD–		PC+		None
General ability	I0	C+	A+	V+	S0								None
Language development		C+		V+	S0	Sen–			BD–				None
Reasoning		C+	A+		S0		OA–						None
Semantic content (Guilford)	I0	C+	A+	V+	S0	Sen–							None

continued

Table 4.8   continued

Ability	Verbal Subtests						Performance Subtests						Strength or Weakness (S or W)
	I	C	A	V	S	Sen	OA	GD	BD	Mz	PC	AP	
Verbal conceptualization (Bannatyne)		C+		V+	S0	Sen–							None
Verbal reasoning		C+			S0								None
Output													
Much verbal expression		C+		V+	S0								S
Influences Affecting Scores													
Cultural opportunities	I0	C+		V+									S
Negativism		C+			S0			GD0			PC+		None
Overly concrete thinking		C+			S0								None

Note. I = Information; C = Comprehension; A = Arithmetic; V = Vocabulary; S = Similarities; Sen = Sentences; OA = Object Assembly; GD = Geometric Design; GD (1–7) = first seven Geometric Design items only; BD = Block Design; Mz = Mazes; PC = Picture Completion; AP = Animal Pegs.

0 = subtest scaled score is equal to mean subtest scaled score.

+ = subtest scaled score is above mean subtest scaled score.

– = subtest scaled score is below mean subtest scaled score.

Guideline 4

Repeat Guidelines 1, 2, and 3 for every other significant strength or weakness (listed in Step 5) that has not been accounted for. Table 4.9 shows Emma's next relative subtest weakness, Object Assembly (Rapid Reference 4.11). After filling in all the symbols for Emma's abilities underlying Object Assembly, we see that some hypothesized abilities appear to explain her weakness in Object Assembly: synthesis and trial-and-error learning. Before including any of these hypothesized abilities in Emma's report, it is necessary to consider whether the behavioral observations, background information, and supplemental test data support these hypotheses. Chapter 7 provides a complete case report of Emma K.'s profile that integrates and interprets her various strengths and weaknesses.

Guideline 5

If no hypothesized strong or weak abilities are uncovered during the process of examining subtests' shared abilities, then consider interpreting the unique abilities that are presumably measured by significantly high or low scores on subtests. However, the primary focus in explaining the peaks and valleys in a subtest profile should be on shared abilities that link several subtests and are also supported by background information, behavioral observations, and supplemental testing. Occasionally, however, no hypothesized strengths or weaknesses in abilities are apparent across subtests. Interpretations that are specific to a particular subtest must then be considered. The unique abilities (denoted with an asterisk) are listed in the subtest-by-subtest description of abilities earlier in this chapter.

It is important to determine the amount of specificity of a subtest before interpreting the unique ability associated with it. Those subtests with ample or adequate amounts of specificity may be interpreted (see Rapid Reference 4.2). However, a unique ability should not automatically be interpreted even if it has "ample" specificity. It is best to have other supportive evidence from background data, behavioral observations, or supplemental testing if you are interpreting a unique ability. Acquiescing to an interpretation of a highly specific and unique strength or weakness should only occur when all hypotheses involving shared abilities have proven useless.

Table 4.9 Example List of Shared Abilities for Object Assembly With Abilities Ruled in or out as Weaknesses Underlying Emma K.'s Profile

Ability	Verbal Subtests						Performance Subtests						Strengths or Weaknesses (S or W)
	I	C	A	V	S	Sen	OA	GD	BD	Mz	PC	AP	
Input													
Simple verbal directions	I (1–6)		A (1–7)				OA–	GD0			PC+		none
Visual-motor channel	I (1–6)		A (1–7)				OA–	GD0	BD–	Mz–	PC+	AP+	none
Visual perception of meaningful stimuli							OA–				PC+		none
Integration/Storage													
Cognition (Guilford)			A+	V+	S0		OA–	GD (1–7)	BD–		PC+		none
Evaluation (Guilford)		C+					OA–	GD (1–7)	BD–		PC+		none
Figural cognition (Guilford)							OA–	GD (1–7)	BD–	Mz–	PC+		none
Figural evaluation (Guilford)			A (1–7)		S (1–6)		OA–	GD (1–7)	BD–	Mz–	PC+	AP+	none
Fluid ability (Horn)			A+		S0		OA–		BD–				none
Holistic (right-brain) processing							OA–	GD0		Mz–	PC+		none
Planning ability							OA–	GD0	BD–	Mz–		AP+	none

Ability	Verbal Subtests						Performance Subtests						Strengths or Weaknesses
	I	C	A	V	S	Sen	OA	GD	BD	Mz	PC	AP	(S or W)
Reasoning		C+	A+		S0		OA–						none
Simultaneous processing							OA–	GD0	BD–	Mz–	PC+		none
Spatial (Bannatyne)							OA–	GD0	BD–	Mz–	PC+		none
Synthesis							OA–	GD0	BD–				W
Trial-and-error learning							OA–		BD–	Mz–			W
Visual processing (Horn)							OA–	GD0	BD–	Mz–	PC+		none
Output													
Visual-motor coordination	I (1–6)		A (1–7)		S (1–6)		OA–	GD0	BD–	Mz–		AP+	none
Influences Affecting Scores													
Ability to respond when uncertain							OA–				PC+		none
Cognitive style (field dependence)							OA–	GD0	BD–	Mz–	PC+		none

continued

Table 4.9 continued

Ability	Verbal Subtests						Performance Subtests						Strengths or Weaknesses
	I	C	A	V	S	Sen	OA	GD	BD	Mz	PC	AP	(S or W)
Influences Affecting Scores (cont.)													
Flexibility					SO		OA–	GD0	BD–	Mz–			none
Persistence							OA–	GD0		Mz–		AP+	none
Visual-perceptual problems							OA–	GD0	BD–	Mz–		AP+	none
Work under time pressure							OA–		BD–	Mz–	PC+	AP+	none

Note. I = Information; I (1–6) = first six Information items only; C = Comprehension; A = Arithmetic; A (1–7) = first seven Arithmetic items only; V = Vocabulary; S = Similarities; S (1–6) = first six Similarities items only; Sen = Sentences; OA = Object Assembly; GD = Geometric Design; GD (1–7) = first seven Geometric Design items only; BD = Block Design; Mz = Mazes; PC = Picture Completion; AP = Animal Pegs.

0 = subtest scaled score is equal to mean subtest scaled score.

+ = subtest scaled score is above mean subtest scaled score.

– = subtest scaled score is below mean subtest scaled score.

STEP-BY-STEP: HOW TO INTERPRET THE WISC-III PROFILE

This section provides a useful, sequential approach to examine the WISC-III profile. The seven steps begin with examination of the most global scores and then move to analysis of the factor indexes before finally addressing the strengths and weaknesses in the subtest profile. It is important to integrate this empirical approach with clinical skill, theoretical understanding, and knowledge of the WISC-III to achieve an in-depth understanding of each child's profile.

Although the steps described here are similar to the sequential process we have described for interpreting the WAIS-III (Kaufman & Lichtenberger, 1999), it is important to note that they are not exactly the same. The process of going from an examination of the most global score (Full Scale IQ) to the most specific (individual subtest scaled scores) is the same, but there is variation in the steps between. What we offer here about the WISC-III differs from what we said about interpreting the WAIS-III in an effort to be consistent with Kaufman's (1994a) text on the WISC-III. We wanted to avoid confusing examiners who use Kaufman (1994a) as a companion source for this book.

A summary of the WISC-III interpretive steps is provided in Appendix C (see WISC-III Interpretive Worksheet), but in the next few pages we explain each of the steps in detail. Further explanation and examples of how to use these steps may be found in Kaufman 1994a.

Step 1. Interpret the WISC-III Full Scale IQ

As is true of all Wechsler instruments, the WISC-III Full Scale IQ is the most reliable score found on the test (average split-half $r = .96$; average test-retest $r = .94$). The strength of the most global WISC-III scale warrants its consideration first. Thus along with the Full Scale IQ, the confidence interval, percentile rank, and descriptive category should be examined. To ensure that you clearly communicate in your report the issue of scores falling within a band of error, we recommend that you include not only the confidence interval of the IQ but also the range of descriptive categories within which the score falls. Although the interpretive process begins with the Full Scale IQ, children's abilities are not often accurately represented by one simple number; thus we must delve further into the profile.

Step 2. Determine if the WISC-III Verbal-Performance IQ Discrepancy Is Statistically Significant

Compute the size of the difference between the Verbal IQ and the Performance IQ. As shown in the WISC-III Interpretive Worksheet (Appendix C), the size of discrepancy needed for significance at the $p < .01$ level is 15 or more points, and at the $p < .05$ level the size of discrepancy needed for significance is 11 points. These point values are based on the information in the WISC-III manual (Wechsler, 1991) for the average of all age groups. Each examiner must decide for each examinee which level of confidence to use (.01 or .05). For most testing purposes, when considering difference scores the level should be at least 95%, which allows for flexible interpretation; but examiners who wish to be more conservative may prefer the 99% level.

If the difference between the WISC-III Verbal IQ and Performance IQ is not significant, then the child's verbal and nonverbal skills are fairly evenly developed. As stated in the Step 2 Decision Box of the WISC-III Interpretive Worksheet, you should explain what the "nonsignificant" difference means and then skip to Step 5. If there is a significant difference between the Verbal IQ and Performance IQ, you should proceed to Step 3 prior to making any interpretation about this difference.

Step 3A. Determine if the WISC-III V-P IQ Discrepancy Is Interpretable — or if the VC and PO Factor Indexes Should Be Interpreted Instead

At times the WISC-III IQs do not represent unitary abilities. In such a case the Verbal Comprehension (VC) and Perceptual Organization (PO) indexes may provide purer measures of verbal and nonverbal abilities. Step 3 shows how to determine whether the global IQ discrepancy is clinically and practically meaningful and should be interpreted, or whether the discrepancy between the two large factors should be considered. The four questions asked in Step 3 help determine whether each of the IQs is measuring a unitary construct (e.g., if the subtest scaled scores vary greatly or the factor indexes that constitute the IQs vary greatly, then the IQ may not be a meaningful construct).

The WISC-III factor indexes can be thought of as pairs: two paired with the verbal abilities (Verbal Scale) and two with the nonverbal abilities (Performance Scale). Verbal Comprehension and Freedom from Distractibility are the Verbal pair, and Perceptual Organization and Processing Speed are the Performance pair. Don't Forget 4.2 shows the meaning of both these pairs.

1. Is there a significant difference ($p < .05$*) between the child's standard scores on the Verbal Comprehension Index and the Freedom from Distractibility Index?*
If the Verbal Comprehension Index (comprising Information, Simi-

DON'T FORGET
4.2 Pairs of Factor Indexes

Verbal IQ

Verbal Comprehension Index

Verbal conceptualization, knowledge, and expression. Answering oral questions that measure factual knowledge, word meanings, reasoning, and the ability to express ideas in words.

Freedom from Distractibility Index

Number ability and sequential processing. Responding to oral stimuli that involve the handling of numbers in a step-by-step, sequential fashion and require a good non-distractible attention span for success.

Performance IQ

Perceptual Organization Index

Nonverbal thinking and visual-motor coordination. Integrating visual stimuli, reasoning nonverbally, and applying visual-spatial and visual-motor skills to solve the kinds of problems that are not school-taught.

Processing Speed Index

Response speed. Demonstrating extreme speed in solving an assortment of nonverbal problems (speed of thinking as well as motor speed).

larities, Vocabulary, and Comprehension subtests) is significantly different from the Freedom from Distractibility Index (comprising Digit Span and Arithmetic), then the Verbal IQ doesn't mean very much. It is not a unitary construct. The WISC-III Interpretive Worksheet provides the discrepancy values necessary for the index to be significantly different from one another. Even if the two indexes do not differ significantly, the IQs still may not be interpretable due to scatter within the scales.

2. Is there abnormal scatter (highest minus lowest scaled score) among the five Verbal subtests used to compute the Verbal IQ?
The range of scaled scores on each IQ helps to determine whether the IQ is measuring a unitary construct. This range is computed by subtracting the lowest Verbal subtest scaled score from the highest. Only the subtests that are used in the computation of the Verbal IQ should be used to determine the range. If a significant amount of scatter (e.g., a range of 7 or more scaled score points) is found on the Verbal Scale, then the Verbal IQ represents nothing more than a summary of diverse abilities and does not represent a unitary entity. This IQ score should probably not be interpreted.

3. Is there a significant difference (p <.05) between the child's standard scores on the Perceptual Organization Index and the Processing Speed Index?
The question asked about the factor indexes that constitute the Performance Scale follows the same logic as presented with the Verbal Scale. If the Perceptual Organization Index (comprising Picture Completion, Picture Arrangement, Block Design, and Object Assembly) is significantly different from the Processing Speed Index (comprising Coding and Symbol Search), then the Performance IQ is not meaningful and is not a unitary construct. (See the WISC-III Interpretive Worksheet in Appendix C for discrepancy values needed for significance).

4. Is there abnormal scatter (highest minus lowest scaled score) among the five Performance subtests used to compute the Performance IQ?
Similar to the process explained in determining scatter on the Verbal Scale, the range of Performance subtest scaled scores should be calculated. If the range of scores is abnormally large (e.g., 9 or more scaled score points), then the Performance IQ does not represent a unitary construct.

To determine whether the Verbal IQ versus the Performance IQ discrepancy can be interpreted, the four questions asked about the Verbal and Performance IQs in the preceding paragraphs must be answered (see Step 3 and the Step 3 Decision Box in the WISC-III Interpretive Worksheet). If the Verbal IQ has not been found to be a meaningful unitary construct (either because of discrepancy between the Verbal Comprehension and Freedom from Distractibility indexes or because of Verbal scatter), then the discrepancy between the Verbal and Performance IQs should probably not be interpreted. Likewise if the Performance IQ has not been found to be a meaningful unitary construct (either because of discrepancy between the Perceptual Organization and Processing Speed indexes or because of Performance scatter), then the discrepancy between the Verbal and Performance IQs should probably not be interpreted.

In summary, if all four of the questions asked in Step 3 are answered "no," then both the Verbal IQ and Performance IQ are meaningful unitary constructs and therefore the discrepancy between these IQs may be meaningfully interpreted. This discrepancy is a way to represent the difference between a child's verbal and nonverbal abilities. However, if the answer to at least one of the Step 3 questions is "yes," then the Verbal-Performance IQ discrepancy is probably not interpretable and the difference between the Verbal IQ and Performance IQ should probably not be interpreted. If either of the IQs is uninterpretable, for any reason, move to the next part of Step 3 in which the Verbal Comprehension Index and the Perceptual Organization Index are examined.

Step 3B. Examine the WISC-III Verbal Comprehension–Perceptual Organization Factor Index Discrepancy

A second way to examine the verbal and nonverbal abilities of children on the WISC-III is via the Verbal Comprehension Index and the Perceptual Organization Index. These are sometimes considered "purer" measures of verbal and nonverbal intelligence because they use the subtests that measure sequential processing, short-term memory, and number ability removed from the Verbal Comprehension Index and the two subtests that measure mental and motor speed removed from the Perceptual Organization Index.

The process of determining whether the Verbal Comprehension Index and Perceptual Organization Index are interpretable is similar to that done with the Verbal and Performance IQ. Questions about scatter on each of the indexes are answered to determine if each index represents unitary dimensions: (a) Is there abnormal scatter among the four Verbal Comprehension subtests? and (b) Is there abnormal scatter among the four Perceptual Organization subtests? If the range of scaled scores on the Verbal Comprehension Index subtests is 7 or more points, then the index is said to have abnormal scatter. If the range of scaled scores on the Perceptual Organization Index subtests is 8 or more points, then the index is said to have abnormal scatter.

If abnormal scatter is present on either the Verbal Comprehension or Perceptual Organization Index, then you probably should not interpret the Verbal Comprehension Index versus Perceptual Organization Index discrepancy. The presence of abnormal scatter on either index means that the index cannot be meaningfully interpreted, as it is not a unitary factor. However, if both indexes are found to be unitary factors (abnormal scatter is not present in either factor), then the difference between the Verbal Comprehension Index and the Perceptual Organization Index may be interpreted.

Step 4. Determine if the WISC-III Verbal IQ Versus Performance IQ Discrepancy or Verbal Comprehension Versus Perceptual Organization Discrepancy Is Abnormally Large

Although we have determined whether the size of the discrepancy between the verbal and nonverbal dimensions (either the Verbal IQ and Performance IQ or the Verbal Conceptualization Index) is significant, it is important to look one step further. Step 4 examines the frequency with which discrepancies of various magnitudes occur within the normal population. In the standardization population, the mean discrepancy between the Verbal and Performance IQs is 10.0 and the mean discrepancy between the Verbal Comprehension Index and the Perceptual Organization Index is 10.3 (Wechsler, 1991, Table B.1). These differences are just shy of the difference needed for significance (11 points for the IQs and 12 points for the indexes). About 25% of the children in the standardization have Verbal-Performance IQ discrepancies that are significantly different (11 points or greater).

Although a difference is significant (and therefore meaningful), it may not be unusual or abnormal. To determine how unusual the size of a given discrepancy is, examiners should look at the frequency of occurrence of a discrepancy. The tables in Step 4 of the WISC-III Interpretive Worksheet provide the size of the discrepancies necessary to be considered abnormal. For either a Verbal-Performance IQ discrepancy or a Verbal Comprehension–Perceptual Organization discrepancy to be considered abnormal, it must be at least 19 points (this occurs in 15% or less of the normal population). The Step 4 tables also present the extreme 1%, 2%, 5%, and 10% so that examiners can determine more specifically how rare a given discrepancy is.

If an abnormally large discrepancy between a child's verbal and nonverbal abilities (IQs or indexes) is found, then that discrepancy should be addressed and interpreted. The abnormal discrepancy should be interpreted even if an abnormal amount of scatter is found to exist within the IQs or indexes. As outlined in the Step 4 Decision Box (WISC-III Interpretive Worksheet), the abnormal discrepancy should be interpreted. But if no abnormal differences between the verbal and nonverbal dimensions are found, then the subtest scatter and discrepancy between indexes (Verbal Comprehension vs. Freedom from Distractibility, and Perceptual Organization vs. Processing Speed) should be reviewed prior to making global interpretations.

Step 5. Interpret the Meaning of the Global Verbal and Nonverbal Dimensions and the Meaning of the Small Factors

Just as the Verbal IQ, Performance IQ, Verbal Comprehension Index, and Perceptual Organization Index have been examined to determine if they are unitary dimensions, the smallest factors must be checked for abnormal scatter. Part of Step 5 involves examining the difference between Arithmetic and Digit Span to determine if the Freedom from Distractibility Index is interpretable. If the difference is 4 or more points, there is abnormal scatter and the index should not be interpreted. The difference between Coding and Symbol Search should also be calculated to determine if the Processing Speed Index is interpretable. If the difference is 4 or more points, there is abnormal scatter and this index should not be interpreted. If abnormal scatter is not present on these indexes, then they should be considered unitary dimensions and may be meaningfully interpreted. Step 5 of the WISC-III Interpretive Worksheet reviews the values necessary to determine abnormal scatter on the Freedom from Distractibility Index and the Processing Speed Index.

If you have found that the IQs and/or indexes are meaningful and warrant interpretation, then you must explore the many available interpretive hypotheses. As with the WPPSI-R, such hypotheses are derived from clinical, theoretical, and research-based sources. Many sources are available for deriving hypotheses, and we provide only a brief overview here (see also Flanagan, McGrew, & Ortiz, in press; Kaufman, 1994a; Prifitera & Saklofske, 1998). Possible interpretations of Verbal > Performance profiles and Performance > Verbal profiles were presented earlier in this book during discussion of WPPSI-R interpretation (pp. 133–136). Like the global verbal and nonverbal factors, the small factors on the WISC-III have numerous possible interpretations.

Freedom from Distractibility Index

The two subtests that constitute the Freedom from Distractibility Index, Arithmetic and Digit Span, are not simply measures of a child's level of distractibility (as the name of the index suggests). To truly understand how to interpret this index, examiners must look beyond the factor index score and the scaled scores of the subtests that constitute it. Interpretation must be done by examining behavioral observations, background information, and the nuances of the child's performance (e.g., analysis of errors on Arithmetic and comparing forward vs. backward span on Digit Span).

The possible interpretations of the Freedom from Distractibility Index are diverse. They may include such hypotheses as attention, concentration, anxiety, sequencing ability, sequential processing, number ability, planning ability, short-term memory, executive processing, and visualization (see Don't Forget 4.3). Hypothetical interpretations of the Freedom from Distractibility Index include those that are behaviorally driven as well as

> **DON'T FORGET**
>
> ### 4.3 Possible Interpretations of the Freedom from Distractibility Index
>
> - attention
> - concentration
> - anxiety
> - sequencing ability
> - number ability
> - planning ability
> - short-term memory
> - executive processing or planning
> - visualization

those that are cognitive. In some cases a child's performance on this index may have multiple interpretations.

Deciding what a child's performance on the Freedom from Distractibility Index means requires good clinical skill and the ability to integrate data from diverse sources. For example, to accept a behavioral explanation as the main source of a child's performance, you must have clinical support. Distractibility, poor concentration, inattention, hyperactivity, and anxiety cannot be assumed to be present without some behavioral symptoms. If a child cannot remain seated for more than 10 minutes, touches everything that is within arm's reach, and asks you questions about everything except the task at hand, this may be powerful evidence for distractibility and hyperactivity. Likewise, if a child's parent presents background information including reports of inattention and "spacing off" during classes in school and you notice that during the evaluation session the child is only able to hold his attention sporadically, then you clearly have evidence supportive of poor attention as an explanation of a low index.

Anxiety may manifest itself during the evaluation session in the form of excess motor activity, excessive talking, or distractibility. Such anxiety may especially affect highly speeded WISC-III tasks. Other factors such as the child's background history and referral question should be considered when deciding whether anxiety may have influenced performance on the index.

Another possible explanation performance on the Freedom from Distractibility Index is number ability. If a child has not adequately mastered basic computational skills, compensatory strategies such as counting on fingers or writing with fingers may be observed. Children may verbalize anxiety about working with numbers or about their math class in school. Although difficulties will be most apparent during the Arithmetic subtest, some problems may also be noticeable during Digit Span. Specifically during the Digits Backward portion of the task, difficulties may be noted because it involves manipulation of numbers. Even if Digits Forward is found to be adequate (as it only involves simple rote memory), Digits Backward may cause difficulty for a child who has poorly developed number skills or is insecure about his or her number ability. Of course the opposite explanation should be considered for children who perform extremely well on the Freedom from Distractibility Index. Children who are strong in mathematics and feel confident in their numerical abilities may show exceptional skill on the tasks that constitute this index.

Memory is another influencing factor for the Freedom from Distractibility Index. The cognitive demands for the earlier items of Arithmetic are not as memory-intensive as the later items. The later items require children to hold in their memory the necessary facts and then manipulate the numerical values to come up with a correct response. Similarly, the two portions of Digit Span (Forward and Backward) have different demands on the memory. Digits Forward requires simple rote memory, whereas Digits Backward requires visualization of the numbers and manipulation of them while they are held in memory. Examination of the Coding subtest may also help to rule in or rule out a memory hypothesis. On Coding children benefit from remembering the visual stimuli, so examination of this variable may be helpful.

Processing Speed Index

As with the Freedom from Distractibility Index, to accurately interpret the Processing Speed Index multiple sources of data must be integrated. The most obvious interpretation of the Processing Speed Index is, of course, processing speed. However, other factors may also come into play during the two subtests on this index: Coding and Symbol Search. Other factors include fine motor coordination, motivation, reflectiveness, compulsiveness, visual memory, and planning ability (see Don't Forget 4.4).

The types of speed measured by the two subtests of the Processing Speed Index differ. Mental speed is tapped considerably during Symbol Search, whereas psychomotor speed is tapped during Coding. Either or both of these aspects of speed may influence a score on the Processing Speed Index. The effect of visual-motor coordination is also important in evaluation of performance on this index. Observe children as they hold the pencil. Awkward, clumsy grips and pencil strokes that are not fluid may indicate poor visual-motor coordination. Visual-motor coordination may also be observed during other

> ## DON'T FORGET
> ....
> ### 4.4 Possible Interpretations of the Processing Speed Index
>
> • processing speed
> • visual-motor coordination
> • motivation
> • reflectiveness
> • compulsiveness
> • visual memory
> • planning ability

Performance subtests such as Block Design, Object Assembly, and Picture Arrangement. Each of these subtests requires children to manipulate some sort of object. Visual-perceptual problems may also be evident from how a child draws the symbols during the Coding subtest, errors made during Block Design and Object Assembly, or distortions seen on Picture Completion items.

Noncognitive factors may impact a child's performance on the Processing Speed Index too. For example, level of motivation, anxiety, and perfectionism may all play a role in performance. Some children have a reflective, careful style of processing information, and they are therefore reluctant to work quickly. Other children with perfectionistic tendencies may work very slowly and carefully to ensure that they do not draw any of the symbols inaccurately on Coding or make a messy slash mark on Symbol Search. Anxiety may interfere with a child's ability to remain focused on the task at hand, and this might affect performance as well.

Planning ability and visual memory are two other influences to consider in interpretation of the Processing Speed Index. Good or poor planning ability may be especially evident on the Symbol Search subtest. Children are required to efficiently handle one or two abstract symbols during this task. If children have good planning abilities you may see better performance on Symbol Search than on Coding, but if they are poor in planning ability Symbol Search may be weaker. Performance on both Coding and Symbol Search can be enhanced by strong visual memory skills. If children can remember either the target symbols in Symbol Search or the pairs of symbols and numbers in Coding without having to repeatedly look back at the key, then they will be able to perform more efficiently.

Step 6. Interpret Significant Strengths and Weaknesses in the WISC-III Subtest Profile

Step 6 looks at the finest level of the profile—the subtest profile. It is at the subtest level that an understanding of each unique child is developed. Hypotheses about children's relative individual strengths and weaknesses in cognitive abilities are derived from the peaks and valleys in the subtest profile.

Step 6 requires an ipsative comparison of a child's mean performance on all subtests with each test administered. In contrast to comparing a child's subtest score to that of the normative group, an ipsative comparison examines how well a child is performing relative to his or her own average subtest score. Although a child may earn a subtest scaled score of 11, which is in the Average range compared to the normative group, if the child's own *mean* subtest scaled score is 7, then relative to his or her own performance that subtest scaled score of 11 is high and demonstrates a personal strength.

There are two possible ways by which a mean subtest scaled score can be obtained for Step 7: determine the mean of all subtests administered, or calculate the mean of the Verbal subtests and the mean of the Performance subtests separately. Rapid Reference 4.17 reviews the rules governing which mean to use. Generally, if a child's Verbal IQ versus Performance IQ discrepancy is abnormally large (19 points or more), then you should use two separate means (the mean of all Verbal subtests administered and the mean of all Performance subtests administered). However, if the discrepancy between the Verbal IQ and the Performance IQ is not abnormally large (less than 19 points), then the mean of all subtests administered may be used. If the Verbal

≡ Rapid Reference

4.17 Determining Which Mean to Calculate During Step 6

Mean of What	Includes These Subtests	Total # of Subtests in Calculation of Mean[a]
All subtests administered	5 Verbal subtests + Digit Span + 5 Performance subtests + Symbol Search	12
All Verbal Scale subtests administered	5 Verbal subtests + Digit Span	6
All Performance Scale subtests administered	5 Performance subtests + Symbol Search	6

[a]If all of these subtests were not administered, just include *all* that were administered (e.g., 10, 5, or 5).

and Performance scales show abnormal differences, it makes more sense to compare the subtests on each of the scales just to the mean of that particular scale. But if there is not an unusual difference between the scales, the mean of all the subtests together is the best point of comparison for every subtest.

The mean(s) that are used should be rounded to the nearest whole number (see WISC-III Interpretive Worksheet). Working with whole numbers during the next calculations reduces the chance of examiner error but does not compromise your statistical examination. The difference between each of the individual subtests' means and the overall subtest mean(s) should be calculated. Subtest means that are higher than the overall mean should be recorded with a plus sign (+), and those that are lower than the overall mean should be recorded with a minus sign (−) on the WISC-III Interpretive Worksheet.

To determine whether a particular subtest significantly deviates from the mean of subtests, examine the column on the WISC-III Interpretive Worksheet labeled "Size of Difference Needed for Significance." The values are summarized in this column of the Worksheet but may also be found in the WISC-III manual (Wechsler, 1991, pp. 263−264). We provide an overview with rounded values that are sufficient to calculate strengths and weaknesses. However, if you wish, you may use the exact values presented in the WISC-III manual.

If the difference between a particular subtest and the child's mean is large enough to be statistically significant, then it may be considered a relative strength (if above the mean) or weakness (if below the mean). On the WISC-III Interpretive Worksheet, the strengths and weaknesses may be denoted by the letters *S* and *W*, respectively. However, if differences are not large enough to be considered statistically significant, then they must be considered chance fluctuations. Nonsignificant differences should not be interpreted as strengths or weaknesses. However, performance on these subtests may be used to support hypotheses, as discussed in Step 7.

Similar to Step 6 of WPPSI-R Interpretation, the subtest scaled scores should be converted to percentile ranks. Table 4.5 lists the percentile ranks that correspond to each scaled score. Parents, teachers, and other laypeople, as well as professionals, are likely to understand the metric of percentile rank (but most likely will not be familiar with the scaled score's metric of a mean of 10 and a standard deviation of 3). In writing the test interpretation section of a case report, examiners may find it useful to discuss performance on subtests by including percentile ranks.

Step 7. Generate Hypotheses About the Fluctuations in the WISC-III Subtest Profile

Step 7 is critical in determining what underlies the pattern of subtest strengths and weaknesses. This step requires examiners to pull data not only from the WISC-III itself but also from behavioral observations, background information, and supplemental testing in order to support or reject potential hypotheses about a child's abilities. Unless an interpretation is supported by multiple pieces of data, it may not be strongly validated. Only from validated interpretive hypotheses are strong recommendations made.

The goal of Step 7 in WISC-III interpretation is similar to the final step of WPPSI-R interpretation. To create the most meaningful hypotheses, abilities shared by two or more subtests should be found. When each strength or weakness is supported by two or more subtests—plus clinical observations, background information, and supplementary testing—examiners can feel confident in what they report about a child's abilities. If examiners choose to simply list the abilities associated with each subtest in isolation, they risk missing important information that may be present in the overall pattern of subtests in the profile.

WISC-III Subtest Interpretive Tables

Rapid Reference 4.18 lists the abilities underlying WISC-III subtests that are shared by at least two of the subtests. The information included in this Rapid Reference is a summary of the material that was included in the subtest-by-subtest analysis at the beginning of this chapter. Hypothesis generation may be facilitated by using these shared abilities.

The organization of Rapid Reference 4.18 is similar to that of Rapid Reference 4.15. The WISC-III shared abilities are organized according to the Information Processing Model: Input-Integration/Storage-Output. In the far right column of Rapid Reference 4.18, the split-half and test-retest reliabilities for the combinations of subtests are provided. These values are based on the average reliability values and the subtests' intercorrelations presented in the WISC-III man-

≡ Rapid Reference

4.18 Abilities Shared by Two or More WISC-III Verbal and Performance Subtests

Ability	Verbal Subtests						Performance Subtests						Reliability[a]	
	I	S	A	V	C	D	PC	Cd	PA	BD	OA	SS	r_{xx}	r_{12}
Input														
Attention-concentration			A			D	PC	Cd				SS	.91	.90
Auditory-vocal channel	I	S	A	V	C	D							.95	.94
Complex verbal directions								Cd	PA	BD		SS	.90	.87
Distinguishing essential from nonessential detail		S					PC		PA			SS	.89	.88
Encode information for processing			A			D		Cd				SS	.90	.88
Simple verbal directions							PC				OA		.82	.82
Understanding long questions	I		A		C								.90	.89
Understanding words		S		V		D							.92	.90
Visual-motor channel							PC	Cd	PA	BD	OA	SS	.92	.91
Visual perception of abstract stimuli								Cd		BD		SS	.89	.87

continued

Ability	Verbal Subtests						Performance Subtests						Reliability[a]	
	I	S	A	V	C	D	PC	Cd	PA	BD	OA	SS	r_{xx}	r_{12}
Input (cont.)														
Visual perception of complete meaningful stimuli							PC		PA				.83	.80
Visual perception of meaningful stimuli							PC		PA		OA		.86	.84
Integration/Storage														
Achievement (Horn)	I	S	A	V	C				PA				.92	.90
Acquired knowledge	I		A	V									.92	.92
Cognition (Guilford)		S	A	V	C		PC			BD	OA		.94	.94
Common sense					C				PA				.83	.77
Concept formation		S		V						BD			.93	.92
Convergent production (Guilford)								Cd	PA			SS	.87	.84
Crystallized ability (Horn)	I	S		V	C				PA				.91	.90
Culture-loaded knowledge	I				C								.88	.87
Evaluation (Guilford)					C		PC	Cd	PA	BD	OA	SS	.93	.92
Facility with numbers (ages 8+)			A			D		Cd					.88	.84

Ability	Verbal Subtests						Performance Subtests						Reliability[a]	
	I	S	A	V	C	D	PC	Cd	PA	BD	OA	SS	r_{xx}	r_{12}
Integration/Storage (cont.)														
Figural cognition (Guilford)							PC			BD	OA		.89	.88
Figural evaluation (ages 6–7) (Guilford)							PC	Cd		BD	OA	SS	.90	.88
Figural evaluation (ages 8+) (Guilford)							PC			BD	OA	SS	.90	.89
Fluid ability (Horn)		S	A						PA	BD	OA		.92	.90
Fund of information	I			V									.91	.92
General ability	I	S	A	V	C					BD			.95	.95
Handling abstract verbal concepts		S		V									.91	.91
Holistic (right-brain) processing							PC				OA		.82	.82
Integrated brain function		S						Cd	PA	BD		SS	.90	.87
Language development		S		V	C								.92	.92
Learning ability				V				Cd				SS	.89	.89
Long-term memory	I		A	V									.92	.92
Memory (Guilford)	I		A			D							.91	.88
Nonverbal reasoning									PA	BD	OA		.80	.74
Planning ability								Cd	PA	BD	OA	SS	.82	.77

continued

Ability	Verbal Subtests						Performance Subtests						Reliability[a]	
	I	S	A	V	C	D	PC	Cd	PA	BD	OA	SS	r_{xx}	r_{12}
Integration/Storage (cont.)														
Reasoning		S	A		C				PA		OA		.91	.89
Reproduction of models								Cd		BD			.87	.82
Semantic cognition (Guilford)		S	A	V									.92	.91
Semantic content (Guilford)	I	S	A	V	C				PA				.95	.94
Sequential (Bannatyne)			A			D		Cd					.88	.84
Short-term memory (auditory or visual)						D		Cd				SS	.88	.85
Simultaneous processing							PC			BD	OA		.89	.88
Social comprehension					C				PA				.83	.77
Spatial (Bannatyne)							PC			BD	OA		.89	.88
Spatial Visualization										BD		SS	.87	.83
Symbolic content (Guilford)			A			D		Cd					.88	.84
Synthesis									PA	BD	OA		.88	.84
Trial-and-error learning										BD	OA		.86	.82
Verbal concept formation		S		V									.91	.91

Ability	Verbal Subtests						Performance Subtests						Reliability[a]	
	I	S	A	V	C	D	PC	Cd	PA	BD	OA	SS	r_{xx}	r_{12}
Integration/Storage (cont.)														
Verbal conceptualization (Barnatyne)		S		V	C								.92	.92
Verbal reasoning		S			C								.87	.86
Visual memory							PC	Cd				SS	.87	.87
Visual processing (Horn)							PC		PA	BD	OA		.89	.88
Visual sequencing								Cd	PA				.82	.81
Output														
Much verbal expression		S		V	C								.92	.92
Simple vocal expression	I		A			D							.91	.88
Visual organization							PC		PA				.83	.80
Visual-motor coordination								Cd		BD	OA	SS	.90	.88
Influences Affecting Scores														
Ability to respond when uncertain							PC				OA		.82	.82
Alertness to environment	I						PC						.87	.88
Anxiety			A			D		Cd				SS	.90	.88
Attention span			A			D						SS	.88	.85

continued

Influences Affecting Scores (cont.)

Ability	Verbal Subtests							Performance Subtests					Reliability[a]	
	I	S	A	V	C	D	PC	Cd	PA	BD	OA	SS	r_{xx}	r_{12}
Cognitive style (field dependence)							PC			BD	OA		.89	.88
Concentration			A				PC	Cd				SS	.89	.89
Cultural opportunities	I			V	C				PA				.92	.91
Distractibility			A			D		Cd				SS	.90	.88
Flexibility		S		V		D			PA	BD	OA		.92	.89
Foreign language background	I			V									.91	.92
Hearing difficulties			A			D							.88	.85
Intellectual curiosity and striving	I			V									.91	.92
Interests	I	S		V									.93	.94
Learning disabilities			A			D		Cd				SS	.90	.88
Motivation level								Cd				SS	.85	.84
Negativism		S			C	D	PC	Cd					.91	.89
Obsessive concern with detail and accuracy								Cd				SS	.85	.84

Ability	Verbal Subtests						Performance Subtests						Reliability[a]	
	I	S	A	V	C	D	PC	Cd	PA	BD	OA	SS	r_{xx}	r_{12}
Influences Affecting Scores (cont.)														
Outside reading	I	S		V									.93	.94
Overly concrete thinking		S			C								.87	.86
Persistence								Cd			OA	SS	.86	.84
Richness of early environment	I			V									.91	.92
School learning	I		A	V									.92	.92
Visual-perceptual problems								Cd		BD	OA	SS	.90	.88
Work under time pressure			A				PC	Cd	PA	BD	OA	SS	.93	.92

Note. I = Information; S = Similarities; A = Arithmetic; V = Vocabulary; C = Comprehension; D = Digit Span; PC = Picture Completion; Cd = Coding; PA = Picture Arrangement; BD = Block Design; OA = Object Assembly; SS = Symbol Search.

[a] r_{xx} = split-half reliability; r_{12} = test-retest reliability.

ual (Wechsler, 1991). Keep in mind that the lists of abilities and influences on the subtests are not exhaustive and may be added to by examiners.

Guidelines for Using the Information in the WISC-III Shared Abilities Tables (Rapid Reference 4.18)

The five guidelines provided in this section will help examiners wade through the information available about each subtest. This will help in identifying potential strong and weak abilities to investigate in a systematic manner.

Guideline 1

Choose one of the subtests that was found to be a significant strength (S) or weakness (W). Write down all the shared abilities and influences that involve this subtest. Next to each of the listed abilities or influences associated with the subtest, write down the other subtests that are also associated with the ability or influence.

Guideline 2

One by one, examine each ability or influence associated with the subtest being evaluated (chosen in Guideline 1) to determine how the child performed on the other subtests that also measure the ability. In order to decide what abilities explain the relative strength or weakness in a subtest, consider whether a child has scored above, below, or equal to his or her own mean score on all pertinent subtests for an ability. This information can be obtained directly from Step 6 of the WISC-III Interpretive Worksheet that you already completed. Whether the value recorded in the subtest average score minus subtest "Difference" column of Step 6 is negative, positive, or neutral, this should be recorded. Simply write the following notations next to each subtest in the list that was derived in Guideline 1:

- − (indicating performance below the child's mean subtest scaled score)
- + (indicating performance above the child's mean subtest scaled score)
- 0 (indicating performance exactly at the child's mean subtest scaled score).

Guideline 3

To determine whether each ability should be considered a hypothesized strength (or weakness), examine the pattern of pluses, minuses, and zeros written next to each of the subtests that underlie a shared ability. In general, shared strengths are those in which a child has scored above his or her own mean score on all pertinent subtests, with at least one discrepancy reaching statistical significance. There are exceptions to consider beyond this general rule, however. These exceptions are described in Don't Forget 4.1 on page 156. It is important to note that the rules about whether to accept or reject abilities as strengths or weaknesses are not rigid principles but rather rules of thumb. For instance, if there is a large amount of clinical data from the background information or behavioral observations that support a shared ability as a strength or weakness, you may want to consider this ability even if the guidelines in Don't Forget 4.1 are not met. An ability may be accepted and interpreted as a relative strength or weakness if multiple sources of information support it.

Guideline 4

For every other subtest determined to be a significant strength or weakness in Step 6, repeat Guidelines 1, 2, and 3. It is important not only to follow the rules for accepting and rejecting potential hypotheses (Don't Forget 4.1) but to also evaluate all the behavioral observations, background information, and supplemental testing to determine whether they support or contradict the findings in the WISC-III profile. When multiple pieces of data support the same hypothesis, examiners can be confident in their interpretations.

Guideline 5

In some situations, no hypothesized strong or weak abilities are uncovered while examining subtests' shared abilities. If this occurs, then you may need to consider interpreting the unique abilities that are measured by high or low subtest scores. Prior to interpreting unique abilities, every attempt should be made to explain the strengths and weaknesses by evaluating abilities shared by two or more subtests and supported by other information (background, behaviors, supplemental testing). If it is necessary to consider the abilities that are unique to one subtest only, the psychometric qualities of that subtest must be considered. Rapid Reference 4.2 lists the amount of specificity and error of each WISC-III subtest. Those subtests with ample or adequate amounts of specificity may be interpreted. Object Assembly is the only WISC-III subtest that is deemed to have an inadequate amount of subtest specificity. Even those subtests with ample or adequate specificity must be evaluated in light of other supportive evidence prior to making a unique interpretation. The unique abilities of each subtest are listed in the subtest-by-subtest description of abilities (denoted with an asterisk) earlier in this chapter. When investigation of shared abilities proves fruitless and the unique subtest specific abilities are supported with ample additional data, these unique abilities may be useful in interpretation.

 TEST YOURSELF

1. **The approach to test interpretation for the WPPSI-R and the WISC-III advocated in this chapter requires examiners to focus on**

   (a) unique abilities of subtests.

   (b) shared abilities across two or more subtests.

   (c) shared abilities across two or more subtests plus behavioral observations.

   (d) shared abilities across two or more subtests plus behavioral observations, background information, and supplemental testing.

2. **You have been analyzing Annie's profile and have found that there are no abilities shared by two or more subtests. Before interpreting the unique ability for a specific subtest, what should you consider?**

   (a) the g loading

   (b) throwing out the entire assessment

   (c) the amount of subtest specificity

   (d) the intercorrelations between all subtests

3. **The most reliable score on both the WPPSI-R and the WISC-III is the**

   (a) Full Scale IQ.

   (b) Verbal IQ.

   (c) Performance IQ.

4. **In completing Step 4 of the WISC-III Interpretive Worksheet (Appendix C), you find that there is a 22-point discrepancy between Jon's Verbal IQ and his Performance IQ. Because this is considered an abnormally large discrepancy,**

   (a) Jon should be deemed abnormal.

   (b) Jon's profile should be considered invalid.

   (c) this unusually large discrepancy should be interpreted even if there is significant scatter in either the Verbal or Performance scales.

   (d) you must check to see whether there are significant discrepancies between the factor index before being able to interpret this abnormally large discrepancy.

5. **An ipsative comparison is one that**

   (a) compares an individual's scores to those in the normative group that are the same age as the individual.

   (b) compares an individual's subtest scaled score to the mean of his or her own mean scaled score.

   (c) should only be made on rare occasions.

   (d) can only be made with children ages 3 to 5 years.

6. **A hypothesis that a child has difficulty understanding pictorial stimuli may be supported if a young child has made many errors *only* on the first few items on which of the following WPPSI-R subtests?**

   (a) Information, Arithmetic, Similarities, Geometric Design, Vocabulary

   (b) Sentences, Comprehension, Information, Object Assembly

   (c) Animal Pegs, Object Assembly, Block Design, Mazes

7. **The "Rules for Accepting and Rejecting Potential Hypotheses" for using the shared abilities tables in WPPSI-R and WISC-III profile interpretation should be considered rigid rules that are not ever to be broken.** True or False?

8. **The constructs central to Horn and Cattell's (1967) theory are**

   (a) Verbal and Performance IQ.

   (b) Crystallized (Gc) and Fluid (Gf) Intelligence.

   (c) creativity and practical intelligence.

   (d) visual and auditory memory.

continued

9. **A low score on the WISC-III Freedom from Distractibility Index may be interpreted as all of the following except**

   (a) distractibility or attentional difficulties.

   (b) difficulty with numbers.

   (c) poor motor ability.

   (d) excessive anxiety.

10. **The suggestion to replace Symbol Search with Coding when calculating the Performance IQ and Full Scale IQ was made because**

    (a) Coding is a boring test for most children.

    (b) Symbol Search is a newer subtest.

    (c) the psychometric qualities of Symbol Search are stronger than those of Coding.

    (d) most children perform better on Symbol Search than on Coding.

11. **A low score on the Processing Speed Index of the WISC-III may be interpreted as all of the following except**

    (a) fine motor control difficulty.

    (b) reflective processing style.

    (c) poor visual memory.

    (d) poor nonverbal reasoning.

12. **The goal of the detective work involved in deciphering the strong and weak areas in either the WPPSI-R or WISC-III profile is to find information that is consistent across the entire profile.** True or False?

Answers: 1. d; 2. c; 3. a; 4. c; 5. b; 6. a; 7. False; 8. b; 9. c; 10. c; 11. d; 12. True

Five

STRENGTHS AND WEAKNESSES OF THE WISC-III AND WPPSI-R

S ince the Wechsler instruments' inception, there have been many published opinions about their strengths and weaknesses. In this chapter we highlight what we feel are the tests' *major* strengths and weaknesses. For the WPPSI-R and the WISC-III we list strengths and weaknesses of test development, administration and scoring, reliability and validity, standardization, and interpretation. We choose the Rapid Reference format to present this information most efficiently.

OVERVIEW OF ADVANTAGES AND DISADVANTAGES OF THE WPPSI-R

The strengths and weaknesses of the WPPSI-R have been identified from our own clinical experience with the instrument as well as from published reviews (Bracken, 1992; Delugach, 1991; Glutting & McDermott, 1989; Kaufman, 1990b, 1992; Kaufman & Lichtenberger, 1998; Sattler, 1992) and are summarized in Rapid References 5.1 through 5.5.

We have found several major strengths of the WPPSI-R: The reliability is excellent for all IQ scales, stability coefficients for IQ scales are quite strong, and factor analytic results demonstrate construct validity of the test. In addition, the normative group on which the test was based was well stratified and an excellent overall sample. Weaknesses of the WPPSI-R include the overemphasis on speed of processing and inclusion of some concepts that are too advanced for preschool-age children. The floor of some of the WPPSI-R subtests is unsatisfactory for the youngest children, and certain subtests have poor stability coefficients.

OVERVIEW OF ADVANTAGES AND DISADVANTAGES OF THE WISC-III

The strengths and weaknesses of the WISC-III have been identified from our own clinical experience with the instrument as well as from published reviews (Alfonso, Johnson, Patinella, & Rader, 1998; Blumberg, 1995; Braden, 1995; Kaufman, 1992, 1993, 1994a; Kaufman & Lichtenberger, 1998; Prifitera & Saklofske, 1998; Sandoval, 1995, Sattler, 1992; Slate, 1998) and are summarized in Rapid References 5.6 through 5.10.

The psychometric qualities of the WISC-III are included among its major strengths. The split-half reliability coefficients are strong for all IQ scales, and the validity of the instrument is well documented through numerous studies. The WISC-III normative sample was excellent and well stratified. The clinical usefulness and interpretability of the test are aided by the four-factor structure of the WISC-III. We do note some weaknesses, but none that we consider *major*.

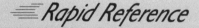

Rapid Reference

5.1 Strengths and Weaknesses of WPPSI-R Test Development

Strengths

- Artwork, including color, is appealing to young children.
- Tabbed format of the manual and "bent" cover are user friendly.

Weaknesses

- The test does not provide a factor solution that is similar to that of the WISC-III and WAIS-III.
- The new Similarities picture items can be confusing because the target stimuli (top) and the choice stimuli (bottom) are not separated by a line of any sort.
- Too much emphasis is placed on speed (e.g., bonus points for Block Design and Object Assembly) for an age group that is not generally attuned to the need to respond quickly.

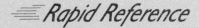

Rapid Reference

5.2 Strengths and Weaknesses of WPPSI-R Administration and Scoring

Strengths

- The record form is well designed and facilitates administration.
- Inclusion of teaching items facilitates administration to the youngest children.

Weaknesses

- Many directions are too long and wordy.
- Some directions include concepts that may be too advanced for some preschoolers (e.g., *farther, inside, middle, skip*).
- Extreme detail in scoring Geometric Design costs examiners a lot of time.
- Directing a young child to "Now HURRY!" places undue stress on a youngster who doesn't understand the concept of needing to work quickly.
- The 75-minute administration time is inappropriate for many very young children.

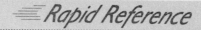

5.3 Strengths and Weaknesses of WPPSI-R Reliability and Validity

Strengths

- Reliability coefficients for IQs are strong (Verbal, Performance, and Full Scale IQs averaged .95).
- Stability coefficients for the three IQs are good (.88 to .91).
- Factor analytic results offer strong support for the construct validity of the battery across all age groups.

Weaknesses

- The floor of half of the 12 subtests is poor for the youngest children (raw scores of 1 translate to 8 for Comprehension, 7 for Similarities, and 6 for other tasks).
- For 7-year-olds, the ceiling of some of the tasks is marginal (maximum scaled score of 16 for Object Assembly, Geometric Design, and Arithmetic).
- Stability coefficients for individual subtests are highly variable with some values below .75. Average test-retest values are low for Object Assembly (.59), Geometric Design (.67), Mazes (.52), Animal Pegs (.66), Arithmetic (.71), and Similarities (.70).

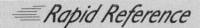

Rapid Reference

5.4 Strengths and Weaknesses of WPPSI-R Standardization

Strengths

- Age range was expanded to span 3 years 0 months and 7 years 3 months.

- The excellent, large normative group was well stratified to match U.S. Census data.

Weaknesses

- There are no major weaknesses.

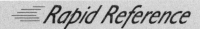

Rapid Reference

5.5 Strengths and Weaknesses of WPPSI-R Interpretation

Strengths

- The manual includes tables that display significant differences between the child's subtests and mean scores as well as frequency of occurrence of significant differences.

Weaknesses

- The inclusion of different types of items on the same subtest complicates interpretation (e.g., there are both picture and verbal items on Information, Similarities, Vocabulary, and Arithmetic; and Geometric Design contains recognition and reproduction items).

≋ Rapid Reference

5.6 Strengths and Weaknesses of WISC-III Test Development

Strengths

- Artwork in the WISC-III is colorful and appealing to children.
- A rigorous approach was taken to remove biased items.

Weaknesses

- In light of its poor psychometric properties, Coding should have been replaced by Symbol Search as a regular subtest in calculation of the IQs.
- Despite the good attempts to remove biased items, the Comprehension subtest still appears to be rather culturally loaded.
- Mazes should have been excluded from the WISC-III; this subtest has poor psycho- metric properties and is not included on any of the four factors.

≋ Rapid Reference

5.7 Strengths and Weaknesses of WISC-III Administration and Scoring

Strengths

- Scoring systems of subjective subtests (Vocabulary, Comprehension, and Similarities) have been improved.
- The "bent" cover of the manual allows it to stand independently, thereby easing administration.

Weaknesses

- There is an unfair increase in the role of bonus points for speed in determining the child's IQ.
- Inadequate floors are present for 6-year-olds for Similarities, Block Design, Picture Arrangement, and Information.
- The ceiling for Picture Completion and Information at age 16 is insufficient, yielding a maximum scaled score of 17.

≋ Rapid Reference

5.8 Strengths and Weaknesses of WISC-III Reliability and Validity

Strengths

- Mean split-half reliability coefficients for the IQs are strong, ranging from .91 to .96.
- Numerous studies supporting the validity of the WISC-III are presented in the manual (e.g., factor structure; correlations with other Wechsler scales; correlations with tests of ability, achievement, and neuropsychological ability, and with school grades).

Weaknesses

- Stability coefficients for Object Assembly (.66), Mazes (.57), and Picture Arrangement (.64) are weak.
- Several Verbal subtests are strongly school related and culturally loaded, making them potentially unfair to ethnic groups such as Hispanics, African Americans, and Native Americans, as well as to children who are referred for learning disabilities.

≡ *Rapid Reference*

5.9 Strengths and Weaknesses of WISC-III Standardization

Strengths

- The WISC-III was stratified according to a broad base of variables closely matching U.S. Census data.
- The WISC-III was conormed with the Wechsler Individual Achievement Test, allowing practitioners to identify discrepancies between aptitude and achievement while correcting for regression effects using conormed tests.

Weaknesses

- There are no major weaknesses.

≡ *Rapid Reference*

5.10 Strengths and Weaknesses of WISC-III Interpretation

Strengths

- Helpful tables for interpreting the IQ and subtest profile are available in the manual (e.g., statistical significance and abnormality of Verbal-Performance differences).
- The four-factor structure aids in interpretation of the battery.

Weaknesses

- Removal of some of the "clinical" items in the revision from the WISC-R to WISC-III may inhibit clinical value.
- The name of the Freedom from Distractibility factor index can be misleading to those who are unfamiliar with the multiple interpretations of this factor.

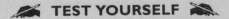

🖋 TEST YOURSELF 🖎

1. **The emphasis on speed on the WPPSI-R and WISC-III**
   (a) is positive because all children like to work quickly.
   (b) is problematic on both tests because children are unfairly penalized due to noncognitive factors such as reflectiveness or motor problems.
   (c) is problematic only on the WPPSI-R.
   (d) is problematic only on the WISC-III.

2. **The standardization samples of the WPPSI-R and the WISC-III are poorly stratified and not adequately representative of U.S. Census data.** True or False?

3. **The floor how many WPPSI-R subtests is inadequate?**
   (a) none
   (b) one
   (c) three
   (d) six

4. **Although the ceiling of the WISC-III was greatly improved, which subtests should be considered carefully in terms of ceiling effects when testing 16-year-olds?**
   (a) Picture Completion and Information
   (b) Similarities and Digit Span
   (c) Block Design and Object Assembly
   (d) Symbol Search and Coding

5. **The WISC-III's Coding subtest has much stronger psychometric properties than Symbol Search does.** True or False?

6. **The poor floor for about half of the WPPSI-R subtests has implications for testing what population?**
   (a) gifted children
   (b) mentally retarded children
   (c) blind children
   (d) normal children age 7 years 3 months

continued

7. **Some of the questions on which WISC-III Verbal subtest may be viewed by children from the nondominant culture as unfair?**

(a) Comprehension

(b) Vocabulary

(c) Similarities

(d) Digit Span

8. **The four-factor structure of the WISC-III may make which process easier for examiners?**

(a) administration

(b) scoring

(c) interpretation

Answers: 1. b; 2. False; 3. d; 4. a; 5. False; 6. b; 7. a; 8. c

Six

CLINICAL APPLICATIONS OF THE WISC-III AND WPPSI-R

This chapter focuses on common clinical applications of the WPPSI-R and the WISC-III, including the assessment of learning disabilities, attention-deficit hyperactivity disorder (ADHD), giftedness, and mental retardation. In addition, we discuss the relationship of the WPPSI-R and WISC-III to other measures of cognitive ability and achievement. Because the literature on these topics is vast, we only highlight some of the major findings. Rapid Reference 6.1 provides a listing of references to some of the recent research on these topics.

≡ Rapid Reference

6.1 Recent References on Clinical Applications of the WISC-III and WPPSI-R

Learning Disabilities

Daley & Nagel (1996)

Gaskill & Brantley (1996)

Kaufman (1994a)

Kush (1996)

Mayes, Calhoun, & Crowell (1998)

Prifitera & Dersh (1993)

Raviv, Rahmani, & Ber (1986)

Reynolds & Kaufman (1990)

Rourke (1998)

Sandoval (1984)

Slate (1995)

Ward, Ward, Hatt, & Young (1995)

continued

Learning Disabilities (cont.)
Watkins (1996)
Watkins, Kush, & Glutting (1997a)
Watkins, Kush, & Glutting (1997b)

Attention-Deficit Hyperactivity Disorder
Anastopoulos, Spitsto, & Maher (1994)
Barkley (1990)
Glutting, Robins, & DeLancy (1997)
Kaufman (1994a)
Mayes, Calhoun, & Crowell (1998)
Prifitera & Dersh (1993)
Ricco, Cohen, Hall, & Ross (1997)
Schwean & Saklofske (1998)
Schwean, Saklofske, Yackulic, & Quinn (1993)
Seidman, Biederman, Faraone, & Weber (1997)
Tiholov, Zawallich, & Janzen (1996)

Gifted
Fishkin, Kampsnider, & Pack (1996)
Harrington (1982)
Kaplan (1992)
Kaufman (1992)
Kaufman (1993)
Sparrow & Gurland (1998)
Sternberg (1982)
Tyerman (1986)

Mental Retardation
Das & Naglieri (1996)
Gerken & Hodapp (1992)
Lukens & Hurrell (1996)
Prewett & Matavich (1993, 1994)
Sapp, Abbott, & Hinkley (1997)
Sattler (1992)
Slate (1995)
Spruill (1998)

APPLICATION OF THE WPPSI-R AND WISC-III IN ASSESSMENT OF LEARNING DISABILITIES

One of the largest referral populations in the field of assessment is children with learning disabilities (LDs; Culbertson & Edmonds, 1996). There are a variety of definitions of learning disabilities, which has led to some inconsistency in sampling in the literature on this population. The generic definition of LD that characterizes most children with this diagnosis involves a child's achievement on standardized tests being substantially below what would be expected for his or her age and level of intelligence (American Psychiatric Association, 1994). An LD may occur concomitantly with other handicapping conditions (e.g., sensory impairment) or environmental influences (e.g., cultural influences), but it may not be the direct result of those conditions or influences. The presentation of symptoms associated with LD varies according to the developmental level of the child. Some symptoms (or precursors) of LD may be present in the preschool age range, but typically an LD diagnosis is not made during the preschool years. Thus the findings discussed here focus on school-age children and adolescents.

The use of profiles within the WISC-III (and its precursors, the WISC and WISC-R) to define LD has been studied by many researchers (Kaufman, 1994a). Whether they examine the Verbal IQ in relation to the Performance IQ or look at specific profiles involving combinations of subtests, such as Arithmetic-Coding-Information-Digit Span (ACID) or Symbol Search-Coding-Arithmetic-Digit Span (SCAD), the consensus has been that although such profiles are consistently found in LD populations, these profiles *alone* cannot clearly distinguish normality from abnormality and identify special populations.

The WISC profile most commonly associated with LD is the ACID profile. Researchers have consistently reported findings of the ACID profile in the LD population (Reynolds & Kaufman, 1990; Sandoval, 1994). Prifitera and Dersh (1993) investigated the ACID profile in the WISC-III standardization sample and for samples of LD and ADHD students, finding that although a larger percentage of the LD and ADHD students showed the ACID profile than did those in the standardization sample, students who demonstrated it represented only a fraction of the total group. Ward, Ward, Hatt, Young, and Mollner (1995) followed up Prifitera and Dersh's study in a sample of 719 students and also found the percentage of students displaying the ACID profile to be more prevalent in the LD sample than in the standardization sample, but it was still rather low (4.7%).

The SCAD profile has been examined in relationship to children's performance on the Perceptual Organization Index (Kaufman, 1994a). Findings have shown that the magnitude of difference between the SCAD profile and the Perceptual Organization Index is greater for children with LD and ADHD than for those without. Ward et al. (1995) found the SCAD profile to be more prevalent than the ACID profile in their LD sample, but they did not find the SCAD profile to be more prevalent in their LD sample than in the standardization sample. These findings did not provide support for those reported by Prifitera and Dersh (1993), who found that a significantly higher percentage of children with LD had demonstrated the SCAD profile than did the standardization sample. Other researchers have reported that the SCAD profile is neither a valid diagnostic indicator of learning disabilities nor an important predictor of achievement (Watkins, Kush, & Glutting, 1997b).

Watkins, Kush, and Glutting (1997a) took investigation of the WISC-III ACID profile one step further. The authors examined the discriminant and predictive validity of the ACID profile among 612 students with learning disabilities. Similar to what had been found before, the ACID profile was seen to be more prevalent in the LD sample than in non-LD samples. However, when the ACID profile was used to classify students into disabled and nondisabled groups, only 51% of the children identified by a positive ACID profile were previously diagnosed with a learning disability. In addition, the ACID profile was not found to be a robust predictor of academic achievement among children with LD. Other recent studies have also found that although WISC-III identifiable profile types are present in LD group data, children with and without LD are often indistinguishable on the WISC-III (Mayes, Calhoun, & Crowell, 1998).

In addition to specific combinations of WISC-III subtests to form profiles, researchers have long been investigating the Verbal and Performance IQ discrepancies for patterns in specific populations, such as children with learning disabilities. In a sample of 202 children diagnosed with specific learning disabilities, 115 diagnosed with mental retardation, and 159 with no diagnosis, discrepancy scores on the WISC-III IQs and indexes were examined

(Slate, 1995). Findings supported what had been reported in earlier research on the WISC-R. IQ and index score discrepancies were present for all children in the sample, with diagnoses and without. Evidence supported the fact that mean Performance IQs were significantly higher than the mean Verbal IQ for all three groups. Although the group with specific learning disabilities had the largest mean group difference between Verbal and Performance IQs (4.8 points vs. 3.8 points for the mentally retarded group, and 1.4 points for the group with no diagnosis), the authors noted that the discrepancies were not large enough to be useful in making a differential diagnosis of a learning disability.

Rourke (1998) reported a summary of research on Verbal IQ versus Performance IQ discrepancies on the WISC. The studies he summarized compared children with LD that fit one of three categories: either low Performance IQs and high Verbal IQs, low Verbal IQs and high Performance IQs, or approximately equivalent Verbal and Performance IQs (all three groups had equivalent Full Scale IQs). Rourke reported that his research suggests it is possible to define subgroups of learning disabilities on the basis of WISC Verbal-Performance discrepancy in combination with supplemental data. One group he defined as having a Basic Phonological Processing Disorder and the other as having Nonverbal Learning Disabilities. In terms of the WISC profile, children who are classified as having Basic Phonological Processing Disorder have a Verbal < Performance (by at least 10 points) profile, whereas children with Nonverbal Learning Disabilities have a Performance < Verbal (by at least 10 points) profile.

In summary, although some patterns on the WISC-III are reported fairly consistently for children with learning disabilities, these patterns do not have adequate power on which to base differential diagnoses. The ACID and SCAD profiles may provide useful information about a child's cognitive abilities on a case-by-case basis, but the presence or absence of these profiles cannot justify making a diagnosis of LD. Likewise, the Verbal > Performance or Performance > Verbal profiles do not provide evidence in and of themselves of a learning disability. Many variables—including performance on standardized measures of achievement, academic history, developmental history, medical history, family history, and behavioral observations—must be combined to properly evaluate a child with a potential learning disability. Although it seems as though a cut-and-dry cognitive profile of a typical learning disabled child would ease the process of diagnosis, characterizing a child by means of a single score or combination of scores can never provide adequate information about his or her abilities.

APPLICATION OF THE WPPSI-R AND WISC-III IN ASSESSMENT OF ATTENTION-DEFICIT HYPERACTIVITY DISORDER

The study of cognitive abilities in children with attention-deficit hyperactivity disorder (ADHD) has grown tremendously within the past 20 years (Weiss & Hechtman, 1993). Similar to what is found in the study of learning disabilities, most often children are not diagnosed with ADHD until they move beyond the preschool years and enter grade school. Because the WISC-III (and WISC-R) is one of the most commonly utilized measures of school-age children's ability, it has been reported in many studies of children with ADHD. Schwean, Saklofske, Yackulic, and Quinn (1993) have shown that the WISC-III has patterns of correlations among subtests, index scores, and IQs for children with ADHD that are similar to those of children in the general population. These results provide evidence of the WISC-III's validity in assessing an ADHD population.

The diagnostic utility of profile analyses in the WISC-III has been investigated. Schwean and Saklofske (1998) summarize the findings of three studies (Anastopoulos, Spitsto, & Maher, 1994; Prifitera & Dersh, 1993; Schwean et al., 1993) using the WISC-III with an ADHD population. Across these three studies, the children with ADHD performed the most poorly on the Freedom from Distractibility Index, with the Processing Speed factor being almost equally low. The strongest performance of the children with ADHD was on Perceptual Organization subtests. Generally, a pattern was observed in the WISC-III indexes of stronger Perceptual Organization than Verbal Conceptualization. Authors hypothesize that the Verbal Conceptualization Index score is lower due to the learning difficulties often exhibited by the children in this group. In contrast to their performance on the Perceptual Organization Index, children with ADHD scored almost a standard deviation lower on both the Freedom from Distractibility and Processing Speed indexes. However, it is important to note that because of variability within the ADHD groups, such global patterns of performance are not necessarily seen when children are examined individually. Kaufman (1994a, pp. 220–221) provides tables to compare children's performance on the SCAD subtests to the Perceptual Organization Index. Significant differences between these scores cannot diagnose exceptionality but may help to explain how an individual child is functioning compared to a group of "normal" children (Kaufman, 1994a). Each child must be studied as a separate individual to best understand his or her abilities.

Schwean and Saklofske (1998) offer a list of suggestions to improve the testing outcome for children with ADHD. Many of their suggestions correspond to what we have recommended in Chapter 2 on administration, so we highlight those that were not already mentioned and that are specific to this unique population. Cognitive impulsivity may be evident during an ADHD child's test performance. Thus examiners should be attuned to the child's cognitive style and provide cues to help the child slow down. Transitions are especially difficult for children with ADHD. To minimize the negative impact of this difficulty, prior to scheduling the testing examiners should take into account children's activities that precede the testing. Children with ADHD have variable ability to remain focused and on task. Examiners may find it useful to consistently employ strategies such as verbally cueing the child that an activity is about to start, making clear eye contact with the child before beginning a task, or providing brief breaks if the child cannot maintain attention.

Studies using the WISC-III with samples of ADHD children do show that WISC-III scores provide useful information about these children's intellectual abilities and cognitive strengths and weaknesses. However, the research findings do *not* indicate that the WISC-III can be used as a diagnostic test for ADHD (Schwean & Saklofske, 1998). Many disorders (e.g., learning disabilities, conduct disorder, anxiety, depression, or mental retardation) have features that overlap with some of the symptoms of ADHD, so the WISC-III may be a useful tool in helping to rule out the presence of other disorders. Clearly the WISC-III should be used as part of a broad-based, multimethod assessment when the diagnosis of ADHD is to be made. Critical to making the diagnosis are behavioral observations in the testing situation as well as in other contexts.

GIFTEDNESS

Gifted children have historically been identified by a cut-off score on an intelligence test (Sparrow & Gurland, 1998). Although this means of identification has recognizable problems such as cultural bias (Tyerman, 1986), ceiling effects (Harrington, 1982; Kaplan, 1992; Kaufman, 1993) and over-emphasis on speed (Kaufman, 1992; Sternberg, 1982), psychologists typically do conduct an intellectual assessment if a child is suspected of intellectual giftedness. The key to making appropriate decisions about giftedness is to consider more than a simple cut-off score (such as a Full Scale IQ of above 125). Important issues must be considered, such as the appropriateness of a particular test for a child of a certain cultural background, the ceiling effects, the effect of speed on a child's score, and the scatter within a child's profile.

One commonly noted problem with the WPPSI-R and the WISC-III in the assessment of gifted children is the significant emphasis on the speed of a child's response (Kaufman, 1992; Sparrow & Gurland, 1998). On the WPPSI-R, a child's score on two of the ten subtests (Object Assembly and Block Design) is impacted if the child cannot respond with exceptional speed. On the WISC-III, in addition to the Processing Speed subtests, Arithmetic, Picture Arrangement, Block Design, and Object Assembly are impacted when a child is slow to respond. Depending on the child's age, if he or she obtains a perfect performance but no bonus points for speed on the aforementioned WISC-III subtests, the maximum scaled score may be as low as 6 or 7 (Kaufman, 1993). Children may respond slowly if they have a reflective problem-solving style or a mild coordination problem, or even if they are intellectually gifted. Thus the WISC-III and WPPSI-R may both be impacted by "nonintellectual" variables, such as speed of response, when a child's *cognitive* ability is supposedly being measured. When an examiner feels a child's scores have been impacted by reflective style or coordination problems, appropriate steps may be taken to clarify why the scores are depressed. For example, supplementary tests may be given that do not emphasize speed of responding, or tests of motor coordination may be administered to demonstrate what variables impacted performance on the Wechsler scales.

Examination of the WISC-III standardization sample of 2,200 children showed that 118 children had Full Scale IQs that were greater than or equal to 125 (the typical cut-off point for determining giftedness). Sparrow and Gurland (1998) reported that 45.8% of those 118 children in the standardization sample had Verbal IQ versus Performance IQ discrepancies that were statistically significant at the .05 level (≥ 11 points). A difference of 16 or more points was found in 27.1% of the gifted sample. Thus from these data it is clear that significant Verbal IQ–Performance IQ discrepancies are common among gifted children. Such discrepancies raise questions about whether the Full Scale IQ–defined criteria for giftedness are adequate. Subtest scatter is reported in greater frequency in gifted samples than in the normative sample (Fishkin, Kampsnider, & Pack, 1996). In this book and others (e.g., Kaufman, 1994a) it is suggested that careful consideration be made as to whether the Full Scale IQ can be meaningfully interpreted for each individual child.

The WPPSI-R and WISC-III are recommended for use in gifted assessment, but some aspects reveal a need for caution. One of the main drawbacks of these instruments in the assessment of giftedness is the overemphasis on speed of responding. The scatter often reported in WISC-III profiles of gifted samples suggests that caution be made when interpreting global scores. Astute examiners should go beyond simple IQs and try to make sense of why a child scores a certain way. Observation of behaviors during testing, in combination with information from the child's background, can provide important clues to interpreting the profile. Psychologists and educators should take into account these issues and support their WISC-III or WPPSI-R data with supplementary tests, being careful not to interpret one IQ score as *the sole* number that represents the child's ability.

MENTAL RETARDATION

The diagnosis of mental retardation must take into account not only a person's intellectual functioning but also a person's adaptive behavior. To fall in the category of mental retardation, a child's IQ must be less than 70 (American Psychiatric Association, 1994). Thus although we focus in this section on the intellectual component as measured by standardized tests like the WISC-III and WPPSI-R, it is important to keep in mind that assessment of mental retardation must also address adaptive functioning (e.g., the ability to meet the standards of personal behavior and independence expected for individuals of their chronological age). Thus in addition to a finding of low IQ, adaptive functioning must be considered "significantly impaired" for a diagnosis of mental retardation to be made.

The WISC-III manual (Wechsler, 1991) reports the results of a study of 43 children diagnosed with mental retardation. As is typically found in mentally retarded populations, there was very little variability across a given subject's subtest performance. The standard deviations ranged from 8 to 9 points, in contrast to the 15-point standard deviation usually found in the general population. Hishinuma and Yamakawa (1993) reported results that supported the four-factor structure with an exceptional population. However, the Verbal Comprehension and Perceptual Organization factors were more clearly delineated than the Freedom from Distractibility and Processing Speed factors. Generally, performance on the Verbal and Performance scales is reported to be approximately equally depressed for children diagnosed with mental retardation (Slate, 1995; Wechsler, 1991).

The WPPSI-R manual (Wechsler, 1989) also reports data on a sample of children diagnosed with mental retardation ($N = 21$). Although little detail is available about this study in the manual, the results of the study suggest evidence of an "adequate floor" for assessment of young children with "low ability" (Wechsler, 1989). However, it should be noted that according to the study in the WPPSI-R manual, a "few" of the children would be categorized as functioning in the Average to Below Average range, even though they had been previously diagnosed as mentally retarded. In another study with a small sample of children referred for special education services, correlations between the WPPSI-R IQs and Stanford-Binet L-M were found to be strong (ranging from .75 to .85; Gerken & Hodapp, 1992). However, some questions remain about the consistency of different measures of intellectual ability in categorizing preschool-age children as mentally retarded or not.

As discussed earlier in this book, we note that for children ages 6 years 0 months to 7 years 3 months suspected of mental retardation the WPPSI-R is better than the WISC-III in assessing cognitive ability. We recommend that the WPPSI-R be administered to children with these characteristics because it provides a better floor than the WISC-III for children who are functioning at a very low level of ability. On the WISC-III, Similarities, Block Design, and Picture Arrangement have inadequate floors for 6-year-olds (Spruill, 1998). For example, a raw score of 1 earns a 6-year-old child a WISC-III scaled score of 4 on Similarities, Information, Picture Arrangement, or Block Design.

No WISC-III or WPPSI-R profiles of children with mental retardation have been consistently reported (Spruill, 1998). Although there is a slight trend for children with very low ability to perform better on the Performance Scale than on the Verbal Scale, this finding cannot be used as a diagnostic characteristic of the population. Indeed, a diagnosis of mental retardation should only be made after the appropriate instrument has obtained an estimate of a child's level of intellectual ability and an assessment of a child's adaptive functioning has been made. All this information, in combination with relevant clinical data from a child's background (developmental, educational, medical) history and behavioral observations, should be considered in making a differential diagnosis of mental retardation.

CORRELATIONAL STUDIES

Most psychoeducational or neuropsychological evaluations utilize multiple instruments to assess a child's functioning. In order to appropriately interpret these instruments in combination, examiners must have a sense of how such instruments are related. Tables in this section summarize how the WISC-III and WPPSI-R are related to other measures of cognitive ability (see Tables 6.1, and 6.2) and how the WISC-III is related to measures of achievement (see Table 6.3).

A review of comparisons between the WISC-III and other measures of cognitive ability shows strong criterion validity. The correlations range from .53 to .87 with a median of .76. When global IQ scores from other measures of IQ are compared to the Full Scale IQs of the WISC-III, the differences in scores in these studies range from 2.8 to −8.4 and the median difference is −0.9. Comparisons between the WPPSI-R and other measures of cognitive ability also show strong criterion validity. The correlations range from .49 to .82 with a median of .67. When the differences between WPPSI-R Full Scale IQs and other global IQs are computed, the range of discrepancies is from 4.5 to −13.3 with a median difference of −2.1.

The correlations between WISC-III Full Scale IQs and measures of achievement are also strong. Correlations among measures of reading and Full Scale IQ reported in the studies listed in Table 6.3 range from .24 to .76 with a median of .59, and correlations among measures of arithmetic range from .52 to .89 with a median of .72. It is interesting to note, however, that although about half the samples were of learning disabled students, the size of the differences between the standard scores from standardized measures of achievement and WISC-III Full Scale IQ are generally low. The maximum difference reported between achievement and IQ is 10.2 points, but the

Table 6.1   Concurrent Validity Studies of WISC-III and Other Intelligence Tests

Adapted and reproduced with permission of authors and publisher from Zimmerman, I. R., and Woo-Sam, J. M. Review of the criterion-related validity of the WISC-III: The first five years. *Perceptual and Motor Skills,* 1997, 85, 531–546. © Perceptual and Motor Skills 1997.

Instrument	Sample	N	WISC-III FS-IQ	Other IQ	r	Reference
Stanford-Binet–IV	Normal	57	111.3	109.8	.81	Rust & Lindstrom (1996)
	Normal	32	112.6	109.8	.74	Carvajal et al. (1993)
	Normal	40	107.0	108.0	.82	Lavin (1996c)
	ADHD	45	98.0	102.0	.73	Saklofske et al. (1994)
	LD	73	74.6	82.9	.81	Prewett & Matavich (1993)
	MR	31	58.0	65.7	.68	Lukens & Hurrel (1996)
Kaufman Assessment Battery for Children	Normal	67	112.2	112.3	.60	Rust & Yates (1997)
	Language problems	40	71.2	79.2	.79	Phelps et al. (1993)
Kaufman Brief Intelligence Test	Gifted	29	122.9	120.6	.53	Levinson & Folino (1994)
	LD	29	105.2	105.2	.76	Sparrow (1991)
	Psychiatric	63	91.9	90.3	.76	Javorsky (1993)
	Brain damage	47	83.8	92.2	.76	Donders (1995)
	LD	137	81.7	82.4	.87	Canivez (1995)
	LD	50	72.1	76.9	.78	Prewett (1995)
Woodcock-Johnson–Revised Tests of Cognitive Ability	LD	61	107.8	105.4	.71	Barnes et al. (1993)

Note. ADHD = attention-deficit hyperactivity disorder; LD = learning disability; MR = mentally retarded; Psychiatric = psychiatric clinic population.

Table 6.2   Concurrent Validity Studies of WPPSI-R and Other Intelligence Tests

Instrument	Sample	N	WISC-III FS-IQ	Other IQ	r	Reference
Stanford-Binet–IV	Normal	115	105.3	107.2	.74	Wechsler (1989)
	MR	16	75.6	77.93	.82	Gerken & Hodapp (1992)
Kaufman Assessment Battery for Children	Normal	59	96.8	103.1	.49	Wechsler (1989)
McCarthy Scales of Children's Abilities	Normal	93	102.4	104.8	.81	Wechsler (1989)
	Normal	33	106.8	108.1	.67	Faust & Hollingsworth (1991)
Woodcock-Johnson–Revised Tests of Cognitive Ability	Normal	30	120.1	115.6	.66	Harrington et al. (1992)
Kaufman Brief Intelligence Test	Normal	50	95.2	97.3	.63	Lassiter & Bardos (1995)
Leiter International Performance Scale	African American	15	92.6	92.9	na	Lewis & Lorentz (1994)
	Latino	11	84.5	97.8		

Note. MR = mentally retarded.

Table 6.3 Concurrent Validity Studies of WISC-III and Achievement Tests

Adapted and reproduced with permission of authors and publisher from Zimmerman, I. R., and Woo-Sam, J. M. Review of the criterion-related validity of the WISC-III: The first five years. *Perceptual and Motor Skills*, 1997, 85, 531–546. © Perceptual and Motor Skills 1997.

Instrument	Sample	N	Mean WISC-III FS-IQ	Mean Reading	Mean Arithmetic	r Reading	r Arithmetic	Reference
				Achievement				
Woodcock-Johnson–Revised Achievement Tests	LD	61	107.8	102.6	106.7	.61	.71	Barnes et al. (1993)
	LD	32	87.7	86.1	87.4	.68	.68	Zimmerman & Woo-Sam (1990)
	Psychiatric	85	87.5	91.2	90.4	.36	.52	Lavin (1996b)
	LD	32	84.3	92.3	91.2	.66	.75	Zimmerman & Woo-Sam (1990)
	LD	75	82.7	81.2	81.3	.38	.59	Canivez (1996)
	LD	25	77.2	72.9	69.4	.53	.62	Doll & Boren (1993)
Wide Range Achievement Test 3	Normal	100	98.5	97.5	97.5	.66	.73	Zimmerman & Woo-Sam (1972)
	LD	60	87.6	77.4	84.0	.72	.82	Weiss (1995)
	LD	37	78.7	81.0	82.1	.57	.58	Vance & Fuller (1995)
Wechsler Individual Achievement Test	Normal	753	102.6	na	na	.66	.68	Wislar et al. (1993)
	Normal	108	92.5	na	na	.76	.73	Wislar et al. (1993)
	Psychiatric	53	89.0	86.4	88.7	.50	.79	Ponton et al. (1997)
	Normal	137	88.8	na	na	.69	.74	Wislar et al. (1993)
	Emotionally Disturbed	202	84.6	81.7	85.9	.55	.79	Slate & Jones (1995)
	Normal	159	79.9	89.2	87.5	.24	.85	Slate & Jones (1995)
	MR	115	60.0	68.7	70.0	.60	.89	Slate & Jones (1995)

| | | | Mean | Achievement | | | | |
Instrument	Sample	N	WISC-III FS-IQ	Mean Reading	Mean Arithmetic	r Reading	r Arithmetic	Reference
Kaufman Test of Educational Achievement	LD	72	88.9	88.2	85.4	.53	.65	Lavin (1996a)
Kaufman Functional Academic Skills Test	Psychiatric	30	93.5	97.5	91.0	.45	.69	Connery et al. (1996)

Note. ADHD = attention-deficit hyperactivity disorder; LD = learning disability; MR = mentally retarded; Psychiatric = psychiatric clinic population.

median difference is a negligible 1-point discrepancy. Zimmerman and Woo-Sam (1997) note that these small differences may result in fewer children meeting the requirement for identification as learning disabled.

Understanding how the WISC-III and WPPSI-R relate to other measures of cognitive ability and/or achievement is important in interpreting a battery of tests. Although the data summarized here demonstrate only relationships across *groups* of children and do not necessarily represent one *individual* child, they provide a baseline by which to understand how such measures relate. This information is an important backdrop to the interpretation of a child's unique profile of scores from multiple tests.

✐ TEST YOURSELF ✐

1. **Aimee has a clear and distinctive ACID profile. This means that**
   (a) she has a learning disability.
   (b) she has attention-deficit hyperactivity disorder.
   (c) she performed more poorly on Arithmetic, Coding, Information, and Digit Span than on other subtests.
   (d) she is mentally retarded.

2. **Jack has been diagnosed as moderately mentally retarded. This diagnosis can be confirmed with which of the following?**
   (a) a Verbal IQ that is significantly lower than his Performance IQ
   (b) a Performance IQ that is significantly lower than his Verbal IQ
   (c) a measure of significantly impaired adaptive functioning in addition to IQ of less than 70
   (d) evidence of a SCAD profile

3. **Gifted children rarely show scatter in their WISC-III or WPPSI-R profile.** True or False?

4. **Poor performance on the Processing Speed Index and Freedom from Distractibility Index of the WISC-III is found in nearly 100% of children diagnosed with ADHD.** True or False?

5. Jamie was found to perform very poorly on subtests that require speed to obtain bonus points, but she performed consistently nearly 2 standard deviations above normal on other subtests. Given that she has been diagnosed as _____, this finding is not surprising.

(a) mentally retarded

(b) gifted

(c) hearing impaired

(d) emotionally disturbed

6. The strong correlations found between the WISC-III and other measures of cognitive ability point to the

(a) validity of the test.

(b) reliability of the test.

7. Which of the following diagnoses have a clearly defined Wechsler profile?

(a) ADHD

(b) learning disabled

(c) mental retardation

(d) gifted

(e) none of the above

Answers: 1. c; 2. c; 3. False; 4. False; 5. b; 6. a; 7. e

Seven

ILLUSTRATIVE CASE REPORTS

This chapter presents case studies of two children who were referred for psychoeducational evaluations. The WPPSI-R profile of Emma K. was included in Chapter 4 to exemplify how to utilize the steps of interpretation. The culmination of that interpretive process appears here in Emma's case report. The other case report describes the profile of a 6-year-old girl with childhood leukemia who was referred to assess the impact that the treatment for her illness was having on her cognitive functioning.

The goal of this chapter is to bring all other facets of this book together to show how the WPPSI-R and WISC-III may be used as part of a comprehensive test battery. The case reports demonstrate the cross-validating of hypotheses with behavioral observations, background information, and supplemental tests. Each report includes the following: information about the child (see Don't Forget 7.1), reason for referral, background information, physical appearance of the client and behavioral observations during the assessment, tests administered, test results and interpretation, summary, and recommendations. For the cases presented here we give all the test data (scores) prior to the text of the report, but in a report for the client we would include this information at the very end in a section labeled Psychometric Summary.

Case Report: Emma K., Age 3, Possibly Gifted

Wechsler Preschool and Primary Scale of Intelligence–Revised (WPPSI-R) Profile

Scale	IQ	90% Confidence Interval	Percentile Rank
Verbal Scale	124	119–129	95
Performance Scale	105	98–111	63
Full Scale	116	111–121	86

Verbal Subtest	Scaled Score[a]	Percentile Rank	Performance Subtest	Scaled Score[a]	Percentile Rank
Information	12	75	Object Assembly	6 (W)	9
Comprehension	16 (S)	98	Geometric Design	12	75
Arithmetic	14	91	Block Design	9 (W)	37
Vocabulary	14	91	Mazes	11	63
Similarities	12	75	Picture Completion	16 (S)	98
Sentences	11	63	Animal Pegs	14	91

[a](S) indicates a significant relative strength, $p < .05$; (W) indicates a significant relative weakness, $p < .05$.

Kaufman Assessment Battery for Children (K-ABC): Achievement Scale

Scale or Subtest	Standard Score	90% Confidence Interval	Percentile Rank
Achievement	105	98–112	63
Expressive Vocabulary	113	102–124	81
Faces and Places	91	77–105	27
Arithmetic	119	109–129	90
Riddles	95	85–105	37

Woodcock-Johnson Tests of Achievement–Revised (WJ-R)

Scale or Subtest	Standard Score	Percentile Rank
Broad Knowledge	115	85
Letter-Word Identification	128	97
Dictation	124	95
Science	124	94
Social Studies	98	46
Humanities	122	93

Reason for Referral

Emma was referred for evaluation by her parents, Mr. and Mrs. K. According to the Ks, Emma seems to be very bright and advanced both motorically and verbally; her parents would like to know if they should be addressing her skills in some special way. They would like to get a better sense of Emma's strengths and weaknesses in order to help direct her and afford her opportunities. The Ks would like to know whether Emma has special talents and what can be done with them to make her happy and achieve the most academically. (See Don't Forget 7.2.)

Background Information

Emma lives with her parents and her brother, Blake. Both parents work, her father full-time and her mother half-time. Blake is a 15-

> **DON'T FORGET**
> ....
> **7.2 Pertinent Information to Include in Reason for Referral Section**
>
> A. Who Referred the Client
>   1. List name and position of referral source.
>   2. List questions of referral source.
> B. Specific Symptoms and Concerns
>   1. Summarize current behaviors and relevant past behaviors.
>   2. List any separate concerns that the client has.

year-old high school student and is described as Emma's "other father." He is reportedly very close to Emma, and she states to her parents that she misses him when he is not there. According to the parents, there appears to be no jealously between the siblings.

Emma was carried for a full-term pregnancy and weighed 7 pounds 2 ounces at birth. Mr. and Mrs. K. stated that there were no complications during pregnancy. Emma achieved all major developmental milestones within normal limits and has suffered no serious illnesses or injuries. According to her parents Emma has experienced minor reoccurring earaches, but these have not been of any concern to the pediatrician. Emma was described by her parents as having some sleeping difficulties, often waking during the night, sitting up, and calling out to them. Her parents reported, however, that she is easily soothed and is becoming better at getting herself back to sleep.

The Ks described Emma as a very verbal and strong-willed little girl. When she does not want to do something she throws a tantrum, although this behavior only occurs with her mom and dad. When limits are set Emma has outbursts, at which time she is put in "time out" in her room. She must then sit and talk with her parents for approximately 15 minutes about the problem and better ways of handling her emotions. This appears to be the most effective discipline for her, although her behavior sometimes escalates in her room. Both parents discipline Emma, and usually whoever starts the discipline finishes it. Both parents reported that Emma's father tends to be a little "tougher" with Emma, not allowing her as many chances, whereas Emma's mother tries to work with her more. Mr. and Mrs. K. indicated that Emma tends to "blow up" more quickly with her father and appears to be more manipulative with her mother. Her brother sets limits with Emma but defers discipline to the parents.

Emma began preschool this year. The program she attended was a full-day program Monday through Friday. Her parents reported that she experienced no separation problems with the transition to school and is one of only four children in her class who attend the program for a full day. According to the Ks, Emma's teacher said she is "wonderful" in the classroom, is very bright, and has good hand-eye coordination.

Emma's parents stated that she is able to write and type on the computer. She can type and write her name, knows her numbers (counting and labeling), and can do some basic arithmetic. Her parents indicated that she likes to do puzzles, read picture books, and create a storyline for the pictures in the books. Emma enjoys listening to things as well as looking at them, and she usually goes to bed at night listening to a tape. She also plays the piano and can ride a tricycle. Other activities that Emma enjoys include going to the park or zoo. Her parents stated that Emma picks things up very quickly if they intrigue her, but no special interests last over time. At present her most consistent interest has been in the television character Barney. Emma also reportedly has a menagerie of make-believe friends with whom she likes to play. Most of the children in the neighborhood with whom she plays are older than her, ranging from age 4 to 8.

Emma has begun to be given responsibilities around the house and has just started to feed and water the dog. She also helps with the cooking and is able to stir, pour, and put cookies on the cookie sheet. She is able to dress and undress herself completely and picks out her own clothes to wear. The Ks stated that Emma refuses to speak on the phone, no matter how much they encourage her to do so. (See Don't Forget 7.3.)

DON'T FORGET

7.3 Pertinent Information to Include in Background Information Section

Present in paragraph form the information you have obtained from all sources, including referral source, client, family members, social worker, teachers, medical records, etc. Only state pertinent information, not needless details.

The following information may be included:

- current family situation (parents, siblings, etc.) (*no* gossip)
- other symptoms
- medical history (including emotional disorders)
- developmental history
- educational history
- previous treatment (educational or psychological)
- new or recent developments (including stressors)
- review of collateral documents (past evaluations)

Appearance and Behavioral Characteristics

Emma is a cute Caucasian 3-year-old who appears her stated age. She has green eyes, brown hair, and fair skin and is tall for her age. When Emma was first introduced to the examiner, she clung to her mother and was rather quiet, appearing shy. Approximately 5 minutes into the first testing session, Emma was able to relax and interact more with the examiner. She joined the examiner in comparing the lace on her dress to the lace on her favorite blanket. As the examiner brought out brightly colored toy plastic necklaces to show her, Emma approached but did not spontaneously speak to the examiner and was a bit resistant to following directions.

Although Emma was able to communicate verbally with the examiner, on many occasions she chose not to, and many tasks were chosen so as to allow responses that involved pointing. On the second day of testing Emma entered the session with her father, kicking and flailing her arms, and she appeared resistant to testing. Emma's father was able to calm her down by drawing a face on a piece of paper for her. Her father attempted to ease the

---

DON'T FORGET

7.4 Pertinent Information to Include in Appearance and Behavioral Characteristics Section

- Talk about significant patterns or themes you see going on during testing.
- Sequence information in order of importance, rather than in order of occurrence. (Don't just make a chronological list.)
- Describe the behavioral referents to your hypotheses (specific examples).
- Describe what makes this client unique. (Paint a picture for the reader.)

Suggested areas to review (note only significant behavior):

Appearance
- size: height and weight
- facial characteristics
- grooming and cleanliness
- posture
- clothing style
- maturity: Does the person look his or her age?

continued

Behavior

- speech articulation, language patterns
- activity level (foot wiggling, excessive talking, nail biting, tension, etc.)
- attention span/distractibility
- cooperativeness or resistance
- interest in doing well
- How does the client go about solving problems?
- Does client use a trial-and-error approach?
- Does client work quickly or reflectively?
- Does client check his or her answers?
- How does the client react to failure or challenge?
- Does client continue to work until time is up?
- Does client ask for direction or help?
- Did failure reduce interest in the task or working on other tasks?
- When frustrated, is client aggressive or dependent?
- What is the client's attitude toward self?
- Does client regard self with confidence, have a superior attitude, feel inadequate, or appear defeated?
- How did client strive to get approval and respond to your praise of effort?

Validity of test results

- "On the basis of John's above behaviors, the results of this assessment are considered a valid indication of his current level of cognitive and academic ability."
- Or if not, state why.

transition and aid in her compliance to testing, but he was only moderately successful. Emma's mother arrived shortly after the session began, and her father left. At that point Emma became much more cooperative. Generally, Emma appeared to have difficulty transitioning and complying with the social demands of the testing situation. Emma displayed the ability to manipulate the situation to her benefit. For example, when her mother promised her a cookie after completing a task, Emma responded, "How about three more cookies?"

Throughout most of the testing, Emma had a rigid approach to problem solving. For example, on a task in which she placed pieces of a puzzle together, Emma tried to forcefully bang the pieces into the wrong slots. When the pieces did not conform to her view of the puzzle, she asked her mother for assistance (her mother did not assist). Emma then continued to attempt the remaining items with the same approach. In another example, when Emma was asked if the examiner had spelled her name correctly as "Emma," she responded no and wrote "EMMA" in all capital letters. Apparently Emma believed her name was correctly spelled only if it contained all capitals.

In general, Emma's gross motor and fine motor coordination were good. She was very observant and watched carefully as the examiner demonstrated various tasks. Her attention to detail was very accurate, leading her to reproduce not only motor activities that were required as part of a task but also the same gestures and other superfluous movements that were not directly part of the task, such as placing her arms on her hips between tasks in order to rest.

Although at times Emma demonstrated some difficulty in complying with the examiner's directions, she was able to eventually complete all the tasks during the assessment. Her initial shyness did dissipate, and rapport was established and maintained throughout the assessment. In light of these and other described behaviors, the results of this assessment are viewed as an accurate estimate of Emma's overall cognitive and early academic abilities. (See Don't Forget 7.4.)

Tests Administered

- Wechsler Preschool and Primary Scale of Intelligence–Revised (WPPSI-R)
- Woodcock-Johnson Tests of Achievement (WJ-R)
- Kaufman Assessment Battery for Children (K-ABC): Achievement Scale
- clinical interview with parents

Test Results and Interpretation

Emma was administered the Wechsler Preschool and Primary Scale of Intelligence–Revised (WPPSI-R), which is an individually administered test of a child's intellectual ability and cognitive strengths and weaknesses. The WPPSI-R comprises 12 subtests and measures both verbal skills and specific nonverbal abilities such as constructing designs with blocks and completing puzzles. On the WPPSI-R Emma earned a Full Scale IQ of 116 ± 5 (86th percentile). However, because there was a significant amount of scatter within Emma's subtest profile, her Full Scale IQ is meaningless, as it is only an average of several very diverse abilities. Likewise, the abnormal amount of scatter within the Performance Scale renders her Performance IQ of 105 ± 6 (63rd percentile) uninterpretable. Emma's performance on the Verbal Scale was not highly variable, making her Verbal IQ of 124 ± 5 (95th percentile) a meaningful and good estimate of her global High Average to Superior verbal abilities. However, because of the variability covering most of her profile, the most meaningful representation of Emma's abilities is found in her individual strengths and weaknesses.

Emma's consistently strong verbal skills were evident throughout the testing. She demonstrated a significant relative strength in her ability to understand long verbal questions as well as to express herself with much verbal expression. This was evident on WPPSI-R subtests that required her to define vocabulary words (91st percentile) and give verbal responses to questions about certain events (98th percentile). Her performance in the High Average to Superior range of cognitive functioning on the WPPSI-R Verbal Scale was further reflected on several other tests administered to her. For example, on a test of expressive vocabulary on the Achievement scale of the Kaufman Assessment Battery for Children (K-ABC), Emma earned a standard score of 113 ± 11 (81st percentile).

In general, on verbal tasks Emma was very literal in her interpretation of instructions and performed best on items that required rote memory and little reasoning or integration of material. On many tasks Emma did not make necessary cognitive associations when reasoning was required. For example, when shown a car and asked which picture "goes with it," she chose a picture of the sun and not the correct answer, a picture of a truck. When asked how a spoon and a fork are alike, she responded, "they have sharp points." Emma appeared firm in her mental set when responding to material about which she possessed acquired information. For example, when asked what type of animals lizards, snakes, and crocodiles are, she answered, "I don't know, but they have sharp teeth." In this way she proved quite resourceful in communicating vast quantities of learned facts, even if her answers were tangential or irrelevant to the questions. Overall, Emma performed better on items that were related to or stressed information that she had received through enrichment and performed less well on novel and/or problem-solving tasks.

Parallel to her strong performance on cognitive verbal tasks, Emma demonstrated relative strengths in areas of academic achievement that involved the verbal channel as well as acquired knowledge. This strength was apparent in Emma's performance on the Woodcock-Johnson–Revised Tests of Achievement (WJ-R), which were administered in addition to the Achievement scale of the K-ABC. Emma demonstrated exceptional performance in the areas of Humanities (93rd percentile), Science (94th percentile), Dictation (95th percentile), and Letter-Word Identification (97th percentile). On tests of mathematical ability on the K-ABC and the WPPSI-R, Emma also showed verbal strength and academic strength in her quantitative abilities, scoring at the 90th and 91st percentiles.

The consistency in Emma's verbal and academic abilities was in contrast to the significant variability in her nonverbal skills. Her performance on the WPPSI-R Performance Scale ranged from the 9th to the 98th percentiles. Within the nonverbal sphere, Emma performed better when she was able to respond verbally to complete visual stimuli than when she had to respond motorically to synthesize visual stimuli. For example, on a task that required Emma to name the missing part of a visually presented picture she performed at the 98th percentile, but on tasks that required her to put together puzzle pieces to form a whole or use blocks to copy designs she had much more difficulty (9th and 37th percentiles). Emma also appeared to have difficulty learning from her mistakes (e.g., trial-and-error learning). On tasks for which she had to correct her errors using the available visual feedback, she tended to persist in making the same errors repeatedly. This was exemplified in her continued efforts to try to fit a puzzle piece into a hole that was not the right size.

Emma appears to be able to display her abilities better when presented with auditory stimuli and when able to utilize verbal expression, in contrast to visual stimuli and nonverbal responding. For example, she scored at the 75th percentile on a WPPSI-R test of general factual knowledge when the stimuli were verbal, but at the 27th percentile on a K-ABC test of general factual knowledge when the stimuli were visual. When shown visual depictions of nursery rhyme characters such as Humpty-Dumpty and Jack and Jill on the K-ABC Faces and Places subtest, Emma was unable to identify the characters; but when asked to complete the verbal rhymes with these same characters on WJ-R tests of achievement, she was able to do so. Also, her score on a WPPSI-R verbal test of social understanding (98th percentile) was notably higher than her score on a WJ-R subtest that assesses similar skills via pictures (46th percentile).

Overall Emma is advanced for her age, especially linguistically and academically, scoring at or above 90 to 98% of her peers. Her abilities on tasks within the visual-motor channel, on average, are about at an age appropriate level. At present, she would not, technically, merit the label of "gifted" based on the current evaluation. Her variety of accomplishments and creative skills

DON'T FORGET

7.5 Pertinent Information to Include in Test Results and Interpretation Section

- Use paragraph form.
- Put numbers in this section, including IQs and index scores with confidence intervals and percentile ranks. When discussing performance on subtests use percentile ranks (most people aren't familiar with a mean of 10 and standard deviation of 3); do not include raw scores.
- Tie in behaviors with results to serve as logical explanations or reminders wherever appropriate.
- With more than one test, find similarities in performances and differences (discrepancies) and try to hypothesize if you have enough information to say.
- Support hypotheses with multiple sources of data, including observed behaviors.
- Do not contradict yourself.
- Be sure that you are describing the subtests, not just naming them. Remember, the reader has no idea what "Picture Completion" means.
- Describe the underlying abilities that the task is tapping.
- Talk about the child's abilities, not the test.
- Be straightforward in your writing. Do not be too literary, and avoid writing in metaphors.

documented by her parents, however, certainly indicate that she has the potential for giftedness. Intelligence and achievement scores at age 3 years 0 months to 3 years 6 months, though reliable, do not always accurately predict cognitive functioning in late childhood (scores begin to stabilize more completely between ages 4 and 5). Also, variability is the hallmark of very young children's test performance, and this seemed to be true in Emma's case. Thus more stable test performance would be anticipated if Emma is retested at age 6; at that time she will also be old enough to be administered reliable tests that tap a wider range of academic and intellectual abilities. (See Don't Forget 7.5.)

Summary and Diagnostic Impressions

Emma is a 3-year-old Caucasian girl referred for an assessment by her parents. The purpose of the referral was to get a better sense of Emma's strengths and weaknesses in order to guide her and make her happy. Emma has had a normal developmental history with no significant illnesses or injuries to speak of. She is currently attending a full-day program for preschool.

Although Emma had difficulty transitioning into the changing social demands of the assessment situation and complying with rules and structure, she ultimately did comply with the examiner. Despite these difficulties, Emma understood the directions and was able to complete all tasks presented to her. Therefore the test results are interpreted as valid and accurate representations of Emma's present cognitive and behavioral functioning.

Emma's cognitive profile, as assessed by the WPPSI-R, contained a significant amount of variability, making her Full Scale IQ and Performance IQ uninterpretable, as they represent diverse skills ranging from the Low Average to Superior levels of ability. Her Verbal IQ of 124 ± 5 (95th percentile) is a good representation of her High Average to Superior verbal skills. Her relative strengths and weaknesses on the WPPSI-R were supported by her performance on the K-ABC Achievement scale and the WJ-R Tests of Achievement. She has significant relative strengths in her ability to understand long verbal questions and in her ability to express herself verbally. Her academic abilities, especially those that are combined with verbal abilities, are also a relative area of strength. In the verbal realm, Emma has more difficulty with tasks that involve reasoning and problem solving than with

> ## DON'T FORGET
> ....
> ### 7.6 Pertinent Information to Include in Summary and Diagnostic Impressions Section
>
> - State summary information early in the body of the report.
> - Include summary of referral, key background, or behavioral observation points.
> - Summarize the most important interpretations of global scores and strengths and weaknesses.
> - Defend your diagnosis if one is made.

tasks that stress information she has previously learned. Emma's relative weaknesses are in the areas of visual-motor synthesis and trial and error learning.

This evaluation suggests that Emma is an advanced child, especially in the verbal realm. Although Emma does not fit the criteria for placement in a gifted program at the present time, she certainly has displayed advanced language development and a great knowledge base compared to other children her age. Presently, Emma's test performance is somewhat variable, as is the performance of most children her age. More stable scores may be found if she is retested within a couple of years. (See Don't Forget 7.6.)

Recommendations

1. A psychoeducational reevaluation is recommended to reassess Emma's abilities when she reaches age 6. At that time her test performance will be more stable and reliable. This reevaluation will allow for assessment of a wider range of cognitive skill and academic areas and will provide a better predictive picture of her childhood cognitive and academic functioning.

2. In light of the tantrums described by Mr. and Mrs. K. and the difficulty Emma evidenced in transitioning to new situations with higher demands, Emma's parents may benefit from augmenting their present disciplinary techniques:

a. Consequences for appropriate and inappropriate behaviors should be consistently administered by both parents. Even though Mr. and Mrs. K. have slightly different parenting styles, it is important that they be in agreement on the consequences of Emma's behaviors and on their ensuing disciplinary action.

b. Because Emma is a highly verbal child, she will benefit from speaking to her parents about negative situations when they arise. Mr. and Mrs. K. should verbally recognize that she is unhappy and suggest appropriate alternative ways to deal with her unhappiness.

c. When Emma has dealt with her frustration in an appropriate manner, she will benefit from being rewarded. Both tangible rewards (snacks, stars) and intangible rewards (verbal praise, smile) will be useful. Use of the time-out periods when her behavior is unacceptable should also be continued.

d. Teaching Emma alternative ways to communicate her unhappiness (besides flailing her arms and legs and crying) will be beneficial. For example, she may nonverbally express her feelings by drawing with crayons or beating a drum, or she may verbally express her feelings by writing her feelings on a piece of paper or talking to her parents about how she feels. The goal should be to have Emma learn to channel her physical, emotional energy into something more constructive.

3. In light of Emma's strong verbal skills and weaker visual-motor synthesis skills, she may benefit from learning how to verbally mediate nonverbal tasks. For example, when trying a puzzle she can be taught to verbally describe the characteristics of the pieces that will help her ("I need a square corner to fit here and a round side to fit here.").

Jose Gonzalez, Yossi Adir, Danica Katz,   *Nadeen Kaufman, Ed.D.*
Paul Randolph   *Supervisor*
Examiners

Although there are numerous formats in which psychological and psychoeducational reports are written, there are standards of writing that are common across most of these report formats. To help you write a reader-friendly report, we have compiled a list of errors that we have noticed examiners making in writing reports (see Caution 7.1). This list may be used as a checklist of sorts to review before submitting your reports.

CAUTION

7.1 Common Errors to Avoid in Report Writing

- including inappropriate detail
- using unnecessary jargon or technical terms
- using vague language
- making abstract statements
- not supporting hypotheses with adequate data
- making gross generalizations from isolated information
- inserting value judgments
- discussing the test itself rather than the person's abilities
- using poor grammar
- presenting behaviors or test scores without interpreting them
- failing to adequately address reasons for referral
- failing to provide confidence intervals or otherwise denote that all obtained test scores include a band of error
- giving test results prematurely (e.g., in the Appearance and Behavioral Characteristics section)

Case Report: Susie O., 6-Year-Old With Childhood Leukemia

Wechsler Intelligence Scale for Children–Third Edition (WISC-III) Profile

Scale/Index	IQ/Index	90% Confidence Interval	Percentile Rank
Full Scale	97	92–102	42
Verbal Scale	84	80–90	14
Performance Scale	113	105–119	81
Verbal Comprehension Index	92	87–98	30
Perceptual Organization Index	116	107–121	86
Freedom from Distractibility Index	69	65–81	2
Processing Speed Index	106	97–113	66

Wechsler Intelligence Scale for Children–Third Edition (WISC-III) Profile (continued)

Verbal Subtests	Scaled Score[a]	Percentile Rank	Performance Subtests	Scaled Score[a]	Percentile Rank
Information	9	37	Picture Completion	10	50
Similarities	9	37	Coding	12	75
Arithmetic	2 (W)	<1	Picture Arrangement	17 (S)	99
Vocabulary	10 (S)	50	Block Design	12	75
Comprehension	6	9	Object Assembly	11	63
Digit Span	7	16	Symbol Search	10	50

[a](S) indicates a significant relative strength, $p < .05$; (W) indicates a significant relative weakness, $p < .05$.

NEPSY

Core Domain Subtest	Standard Score	90% Confidence Interval	Percentile Rank
Attention-Executive	92	85–102	30
Tower	6		9
Auditory Attention and Response Set	10		50
Visual Attention	11		63
Language	95	88–103	37
Phonological Processing	7		16
Speeded Naming	8		25
Comprehension of Instructions	13		84
Sensori-Motor	87	81–98	19
Fingertip Tapping	3		1
Imitating Hand Positions	7		16
Visuomotor Precision	15		95

continued

NEPSY (continued)

Core Domain Subtest	Standard Score	90% Confidence Interval	Percentile Rank
Visuo-Spatial	92	85–102	30
Design Copying	9		37
Arrows	8		25
Memory	105	97–112	63
Memory for Faces	13		84
Memory for Names	9		37
Narrative Memory	10		50

Kaufman Assessment Battery for Children (K-ABC): Achievement Scale

Achievement Subtest	Standard Score ± 90% Confidence Interval	Percentile Rank
Faces and Places	99 ± 13	47
Arithmetic	88 ± 11	21
Riddles	94 ± 11	34
Reading/Decoding	81 ± 5	10

Reason for Referral

Susie O. was referred for psychoeducational evaluation by her parents, who were concerned that her medical condition (leukemia) was affecting her learning and adjustment at school. Susie was diagnosed with acute lymphoblastic leukemia (ALL) last November during her kindergarten year; thus she has had little formal schooling and is due to begin the first grade next fall.

Background Information

Susie, a 6-year-old child who does not have any siblings, lives at home with her mother, Arlene O., and her father, Harry O. Mr. O. is a professional golfer, and Mrs. O. has recently started working as a food server. Both Mr.

and Mrs. O. attended college for a few years and reported no history of learning disabilities among Susie's maternal or paternal relatives.

Mrs. O. reported that she had an easy pregnancy with Susie. Susie was carried to full term and was delivered without any complications, weighing 6 lb. 12 oz. No behavior or health problems were noted during infancy, and all developmental milestones were reached on time or early. According to her father, Susie has excellent gross and fine motor coordination. She has had no serious injuries or accidents. However, last fall Susie became anemic and was diagnosed with ALL that winter. Currently she is in the maintenance phase of her treatment. Her chemotherapy regime has involved a number of medications, including prednisone, vincristine, L-asparaginase, and intrathecal methotrexate; however, she has not been administered radiation treatment at any time.

Susie attended preschool between the ages of 4 and 5. According to her father, Susie adjusted well to this school both academically and socially. Susie attended 3 months of kindergarten but did not return to school once she was diagnosed with ALL. She did not complete kindergarten, and she began first grade in the next year. However, due to continued severe immune suppression, Susie entered first grade 6 to 8 weeks after the start of the school year. She received about 8 weeks of tutoring toward the end of her kindergarten year, and she was tutored during the first few weeks of first grade when she was unable to attend class.

A review of Susie's kindergarten records indicates that during the fall semester when she attended kindergarten she displayed appropriate social and study skills, worked well with manipulative materials, and could recognize her own written name. In an interview with Mary C., Susie's current first grade teacher, she expressed her concern that Susie is extremely far behind the other first graders academically. She noted that Susie is acquiring skills at a much slower rate than her peers, and that if she continues to progress at this pace she will not be ready for second grade next year. Ms. C. appears concerned about deficits in Susie's ability to work with manipulative materials, and she reported that Susie has not had sufficient prior experience at "seeing how things fit together." Despite these concerns, she reported that Susie is socially appropriate, has made friends with her peers, and does not appear self-conscious about her illness.

According to both her parents, Susie was an extremely sociable young infant and toddler, and she continues to be very outgoing, relating well to people of all ages. They report that Susie is an active young girl who enjoys golfing, dancing, swimming, riding her bike, drawing, and painting.

Appearance and Behavior Characteristics

Susie presented herself as a sweet, verbal, and extremely friendly 6-year-old girl. She is very pale in complexion, and due to her hair loss in mid-April she has only a light covering of hair on her head. She appears of appropriate height and weight for her age. On all testings, Susie was dressed rather flamboyantly in a bright sundress and a large colorful hat. Susie was enthusiastic about meeting with the examiner and greeted the examiner with a big smile and an affectionate hug. Rapport was immediately established, and Susie made good eye contact at all times during the testing and displayed excellent verbal skills.

Although Susie appeared to exhibit good attention throughout the assessment, she had significant difficulty following instructions on almost all tasks. She frequently asked for instructions to be repeated; however, even with several repetitions Susie was often unable to understand the requirements of a task. She was often only able to complete the task with extensive modeling from the examiner or by working through several of the same type of items and eventually developing an understanding of what was required. This trial-and-error learning led to a great deal of inconsistency in her performance. It appears that Susie's style of solving problems may reflect a difficulty in working with novel tasks and poor planning ability.

It was noted that Susie displayed an impulsive approach to solving problems. She often gave the first answer that came into her mind, and only with encouragement from the examiner did she reconsider the problem and attempt a different solution. There was also some inconsistency in her level of perseverance. On several subtests Susie tended to give up easily when faced with a challenging problem. She quickly stated "I don't know" and did not appear to be concerned that she was unable to answer a question. In contrast, on a subtest requiring her to identify faces that she had previously seen, Susie persevered and did not give up, even when she clearly was unsure about the correct response. Susie's level of perseverance appeared to be related to the content of the task in that she appears to do better when working with meaningful, socially relevant materials rather than abstract concepts.

When unsure of her performance, Susie consistently appeared to look toward the examiner for guidance and reassurance that she was doing a good job. In fact, she had to be encouraged to move ahead without constant assurance that she was doing a good job. Susie therefore appears to rely on social feedback to assess her own progress. She seems to have difficulty working on academic-like tasks alone, and she thrives in a more social setting where she is interacting with others.

Although Susie was cooperative at all times, she clearly became tired as the testing progressed and was eager to take short breaks. However, after the break she willingly accompanied the examiner back to the testing room. On the basis of these behavior observations, this assessment appears to be a valid measure of Susie's current cognitive, neuropsychological, and emotional functioning.

Tests Administered

- clinical interview with Mr. and Mrs. O. (Russell Barkley Parent Interview)
- clinical interview with Susie O.
- interview with Susie's teacher, Mary C.
- Wechsler Intelligence Scale for Children–Third Edition (WISC-III)
- A Developmental Neuropsychological Assessment (NEPSY): Core Battery
- Kaufman Assessment Battery for Children (K-ABC): Achievement Subtests
- Child Behavior Checklist/4-18 (CBCL/4-18)
- Teacher Report Form (TRF)
- review of school records
- review of medical records

Test Results and Interpretation

Susie was administered the Wechsler Intelligence Scale for Children–Third Edition (WISC-III), which is an individually administered test of a child's intellectual ability and cognitive strengths and weaknesses. The WISC-III groups an individual's abilities into two global areas: Verbal IQ, which measures verbal skills, and Performance IQ, which involves the manipulation of concrete materials to solve nonverbal problems. On the WISC-III Susie earned a Verbal IQ (VIQ) of 84 ± 5 (14th percentile), which is in the Below Average range of intellectual functioning; a Performance IQ (PIQ) of 113 ± 6 (81st percentile), which is in the Above Average range of intellectual functioning; and a Full Scale IQ (FSIQ) of 97 ± 5 (42nd percentile), which is in the Average range of intellectual functioning. However, there was a great deal of variability in Susie's scores on the WISC-III, indicating significant inconsistencies in her performance. Therefore Susie's FSIQ of 97 ± 5 is rendered meaningless because it only represents the numerical average of many discrepant abilities. The best description of the distinction between Susie's overall verbal and nonverbal abilities is probably provided by her Verbal Comprehension Index (VCI) of 92 (30th percentile, Average range) and her Perceptual Organization Index (POI) of 116 (86th percentile, High Average ability). The 24-point difference between these indexes is both statistically significant and unusual, occurring in 10% of normal children, and indicates that Susie performs better when solving nonverbal items via the manipulation of concrete materials than when expressing herself orally and solving verbal problems.

It is important to note that there is a significant amount of variability in Susie's verbal abilities. For example, she exhibited a 23-point difference on her VCI of 92 and her Freedom from Distractibility Index (FDI) of 69, the two indexes that make up the Verbal IQ. This significant discrepancy suggests that Susie does better on tasks requiring verbal comprehension and expression than on those requiring short-term auditory memory. However, there is also significant variability in the two tasks that constitute the FDI, making this index meaningless. Therefore in Susie's case, examination of individual subtests on the WISC-III provides a clearer picture of her abilities.

Within the Verbal domain, Susie demonstrated one significant strength and one significant weakness relative to her Below Average verbal ability. She exhibited a significant weakness on a subtest requiring her to respond to auditorally presented arithmetic problems (< 1st percentile), suggesting poor computational skill. Her difficulty on this task appeared to result from an impulsive approach to solving the arithmetic problems, in which she tended to say the first answer that came into her head without thinking through her response. Furthermore, Susie's lack of exposure to a formal academic mathematics program may also account for her difficulty on this task. Susie displayed a significant relative strength on a task in which she was to define vocabulary words (50th percentile), indicating average language development. This is consistent with the good verbal skills she displayed during her interview with the examiner. Moreover, when her performance on this task is combined with tasks assessing similar skills, she is noted to have average crystallized abilities, or skills that depend on acquired knowledge. Thus although she may be struggling academically at school, she is able to adequately apply information she has learned in her home and school environments.

Within the nonverbal domain, Susie displayed a significant relative strength in her temporal and visual sequencing and in her ability to anticipate consequences. This was noted on a subtest requiring her to arrange a set of pictures into a logical story sequence (99th percentile) in which Susie scored in the Very Superior range. Thus she was able to sequence the pictures into a meaningful order quickly and accurately, and she appeared confident about her performance on this task. In contrast, on a verbal subtest of the WISC-III measuring her social judgment and knowledge about social rules, Susie scored at the 9th percentile. This discrepancy indicates that although Susie does have knowledge and understanding about social events, and is able to display common sense, she struggles to verbalize this knowledge.

Because children with leukemia often show neuropsychological deficits, Susie was administered the NEPSY, which is a neuropsychological instrument that measures a child's performance in five areas: (a) Attention and Executive Functions, (b) Language, (c) Sensori-motor Functions, (d) Visuospatial Processing, and (e) Memory and Learning. Overall, Susie performed at the Expected Level of Performance in all five areas; however, she exhibited much variability in performance on several of the domains, suggesting inconsistent abilities and some problem areas. Susie's performance on the NEPSY will be discussed as it relates to her performance on the WISC-III. Thus although not significant strengths or weaknesses for Susie, her performance on several WISC-III tasks is noteworthy when compared to her performance on the NEPSY.

On a WISC-III subtest in which Susie was to replicate two-dimensional geometric patterns using colored cubes, she scored at the 75th percentile. This reflects a strong ability in the area of nonverbal concept formation. It should be noted that this subtest is presented to the child in a graduated fashion in which she is first required to duplicate the examiner's model and then later to duplicate a model depicted on a page. The instructions on this subtest therefore require modeling, which appears to be an efficient method of teaching Susie novel tasks. In contrast, Susie demonstrated a statistically significant weakness on a subtest of the NEPSY in which she was required to move three colored balls to target positions on three pegs in a prescribed number of moves (9th percentile). Her performance on this task indicates below average ability to plan, monitor, self-regulate, and problem solve. Although she was able to complete some of the basic items, on all other items she sat staring at the pegs with clearly no idea where to start working, and she was unaware of her errors. Her low score seems to reflect impairment in her capacity to speculate and generate new solutions to problems, and to plan performance. The discrepancy between Susie's performance on these two similar subtests may result, in part, from the fact that although she has good nonverbal problem-solving skills particularly when working on visual reasoning tasks, she struggles to solve novel problems. This difficulty is especially evident when working on new tasks that require her to plan and self-monitor her performance without the use of modeling.

As was mentioned previously, Susie displayed variable performance in her verbal abilities on the WISC-III. However, her inconsistent performance was noted both between different verbal subtests and within some subtests. For instance, on a WISC-III task on which she was required to indicate the relationship between pairs of concepts (37th percentile), Susie was unable to state how a shirt and a shoe were alike, and she incorrectly replied that what was similar about water and milk is that they "are kind of white . . . clear." However, she was able to correctly answer more difficult items, accurately identifying what was similar between a wheel and a ball. Susie's performance on the Language domain of the NEPSY was similarly inconsistent, ranging from scores in the 16th to 84th percentiles. For example, Susie scored at the 16th percentile on a task in which she was required to identify a picture from an orally presented word segment, and later to create a new word by omitting a word segment or letter sound or by substituting one letter sound for another. Her performance on this task appeared to be impacted by her extreme difficulty in understanding the complex directions involved, and the instructions had to be repeated several times. However, she did seem to benefit from the examiner's feedback, and over time she was able to answer more items correctly. Therefore she got some easier items wrong but was able to successfully complete some more difficult ones. Similarly, Susie obtained a significant strength, relative to her performance on the Language domain, on a task measuring her comprehension of verbal instructions of increasing complexity (84th percentile). Susie appeared to immediately understand the instructions presented on all of the basic items, although she had some difficulty successfully completing many of the higher level items of this task. This is further confirmation that although Susie struggles with complex instruction, she is able to successfully complete tasks with more simple and straightforward directions.

The most significant scatter within a domain on the NEPSY was evident on the Sensori-motor domain, in which Susie's performance ranged from the 1st percentile on a task assessing finger dexterity to the 95th percentile on a task assessing her fine motor skills and hand-eye coordination. These results indicate great discrepancies in Susie's sensorimotor skills. She appears to have good motor control of a pencil and excellent fine motor skills. Her difficulty is with the rate of production of repetitive movements, and she has some difficulty with the fine motor coordination that is required to reproduce positions with her hands, particularly her nonpreferred hand. Her strong fine motor skills, as evidenced on the NEPSY, are consistent with her average scores on WISC-III tasks that assess fine motor skills and require the use of a pencil.

To assess Susie's academic functioning, she was administered the Achievement subtests from the Kaufman Assessment Battery for Children (K-ABC). Susie scored in the Average range on a task measuring her factual learning and acquired knowledge (47th percentile) and on a task measuring her ability to infer the name of a verbal concept when given several of its characteristics (34th percentile). She had more difficulty on an arithmetic task, scoring at the 21st percentile, in the Below Average range, which is not surprising given her significant weakness on an arithmetic subtest of the WISC-III (< 1st percentile). She also scored in the Below Average range on a task measuring her ability to identify letters and to read and pronounce words (10th percentile), a significant weakness for her. The results of the K-ABC Achievement subtests indicate that Susie has not acquired age appropriate skills in reading and math. Furthermore, her Average to Below Average academic skills are significantly lower than her Average to High Average cognitive abilities. Thus she would be expected to have some difficulty keeping up with the other first graders academically, and she may require additional individualized instruction.

Susie's emotional adjustment and psychosocial functioning were assessed by means of a clinical interview, the Child Behavior Checklist (CBCL) and Teacher Report Form (TRF). Susie's parents were asked to separately complete the CBCL to obtain a measure of any behavioral and emotional problems that they may observe in Susie as well as those areas in which Susie is adapting successfully. The CBCL/4-18 is designed to record children's competencies and problems as reported by their parents. The profile generated by both Mr. and Mrs. O.'s reports was not variable, with all scales consistently within the normal range. The only items identified by Susie's parents as potential areas of concern were on the Aggressive Behavior scale, on which they both reported that at times Susie "argues a lot," "demands a lot of attention," and "is easily jealous." On the Social Problems scale, both parents noted that sometimes Susie "clings to adults or is too dependent." Susie's teacher, Mary C., was asked to complete the TRF to obtain a measure of any behavioral and emotional problems that she may observe in Susie, as well as those areas in which Susie is adapting successfully. The TRF is the teacher-completed analogue to the CBCL. The profile generated by Ms. C.'s report on the Problem scales showed scales to be within the normal range. The only area of difficulty noted on the Academic/Adaptive Functioning section was on the Academic Performance scale, and Ms. C. reported that Susie is "Somewhat Below Grade" in all areas.

Susie is clearly an outgoing and engaging young girl who has coped well with all the challenges that she has faced since she became ill. It appears that both Mr. and Mrs. O. view Susie as a competent and social young girl, and that her teacher perceives Susie as being a happy child who works and behaves appropriately despite her academic difficulties.

Summary and Diagnostic Impressions

Susie is a 6-year-old girl in the first grade who was referred for evaluation by her parents. Mr. and Mrs. O. hope to better understand the difficulties their daughter exhibits in her school performance and to learn how to help their daughter adjust to the school environment after her yearlong absence. Susie was diagnosed with ALL last winter and is currently in the maintenance phase of her chemotherapy treatment.

Susie presented as a friendly, outgoing, and verbal young girl who was enthusiastic about the assessment. She displayed good attention throughout the testing sessions and cooperated at all times. Despite her adequate attention, Susie did evidence a degree of impulsivity in that she tended to give the first answer that came into her mind. She was also apt to give up with little effort. She required a great deal of encouragement from the examiner at all times, and she relied on the examiner's feedback and assurances that she was doing a good job. Susie was noted to have difficulty following instructions on several tasks, and she frequently required repetition or modeling of items in order to complete the subtests. She displayed significant problems in understanding complex and multistep directions. This difficulty, along with poor planning ability, tended to impact her performance and contributed to some of the inconsistencies noted in her results.

Although there was a great deal of scatter noted in Susie's scores, some patterns in her performance were evident. On the WISC-III, Susie obtained a Full Scale IQ of 97 ± 5 (42nd percentile), which is in the Average range of intellectual functioning. However, the best measures of her verbal and nonverbal abilities were reflected in her Perceptual Organization Index standard score of 116 (86th percentile, High Average range) and her Verbal Comprehension Index standard score of 92 (30th percentile, Average range). This significant 23-point discrepancy between her verbal and nonverbal scores indicates that Susie appears strong in her abilities to solve nonverbal items via the manipulation of concrete materials, and that she has more difficulty expressing herself verbally. However, it is clear that Susie's lack of exposure to a formal academic program accounts for some of her difficulties on verbal tasks. In fact, Susie is scoring below age expectancy in both reading and arithmetic. She also struggles on all tasks that depend on the ability to monitor one's own performance and problem solve, and on tasks involving an increasing cognitive load that make excessive demands on her working memory. Her difficulties are particularly noted on novel tasks, although when given frequent feedback from the examiner, her performance improves to an age appropriate level.

Susie is clearly viewed by her parents as a competent child who is adapting well to the stresses that she is experiencing. Her teacher, too, views Susie as adapting socially and emotionally; however, she has some concerns about Susie's academic skills. Test results indicate that Susie may benefit from ongoing assessment and support of her emotional and academic functioning to ensure that she continues to succeed socially and to help her succeed academically.

Recommendations

The following recommendations have been made to assist Susie and her parents in dealing with Susie's educational needs and her adjustment to school:

1. Susie should be provided with individual tutoring or small group instruction to help improve her academic skills. This tutoring should focus on developing her basic reading and arithmetic skills to a level that is appropriate for first grade. Furthermore, Susie would benefit from learning by means of concrete, meaningful materials. For example, when learning math she may count photographs of classmates to compare the number of boys versus the number of girls in her class. She should be provided with multisensory learning experiences in which visual, auditory, tactile, and kinesthetic channels are used to reinforce learning whenever possible.

2. Susie clearly has difficulty with complex, multistep directions but is successful at completing tasks involving more simple instruction. She would therefore benefit from having all instruction broken down for her. When giving directions to Susie, it would be useful to stop at various points to ensure that she understands this instruction. Incorporating nonverbal input and visual reinforcement is also important, for example, using gestures, drawing on the board, and modeling the steps of a process.

3. It is evident that Susie benefits from continuous positive feedback and encouragement. Her parents and teachers can therefore assist Susie in maintaining her level of perseverance by providing ongoing positive reinforcement for approved-of behaviors. This can be merely a nod or a smile, or it can be in the form of a positive comment on a paper, small rewards, or a star chart for completing chores at home. Moreover, Susie works best when provided with the feedback and stimulation of others around her in a social setting. Therefore she should be encouraged,

when appropriate, to participate in academic group activities rather than working alone.

4. Although Susie appears to be coping with the stress involved in her illness and consequential isolation from other children, there are indications that she is at risk for some emotional difficulties as a result of these experiences. Her adjustment to school and her social functioning should be monitored, and appropriate counseling support should be sought if necessary.

Shelley Suntup, M.A. *Nadeen Kaufman, Ed.D.*
Examiner   *Debra Broadbooks, Ph.D.*
        Supervisors

 TEST YOURSELF

1. **List five topics to include in the Background Information section of the report.**

2. **Every single behavior that was noticed during the assessment session should be described in detail in the Appearance and Behavioral Characteristics section of the report.** True or False?

3. **Besides a description of the child's physical appearance and behavioral observations, what else should be mentioned in the Appearance and Behavioral Characteristics section of the report?**

   (a) test scores

   (b) referral question

   (c) a statement about the validity of the test results

   (d) brief recommendations

4. **The least meaningful type of score metric and therefore the one that should not be used in case reports is the**

   (a) raw score.

   (b) percentile rank.

   (c) standard score.

   (d) scaled score.

continued

5. **If you forget to mention some of the test results in the Test Results and Interpretation section, there is no need to worry because you can simply write about them in the Summary section of the report.** True or False?

6. **Which of the following are highly recommended in writing your report?**

   (a) using a lot of metaphors

   (b) listing as many observed behaviors as possible without interpreting them

   (c) using a substantial amount of jargon or technical terms

   (d) never providing confidence intervals as they are too confusing

   (e) none of the above

Answers: 1. See Don't Forget 7.3; 2. False; 3. c; 4. a; 5. False; 6. e

Appendix A

Table A–1.   Conversion Table for Calculating the WISC–III Performance IQ When Symbol Search Is Substituted for Coding

Sum of Scaled Scores	IQ	Percentile Rank	Confidence Interval 90%	Confidence Interval 95%
5	44	< 0.1	42–56	41–57
6	46	< 0.1	44–58	43–59
7	47	< 0.1	45–58	44–60
8	48	< 0.1	46–59	45–61
9	49	< 0.1	47–60	45–62
10	51	0.1	49–62	47–63
11	52	0.1	49–63	48–65
12	53	0.1	50–64	49–65
13	54	0.1	51–65	50–66
14	56	0.2	53–67	52–68
15	57	0.3	54–68	53–69
16	58	0.3	55–68	54–70
17	59	0.4	56–69	55–71
18	61	1	58–71	56–72
19	62	1	59–72	57–73
20	63	1	60–73	58–74
21	64	1	60–74	59–75
22	66	1	62–76	61–77
23	67	2	63–77	62–78
24	68	2	64–78	63–79
25	69	2	65–78	64–80
26	71	3	67–80	66–82

continued

Table A–1.   continued

Sum of Scaled Scores	IQ	Percentile Rank	Confidence Interval 90%	Confidence Interval 95%
27	72	3	68–81	66–83
28	73	4	69–82	67–83
29	74	4	70–83	68–84
30	76	5	72–85	70–86
31	77	6	72–86	71–87
32	78	7	73–87	72–88
33	79	8	74–88	73–89
34	80	9	75–89	74–90
35	82	10	77–90	76–92
36	82	12	78–91	77–93
37	83	13	79–92	78–94
38	84	14	80–93	78–94
39	85	18	82–95	80–96
40	87	19	82–96	81–97
41	89	23	83–97	82–98
42	90	25	84–98	83–99
43	92	27	86–100	85–101
44	93	32	87–100	86–102
45	94	34	88–101	87–103
46	95	37	89–102	87–103
47	97	39	91–104	88–104
48	98	45	91–105	90–106
49	99	47	92–106	91–107
50	100	50	93–107	92–108
51	102	55	95–109	94–110

Sum of Scaled Scores	IQ	Percentile Rank	Confidence Interval 90%	Confidence Interval 95%
52	103	58	95–109	95–111
53	104	61	97–110	96–112
54	105	66	98–111	96–112
55	107	68	100–113	98–114
56	108	70	101–114	99–115
57	109	75	101–115	100–116
58	110	77	102–116	101–117
59	112	79	104–118	103–119
60	113	81	105–119	104–120
61	114	84	106–119	105–121
62	115	86	107–120	106–122
63	116	87	108–121	106–122
64	118	90	110–123	108–124
65	119	91	110–124	109–125
66	120	92	111–125	110–126
67	121	94	113–127	112–128
68	123	95	114–127	112–129
69	124	96	115–128	114–130
70	125	96	116–129	115–131
71	126	97	117–130	115–131
72	128	98	119–132	117–132
73	129	98	119–133	118–134
74	130	98	120–134	119–135
75	131	99	121–135	120–136
76	133	99	123–137	122–138
77	134	99	124–137	123–139

continued

Table A–1.   continued

Sum of Scaled Scores	IQ	Percentile Rank	Confidence Interval 90%	95%
78	135	99	125–138	124–140
79	136	99.5	126–139	124–141
80	138	99.6	128–141	126–142
81	139	99.7	129–142	127–143
82	140	99.7	129–143	128–144
83	141	99.8	130–144	129–145
84	143	99.9	132–146	131–147
85	144	99.9	133–147	132–148
86	145	99.9	134–148	133–149
87	146	99.9	135–148	134–150
88	147	> 99.9	136–149	134–151
89	149	> 99.9	138–151	136–152
90	150	> 99.9	139–152	137–153
91	151	> 99.9	139–153	138–154
92	152	> 99.9	140–154	139–155
93	154	> 99.9	142–156	141–157
94	155	> 99.9	143–157	142–158
95	156	>99.9	144–159	143–159

Note. From "Normative tables for calculating the WISC-III Performance and Full Scale IQs when Symbol Search is substituted for Coding," by C. R. Reynolds, S. Sanchez, and V. L. Willson, 1996, *Psychological Assessment, 8,* pp. 378–382. Copyright © 1996 by the American Psychological Association. Adapted and reproduced with permission. All rights reserved.

Table A-2. Conversion Table for Calculating the WISC-III Full Scale IQ When Symbol Search Is Substituted for Coding

Sum of Scaled Scores	IQ	Percentile Rank	Confidence Interval 90%	Confidence Interval 95%
10	41	< 0.1	38–48	38–49
11	42	< 0.1	40–49	39–50
12	42	< 0.1	40–49	39–50
13	43	< 0.1	40–50	40–51
14	44	< 0.1	41–51	41–52
15	44	< 0.1	41–51	41–52
16	45	< 0.1	42–52	41–53
17	46	< 0.1	43–53	42–54
18	46	< 0.1	43–53	42–54
19	47	< 0.1	44–54	43–55
20	48	< 0.1	45–55	44–56
21	48	< 0.1	45–55	44–56
22	49	< 0.1	46–56	45–57
23	50	< 0.1	47–57	46–58
24	50	0.1	47–57	46–58
25	51	0.1	48–58	47–59
26	52	0.1	49–59	48–60
27	52	0.1	49–59	48–60
28	53	0.1	50–60	49–60
29	54	0.1	51–61	50–61
30	54	0.1	51–61	50–61
31	55	0.2	52–61	51–62
32	56	0.2	53–62	52–63
33	56	0.2	53–62	52–63
34	57	0.3	54–63	53–64

continued

Table A-2.   continued

Sum of Scaled Scores	IQ	Percentile Rank	Confidence Interval 90%	95%
35	58	0.3	55−64	54−65
36	58	0.4	55−64	54−65
37	59	0.4	56−65	55−66
38	59	0.5	56−65	55−66
39	60	1	57−66	56−67
40	61	1	58−67	57−68
41	61	1	58−67	57−68
42	62	1	59−68	58−69
43	63	1	60−69	59−70
44	63	1	60−69	59−70
45	64	1	61−70	60−71
46	65	1	62−71	61−72
47	65	1	62−71	61−72
48	66	2	63−72	62−73
49	67	2	64−73	63−74
50	67	2	64−73	63−74
51	68	2	65−74	64−75
52	69	2	65−75	65−76
53	69	2	65−75	65−76
54	70	3	66−76	66−77
55	71	3	67−77	67−78
56	71	3	67−77	66−78
57	72	4	68−78	67−79
58	73	4	69−79	68−80
59	73	4	69−79	68−80
60	74	5	70−80	69−81

Sum of Scaled Scores	IQ	Percentile Rank	Confidence Interval 90%	Confidence Interval 95%
61	75	5	71–81	70–82
62	75	5	71–81	70–82
63	76	5	72–82	71–83
64	77	6	73–83	72–84
65	77	6	73–83	72–84
66	78	7	74–84	73–85
67	79	7	75–85	74–86
68	79	8	75–85	74–85
69	80	9	76–86	75–86
70	81	10	77–86	76–87
71	81	10	77–86	76–87
72	82	12	78–87	77–88
73	82	13	78–87	77–88
74	83	13	79–88	78–89
75	84	14	80–89	79–90
76	84	14	80–89	79–90
77	85	16	81–90	80–91
78	86	18	82–91	81–92
79	86	18	82–91	81–92
80	87	19	83–92	82–93
81	88	19	84–93	83–94
82	88	21	84–93	83–94
83	89	23	85–94	84–95
84	90	25	86–95	85–96
85	90	25	86–95	85–96
86	91	27	87–96	86–97
87	92	30	88–97	87–98

continued

Table A-2.   continued

Sum of Scaled Scores	IQ	Percentile Rank	Confidence Interval 90%	Confidence Interval 95%
88	92	30	88–97	87–98
89	93	32	89–98	88–99
90	94	32	90–99	89–100
91	94	34	90–99	89–100
92	95	37	90–100	90–101
93	96	37	91–101	91–102
94	96	39	91–101	91–102
95	97	42	92–102	91–103
96	98	42	93–103	92–104
97	98	45	93–103	92–104
98	99	47	94–104	93–105
99	100	47	95–105	94–106
100	100	50	95–105	94–106
101	101	53	96–106	95–107
102	102	53	97–107	96–108
103	102	55	97–107	96–108
104	103	58	98–108	97–109
105	104	61	99–109	98–109
106	104	61	99–109	98–109
107	105	63	100–109	99–110
108	105	66	100–109	99–110
109	106	66	101–110	100–111
110	107	68	102–111	101–112
111	107	68	102–111	101–112
112	108	70	103–112	102–113
113	109	73	104–113	103–114
114	109	73	104–113	103–114

Sum of Scaled Scores	IQ	Percentile Rank	Confidence Interval 90%	Confidence Interval 95%
115	110	75	105–114	104–115
116	111	77	106–115	105–116
117	111	79	106–115	105–116
118	112	79	107–116	106–117
119	113	81	108–117	107–118
120	113	81	108–117	107–118
121	114	82	109–118	108–119
122	115	84	110–119	109–120
123	115	86	110–119	109–120
124	116	86	111–120	110–121
125	117	87	112–121	111–122
126	117	88	112–121	111–122
127	118	90	113–122	112–123
128	119	91	113–123	113–124
129	119	92	113–123	113–124
130	120	92	114–124	114–125
131	121	93	115–125	114–126
132	121	93	115–125	114–126
133	122	94	116–126	115–127
134	123	94	117–127	116–128
135	123	95	117–127	116–128
136	124	95	118–128	117–129
137	125	96	119–129	118–130
138	125	96	119–129	118–130
139	126	96	120–130	119–131
140	127	96	121–131	120–132
141	127	97	121–131	120–132
142	128	97	122–132	121–132

continued

Table A-2. **continued**

Sum of Scaled Scores	IQ	Percentile Rank	Confidence Interval 90%	95%
143	129	98	123–133	122–133
144	129	98	123–133	122–133
145	130	98	124–133	123–134
146	130	98	124–133	123–134
147	131	98	125–134	124–135
148	132	99	126–135	125–136
149	132	99	126–135	125–136
150	133	99	127–136	126–137
151	134	99	128–137	127–138
152	134	99	128–137	127–138
153	135	99	129–138	128–139
154	136	99	130–139	129–140
155	136	99	130–139	129–140
156	137	99.5	131–140	130–141
157	138	99.6	132–141	131–142
158	138	99.6	132–141	131–142
159	139	99.7	133–142	132–143
160	140	99.7	134–143	133–144
161	140	99.7	134–143	133–144
162	141	99.8	135–144	134–145
163	142	99.8	136–145	135–146
164	142	99.8	136–145	135–146
165	143	99.9	137–146	136–147
166	144	99.9	137–147	137–148
167	144	99.9	137–147	137–148
168	145	99.9	138–148	138–149

Sum of Scaled Scores	IQ	Percentile Rank	Confidence Interval 90%	Confidence Interval 95%
169	146	99.9	139–149	138–150
170	146	99.9	139–149	138–150
171	147	> 99.9	140–150	139–151
172	148	> 99.9	141–151	140–152
173	148	> 99.9	141–151	140–152
174	149	> 99.9	142–152	141–153
175	150	> 99.9	143–153	142–154
176	150	> 99.9	143–153	142–154
177	151	> 99.9	144–154	143–155
178	152	> 99.9	145–155	144–156
179	152	> 99.9	145–155	144–155
180	153	> 99.9	146–156	145–156
181	153	> 99.9	146–156	145–156
182	154	> 99.9	147–157	146–157
183	155	> 99.9	148–157	147–158
184	155	> 99.9	148–157	147–158
185	156	> 99.9	149–158	148–159
186	157	> 99.9	150–159	149–160
187	157	> 99.9	150–159	149–160
188	158	> 99.9	151–160	150 161
189	159	> 99.9	152–161	151–162
190	159	> 99.9	152–161	151–162

Note. From "Normative tables for calculating the WISC-III Performance and Full Scale IQs when Symbol Search is substituted for Coding," by C. R. Reynolds, S. Sanchez, and V. L. Willson, 1996, *Psychological Assessment, 8,* pp. 378–382. Copyright © 1996 by the American Psychological Association. Adapted and reproduced by permission. All rights reserved.

Appendix B

WPPSI-R Interpretive Worksheet

STEP 1: Interpret the WPPSI-R Full Scale IQ

Scale	IQ	Confidence Interval 90% or 95% (circle one)	Percentile Rank	Descriptive Category
Full Scale				
Performance				
Verbal				

⇨

STEP 2: Is the WPPSI-R Verbal IQ Versus Performance IQ Discrepancy Significant?

V-IQ	P-IQ	Difference	Significant (*p* < .01)	Significant (*p* < .05)	Not Significant	Is there a significant difference?
			15 or more	14–11	0–10	YES NO

⇨

STEP 2 Decision Box

If the answer to Step 2 is **NO**, there is not a significant difference between the V–IQ and P-IQ.	⇨	First explain the meaning of the scales not being significantly different. Then **Skip to STEP 4.**
If the answer to Step 2 is **YES,** there is a significant difference between the V-IQ and P-IQ.	⇨	Continue on to **STEP 3.**

⇨

STEP 3: Is the WPPSI-R V-IQ Versus P-IQ Discrepancy Abnormally Large?

V-IQ vs. P-IQ Discrepancy	Percentage of Normal Children Showing Discrepancy	Size of V-IQ vs. P-IQ Discrepancy Needed to Be Considered Abnormally Large	Is there an abnormally large V-IQ vs. P-IQ discrepancy (at least 20 pts)?	
			YES	NO
	Extreme 15%	20		
	Extreme 10%	22		
	Extreme 5%	26		
	Extreme 2%	32		
	Extreme 1%	36		

⇨

If **ANY abnormal** differences are found ⇨ then this **abnormally** large discrepancy shouldbe interpreted, *even if* significant subtest scatter exists (Step 4). ⇨ Explain the **abnormally large** Verbal and Performance differences. Then **go to STEP 5.**

If **NO abnormal** difference are found ⇨ then you must determine if the noted significant differences between V-IQ and P-IQ are interpretable. ⇨ Review subtest scatter examined in **Step 4** prior to making global interpretations.

STEP 4: Is the WPPSI-R Verbal Versus Performance IQ Discrepancy Interpretable?

A. Is there abnormal Verbal scatter?

High Scaled Score of 5 V-IQ Subtests	Low Scaled Score of 5 V-IQ Subtests	High-Low Difference	Abnormal Scatter	Not Abnormal	Is there abnormal scatter?
			7 or more	0–6	YES NO

B. Is there abnormal Performance scatter?

High Scaled Score of 5 P-IQ Subtests	Low Scaled Score of 5 P-IQ Subtests	High-Low Difference	Abnormal Scatter	Not Abnormal	Is there abnormal scatter?
			8 or more	0–7	YES NO

If the answers to both STEP 4 questions (A and B) are **NO**	⇨	then V-IQ versus P-IQ discrepancy is interpretable.	⇨	Explain the meaningful difference between V-IQ and P-IQ. **Then go to STEP 5.**
If the answers to either STEP 4 question (A or B) are **YES**	⇨	then the V-IQ versus P-IQ difference should probably **not** be interpreted.	⇨	Examine the strengths and weaknesses in **STEP 5.**

Note: If there is a *significant difference* between the component parts of the Full Scale IQ (i.e, the Verbal IQ and the Performance IQ or significant subtest scatter), the Full Scale IQ should *not* be interpreted as a *meaningful* representation of the individual's *overall* performance.

STEP 5: Interpret Significant Strengths and Weaknesses of WPPSI-R Profile

V-IQ–P-IQ discrepancy						
0–19	Then use	⇨	mean of all subtests administered.[a]	⇨	Overall Mean	Rounded Mean
20 or more	Then use	⇦	mean of all Verbal subtests administered.[a] *and also use*	⇨	Verbal Subtests' Mean	Rounded Mean
		⇦	mean of all Performance subtests administered.[a]	⇨	Performance Subtests' Mean	Rounded Mean

[a] After calculating means, round to the nearest whole number.

Verbal Subtest	Scaled Score	Rounded Mean	Difference[b]	Size of Difference Needed for Significance	Strength or Weakness (S or W)	Percentile Rank (see Table 4.5)
Information				±3		
Comprehension				±3		
Arithmetic				±3		
Vocabulary				±3		
Similarities				±3		
Sentences				±3		
Performance Subtest						
Object Assembly				±4		
Geometric Design				±3		
Block Design				±3		
Mazes				±4		
Picture Completion				±3		
Animal Pegs				±4		

[b]Difference = subtest scaled score minus appropriate rounded mean.

STEP 6: Generating Hypotheses About Strengths and Weaknesses

Review information presented on pages _____–_____, which details how to reorganize subtest profiles to systematically generate hypotheses about strengths and weaknesses.

Note. V-IQ = Verbal IQ; P-IQ = Performance IQ.

Appendix C

WISC-III Interpretive Worksheet

STEP 1: Interpret the WISC-III Full Scale IQ

Scale	IQ	90% Confidence Interval	Percentile	Descriptive Category
Full Scale				
Performance				
Verbal				

⇨

STEP 2: Is the Verbal IQ versus Performance IQ Discrepancy Significant?

V-IQ	P-IQ	Difference	Significant (*p* < .01)	Significant (*p* < .05)	Not Significant
			15 or more	11–14	0–10

STEP 2 Decision Box

	Is there a significant difference?
	YES NO

⇨   First explain the meaning of the scales not being significantly
    different. Then **Skip to STEP 4.**

If the answer to Step 2 is **NO**, there is not a significant
difference between the V-IQ and P-IQ.

⇨   Continue on to **STEP 3.**

If the answer to Step 2 is **YES**, there is a significant
difference between the V-IQ and P-IQ.

⇨

STEP 3A: Is WISC-III Verbal Versus Performance IQ Discrepancy Interpretable? Or Should You Interpret the Verbal Comprehension and Perceptual Organization Indexes?

VERBAL SCALE

A. Is there a significant difference between the Verbal Comprehension and Freedom from Distractibility indexes?

VCI	FDI	Difference	Significant ($p < .01$)	Significant ($p < .05$)	Not Significant	Is there a significant difference? YES NO
			17 or more	16–13	0–12	⇨

B. Is there abnormal scatter on the Verbal Scale?

High Scaled Score of 5 V-IQ Subtests	Low Scaled Score of 5 V-IQ Subtests	High-Low Difference	Abnormal Scatter	Not Abnormal	Is there abnormal scatter? YES NO
			7 or more	0–6	⇨

PERFORMANCE SCALE

C. Is there a significant difference between the Perceptual Organization and Processing Speed indexes?

POI	PSI	Difference	Significant ($p < .01$)	Significant ($p < .05$)	Not Significant	Is there a significant difference? YES NO
			19 or more	18–15	0–14	⇨

D. Is there abnormal scatter on the Performance Scale?

High Scaled Score of 5 P-IQ Subtests	Low Scaled Score of 5 P-IQ Subtests	High-Low Difference	Abnormal Scatter	Not Abnormal	Is there abnormal scatter?	
			9 or more	0–8	YES	NO

⇨

STEP 3 Decision Box

If the answers to ALL STEP 3 questions above (A, B, C, and D) are **NO** ⇨ then V-IQ versus P-IQ discrepancy is interpretable. ⇨ Explain the meaningful difference between V-IQ and P-IQ. **Then go to STEP 4.**

If the answers to one or more questions in STEP 3 are **YES** ⇨ then the V-IQ versus P-IQ difference should probably **not** be interpreted. ⇨ Examine VCI versus POI discrepancy in the continuation section of **STEP 3**.

STEP 3B: Is There a Significant Difference Between the Verbal Comprehension and Perceptual Organization Indexes?

VCI	POI	Difference	Significant (p < .01)	Significant (p < .05)	Not Significant	Is there a significant difference?	
			16 or more	12–15	0–11	YES	NO

⇨

A. Is there significant scatter in Verbal Comprehension subtests?

High Scaled Score of 4 VCI Subtests	Low Scaled Score of 4 VCI Subtests	High-Low Scaled Score Difference	Abnormal Scatter	Not Abnormal	Is there abnormal scatter?	
			7 or more	0–6	YES	NO

B. Is there significant scatter in Perceptual Organization subtests?

High Scaled Score of 4 POI Subtests	Low Scaled Score of 4 POI Subtests	High-Low Scaled Score Difference	Abnormal Scatter	Not Abnormal	Is there abnormal scatter?	
			8 or more	0–7	YES	NO

STEP 3 (continued) Decision Box

If there is **not** significant scatter in either the POI or VCI subtests ⇨ then VCI versus POI discrepancy is interpretable. ⇨ Explain the meaningful difference between VCI and POI and **go to STEP 4.**

If there **is** significant scatter in either the POI or VCI subtests ⇨ then the VCI versus POI discrepancy should probably **not** be interpreted. ⇨ Do not interpret VCI versus POI difference and **go to Step 4.**

Note: If there is a *significant difference* between the component parts of the Full Scale IQ (i.e., the Verbal IQ and the Performance IQ—examined in Step 2—or the Verbal Comprehension Index and the Perceptual Organization Index—examined in Step 3) or if there is significant scatter between the subtests, the Full Scale IQ should *not* be interpreted as a *meaningful* representation of the individual's *overall* performance.

STEP 4: Is the WISC-III V-IQ Versus P-IQ or VCI Versus POI Discrepancy Abnormally Large?

V-IQ vs. P-IQ Discrepancy

Percentage of Normal Children Showing Discrepancy	Size of V-IQ vs. P-IQ Discrepancy Needed to Be Considered Abnormally Large	Is there an abnormally large V-IQ vs. P-IQ discrepancy (at least 19pts)?	
		YES	NO
Extreme 15%	19–21		
Extreme 10%	22–24		
Extreme 2%	25–29		
Extreme 2%	30–31		
Extreme 1%	32 and above		

VCI vs. POI Discrepancy

Percentage of Normal Children Showing Discrepancy	Size of VCI vs. POI Discrepancy Needed to Be Considered Abnormally Large	Is there an abnormally large VCI vs. POI discrepancy (at least 19pts)?	
		YES	NO
Extreme 15%	19–21		
Extreme 10%	22–25		
Extreme 2%	26–29		
Extreme 2%	30–32		
Extreme 1%	33 and above		

STEP 4 Decision Box

If **ANY abnormal** differences are found	⇨	then this **abnormally** large discrepancy should be interpreted, *even if* the differences were found uninterpretable in STEP 3.	Explain the **abnormally** large Verbal and Performance differences. Then **go to STEP 5.**
If **NO abnormal** differences are found	⇨	then you must determine if the noted significant differences between V-IQ and P-IQ or VCI and POI are interpretable.	Review subtest scatter and discrepancies between indexes examined in **Step 3** prior to making global interpretations.

⇩

STEP 5: Interpret the Meaning of WISC-III Global Verbal/Nonverbal and Small Factors

Study the information and procedures presented in Chapter 4. The rules below help to determine whether the FDI and PSI have too much scatter to permit meaningful interpretation of these indexes.

1. Is Freedom from Distractibility Index interpretable?

Arithmetic	Digit Span	Difference	Abnormal Scatter	Not Abnormal	Is there abnormal scatter?	
			4 or more	0–3	YES	NO

2. Is Processing Speed Index interpretable?

Symbol Search	Coding	Difference	Abnormal Scatter	Not Abnormal	Is there abnormal scatter?	
			4 or more	0–3	YES	NO

⇩

STEP 6: Interpret Significant Strengths and Weaknesses of WISC-III Profile

V-IQ–P-IQ discrepancy

			Overall Mean	Rounded Mean
0–18	Then use	mean of all subtests administered.[a] ⇧		
19 or more	Then use	mean of all Verbal subtests administered.[a] ⇧	Verbal Subtests' Mean	Rounded Mean
		and also use mean of all Performance subtests administered.[a] ⇧	Performance Subtests' Mean	Rounded Mean

[a] After calculating means, round to the nearest whole number.

Verbal Subtest	Scaled Score	Rounded Mean	Difference[b]	Size of Difference Needed for Significance	Strength or Weakness (S or W)	Percentile Rank (see Table 4.5)
Information				±3		
Similarities				±3		
Arithmetic				±3		
Vocabulary				±3		
Comprehension				±4		
Digit Span				±4		

Verbal Subtest	Scaled Score	Rounded Mean	Difference[b]	Size of Difference Needed for Significance	Strength or Weakness (S or W)	Percentile Rank (see Table 4.5)
Performance Subtest						
Picture Completion				±4		
Coding				±5		
Picture Arrangement				±4		
Block Design				±4		
Object Assembly				±4		
Symbol Search				±4		

[b]Difference = subtest scaled score minus appropriate rounded mean.

STEP 7: Generating Hypotheses About Strengths and Weaknesses

Review information presented on pages 173–188 which details how to reorganize subtest profiles to systematically generate hypotheses about strengths and weaknesses.

Note. V-IQ = Verbal IQ; P-IQ = Performance IQ; VCI = Verbal Comprehension Index; POI = Perceptual Organization Index; FDI = Freedom from Distractibility Index; PSI = Processing Speed Index.

References

Alfonso, V.C., Johnson, A., Patinella, L., & Rader, D. E. (1998). Common WISC-III examiner errors from graduate students in training. *Psychology in the Schools, 35,* 119–125.

American Psychiatric Association. (1994). *Diagnostic and statistical manual of mental disorders:* (4th ed.). Washington, DC: Author.

Anastasi, A., & Urbina, S. (1997). *Psychological testing* (7th ed.). Upper Saddle River, NJ: Prentice-Hall.

Anastopoulos, A. D., Spitsto, M. A., & Maher, M. C. (1994). The WISC-III freedom from distractibility factor: Its utility in identifying children with attention deficit hyperactivity disorder. *Psychological Assessment, 6,* 368–371.

Bannatyne, A. (1974). Diagnosis: A note on recategorization of the WISC scaled scores. *Journal of Learning Disabilities, 7,* 272–274.

Barkley, R. A. (1990). *Attention deficit hyperactivity disorder: A handbook for diagnosis and treatment.* New York: Guilford Press.

Barnes, G., Broeren, J., Newell, L., & Clark, R. D. (1993, April). *A comparison study of the WISC-III and the Woodcock-Johnson Psycho-Educational Battery–R.* Paper presented at the meeting of the National Association of School Psychologists, Washington, DC.

Binet, A., & Simon, T. (1905). Méthodes nouvelles pour le diagnostic du niveau intellectuel des anormaux. *L'Année Psychologique, 11,* 191–244.

Binet, A., & Simon, T. (1908). Le développement de l'intelligence chez les enfants. *L'Année Psychologique, 14,* 1–94.

Blumberg, T. A. (1995). A practitioner's view of the WISC-III. *Journal of School Psychology, 33,* 95–97.

Bracken, B. (1992). Review of the Wechsler Preschool and Primary Scale of Intelligence–Revised. In J. J. Kramer & J. C. Conoley (Eds.), *The eleventh mental measurements yearbook* (pp. 1027–1029). Lincoln, NE: Buros Institute of Mental Measurements.

Braden, J. P. (1995). Review of the Wechsler Intelligence Scale for Children, Third Edition. In J. C. Conoley & J. C. Impara (Eds.), *The twelfth mental measurements yearbook* (pp. 1098–1103). Lincoln, NE: Buros Institute of Mental Measurements.

Canivez, G. L. (1995). Validity of the Kaufman Brief Intelligence Test: Comparisons with the Wechsler Intelligence Scale for Children–Third Edition. *Assessment, 2,* 101–111.

Canivez, G. L. (1996). Validity and diagnostic efficiency of the K-BIT in reevaluation students with learning disabilities. *Journal of Psychoeducational Assessment, 14,* 4–19.

Carvajal, H. H., Hayes, J. E., Lackey, K. L., Rathke, M. L., Wiebe, D. A., & Weaver, K. A. (1993). Correlations between scores on the WISC-III and the General Purpose Abbreviated Battery of the Stanford-Binet-IV. *Psychological Reports, 72,* 1167–1170.

Cattell, R. B., & Horn, J. L. (1978). A check on the theory of fluid and crystallized intelligence with description of new subtest designs. *Journal of Educational Measurement, 15,* 139–164.

Connery, S. L., Katz, D., Kaufman, A. S., & Kaufman, N. L. (1996). Correlations between two short cognitive tests and a WISC-III short form using a sample of adolescent inpatients. *Psychological Reports, 78,* 1373–1378.

Culbertson, J. L., & Edmonds, J. E. (1996). Learning disabilities. In R. L. Adams, O. A. Parsons, J. L. Culbertson, & S. J. Nixon (Eds.), *Neuropsychology for clinical practice: Etiology, assessment, and treatment of common neurological disorders.* Washington, DC: American Psychological Association.

Daley, C. E., & Nagel, R. J. (1996). Relevance of WISC-III indicators for assessment of learning disabilities. *Journal of Psychoeducational Assessment, 14,* 320–333.

Daniel, M. H. (1997). Intelligence testing: Status and trends. *American Psychologist, 52,* 1038–1045.

Das, J. P., & Naglieri, J. A. (1996). Mental retardation and assessment of cognitive processes. In J. W. Jacobson & J. A. Mulick (Eds.), *Manual of diagnosis and professional practice in mental retardation* (pp. 115–126). Washington, DC: American Psychological Association.

Delugach, R. R. (1991). Review of Wechsler Preschool and Primary Scale of Intelligence–Revised (WPPSI-R). *Journal of Psychoeducational Assessment, 9,* 280–290.

Doll, B., & Boren, R. (1993). Performance of severely language-impaired students on the WISC-II, language scales and academic achievement measures. *Journal of Psychoeducational Assessment, 81,* 77–86.

Donders, J. (1995). Validity of the Kaufman Brief Intelligence Test (K-BIT) in children with traumatic brain injury, *Assessment, 2,* 219–224.

Dougherty, E. H. (1992). *Report Writer: WISC-III/WISC-R/WPPSI-R.* Odessa, FL: Psychological Assessment Resources.

Faust, D. S., & Hollingsworth, J. O. (1991). Concurrent validation of the Wechsler Preschool and Primary Scale of Intelligence–Revised (WPPSI-R). *Journal of Psychoeducational Assessment, 9,* 224–229.

Fishkin, A. S., Kampsnider, J. J., & Pack, L. (1996). Exploring the WISC-III as a measure of giftedness. *Roeper Review, 18,* 226–231.

Flanagan, D. P., Genshaft, J. L., & Harrison, P. L. (Eds.). (1997). *Contemporary intellectual assessment: Theories, tests, and issues.* New York: Guilford Press.

Flanagan, D. P., McGrew, K. S., & Ortiz, S. O. (in press). *The Wechsler Intelligence and Memory Scales: A contemporary approach to interpretation.* Boston: Allyn & Bacon.

Flynn, J. R. (1987). Massive IQ gains in 14 nations: What IQ tests really measure. *Psychological Bulletin, 101,* 171–191.

Galton, F. (1869). *Hereditary genius: An inquiry into its laws and consequences.* London: Macmillan.

Galton, F. (1883). *Inquiries into human faculty and its development.* London: Macmillan.

Gaskill, F. W., & Brantley, J. C. (1996). Changes in ability and achievement scores over time: Implications for children classified as learning disabled. *Journal of Psychoeducational Assessment, 14,* 220–228.

Gerken, K. C., & Hodapp, A. F. (1992). Assessment of preschoolers at-risk with the WPPSI-R and the Stanford Binet L-M. *Psychological Reports, 71,* 659–664.

Gesell, A., Ilg, F., & Ames, L. B. (1974). *Infant and child in the culture of today* (Rev. ed.). New York: Harper & Row.

Giordano, F. G., Schwiebert, V. L., & Brotherton, W. D. (1997). School counselors' perceptions of the usefulness of standardized tests, frequency of their use, and assessment training needs. *School Counselor, 44,* 198–205.

Glutting, J. J., & McDermott, P. A. (1989). Using "teaching items" on ability tests: A nice idea, but does it work? *Educational and Psychological Measurement, 49,* 257–268.

Glutting, J. J., McDermott, P. A., Prifitera, A., & McGrath, E. A. (1994). Core profile types for the WISC-III and WIAT: Their development and application in identifying multivariate IQ-achievement discrepancies. *School Psychology Review, 23,* 619–639.

Glutting, J. J., & Oakland, T. (1992). *Guide to the Assessment of Test Session Behavior for the WISC-III and the WIAT.* San Antonio, TX: The Psychological Corporation.

Glutting, J. J., Robins, P. M., & DeLancy, E. (1997). Discriminant validity of test observations for children with attention deficit/hyperactivity. *Journal of School Psychology, 35,* 391–401.

Guilford, J. P. (1967). *The nature of human intelligence.* New York: McGraw-Hill.

Gyurke, J. S. (1991). The assessment of preschool children with the Wechsler Preschool and Primary Scale of Intelligence–Revised. In B. A. Bracken (Ed.), *The psychoeducational assessment of preschool children* (pp. 86–106). Boston: Allyn & Bacon.

Gyurke, J. S., Prifitera, A., & Sharp, S. A. (1991). Frequency of Verbal and Performance IQ discrepancies on the WPPSI-R at various levels of ability. *Journal of Psychoeducational Assessment, 9,* 230–239.

Harrington, R. G. (1982). Caution: Standardized testing may be hazardous to the educational programs of intellectually gifted children. *Education, 103,* 112–117.

Harrington, R. G., Kimbrell, J., & Dai, X. (1992). The relationship between the Woodcock Johnson Psycheducational Battery–Revised (Early Development) and the Wechsler Preschool and Primary Scale of Intelligence–Revised. *Psychology in the Schools, 29,* 116–125.

Hishinuma, E. S., & Yamakawa, E. S. (1993). Construct and criterion-related validity of the WISC-III for exceptional students and those who are "at risk." In B. A. Bracken & R. S. McCallum (Eds.), *Journal of Psychoeducational Assessment monograph series, advances in psychoeducational assessment: Wechsler Intelligence Scale for Children–Third Edition* (pp. 94–104). Germantown, TN: Psychoeducational Corporation.

Horn, J. L. (1989). Cognitive diversity: A framework of learning. In P. L. Ackerman, R. J. Sternberg, & R. Glaser (Eds.), *Learning and individual differences* (pp. 61–116). New York: Freeman.

Horn, J. L. (1991). Measurement of intellectual capabilities: A review of theory. In K. S. McGrew, J. K. Werder, & R. W. Woodcock (Eds.), *Woodcock-Johnson Technical Manual: A reference on theory and current research* (pp. 197–246). Allen, TX: DLM Teaching Resources.

Horn, J. L., & Cattell, R. B. (1966). Refinement and test of theory of fluid and crystallized intelligence. *Journal of Educational Psychology, 57,* 253–270.

Horn, J. L., & Cattell, R. B. (1967). Age differences in fluid and crystallized intelligence. *Acta Psychologica, 26,* 107–129.

Horn, J. L., & Hofer, S. M. (1992). Major abilities and development in the adult period. In R. J. Sternberg & C. A. Berg (Eds.), *Intellectual development* (pp. 44–99). Boston: Cambridge University Press.

Javorsky, J. (1993). The relationship between the Kaufman Brief Intelligence Test and the WISC-III in a clinical sample. *Diagnostique, 19*, 377–385.

Jensen, A. R. (1998). *The g factor: The science of mental ability.* Westport, CT: Praeger.

Kamphaus, R. W. (1993). *Clinical assessment of children's intelligence.* Boston: Allyn & Bacon.

Kaplan, C. (1992). Ceiling effects in assessing high-IQ children with the WPPSI-R. *Journal of Clinical Child Psychology, 21*, 403–406.

Kaufman, A. S. (1983). Intelligence: Old concepts—new perspectives. In G. W. Hynd (Ed.), *The school psychologist: An introduction* (pp. 95–117). Syracuse, NY: Syracuse University Press.

Kaufman, A. S. (1990a). *Assessing adolescent and adult intelligence.* Boston: Allyn & Bacon.

Kaufman, A. S. (1990b). You can't judge a test by its colors. *Journal of School Psychology, 28*, 387–394.

Kaufman, A. S. (1992). Evaluation of the WISC-III and WPPSI-R for gifted children. *Roeper Review, 14*, 154–158.

Kaufman, A. S. (1993). King WISC the third assumes the throne. *Journal of School Psychology, 31*, 345–354.

Kaufman, A. S. (1994a). *Intelligent testing with the WISC-III.* New York: Wiley.

Kaufman, A. S. (1994b). A reply to Macmann and Barnett: Lessons from the blind men and the elephant. *School Psychology Quarterly, 9*, 199–207.

Kaufman, A. S. (in press). Tests of intelligence. In R. J. Sternberg (Ed.), *Handbook of intelligence.* New York: Cambridge University Press.

Kaufman, A. S., & Horn, J. L. (1996). Age changes on test of fluid and crystallized ability for women and men on the Kaufman Adolescent and Adult Intelligence Test (KAIT) at ages 17–94 years. *Archives of Clinical Neuropsychology, 11*, 97–121.

Kaufman, A. S., Kaufman, N. L., Dougherty, E. H., & Tuttle, K. (1996). *Kaufman WISC-III Integrated Interpretive System* (K-WIIS). Odessa, FL: Psychological Assessment Resources.

Kaufman, A. S., & Lichtenberger, E. O. (1998). Intellectual assessment. In A. S. Bellack & M. Hersen (Series Eds.) & C. R. Reynolds (Vol. Ed.), *Comprehensive clinical psychology: Vol. 4. Assessment* (pp. 203–238). Oxford: Elsevier Science Ltd.

Kaufman, A. S., & Lichtenberger, E. O. (1999). *Essentials of WAIS-III Assessment.* New York: Wiley.

Kelley, M. F., & Surbeck, E. (1991). History of preschool assessment. In B. A. Bracken (Ed.), *The psychoeducational assessment of preschool children* (2nd ed., pp. 1–17). Boston: Allyn & Bacon.

Kohs, S. C. (1923). *Intelligence measurement.* New York: Macmillan.

Konold, T. R., Kush, J. C., & Canivez, G. L. (1997). Factor replication of the WISC-III in three independent samples of children receiving special education. *Journal of Psychoeducational Assessment, 15*, 123–137.

Kush, J. C. (1996). Factor structure of the WISC-III for students with learning disabilities. *Journal of Psychoeducational Assessment, 14*, 32–40.

Lassiter, K. S., & Bardos, A. N. (1995). The relationship between young children's academic achievement and measures of intelligence. *Psychology in the Schools, 32*, 170–177.

Lavin, C. (1996a). The relationship between the Wechsler Intelligence Scale for Children–Third Edition and the Kaufman Test of Educational Achievement. *Psychology in the Schools, 33*, 119–123.

Lavin, C. (1996b). Scores on the WISC-III and Woodcock-Johnson Tests of Achievement–Revised for a sample of children with emotional handicaps. *Psychological Reports, 79*, 1291–1295.

Lavin C. (1996c). The WISC-Third Edition and the Stanford Binet Intelligence Scale: Fourth Edition: A preliminary study of validity. *Psychological Reports, 78*, 491–496.

Levinson, E. M., & Folino, L. (1994). The relationship between the WISC-III and the Kaufman Brief Intelligence Test with students referred for gifted education. *Special Services in the Schools, 8*, 155–159.

Lewis, C. D., & Lorentz, S. (1994). Comparison of the Leiter International Performance Scale and the Wechsler Intelligence Scales. *Psychological Reports, 74*, 521–522.

Lipsitz, J. D., Dworkin, R. H., & Erlenmeyer-Kimling, L. (1993). Wechsler Comprehension and Picture Arrangement subtests and social adjustment. *Psychological Assessment, 5*, 430–473.

Lukens, J., & Hurrell, R. M. (1996). A comparison of Stanford Binet-IV and the WISC-III with mildly mentally retarded children. *Psychology in the Schools, 33*, 24–27.

Macmann, G. M., & Barnett, D. W. (1994). Structural analysis of correlated factors: Lessons from the verbal-performance dichotomy of the Wechsler scales. *School Psychology Quarterly, 9*, 161–197.

Matarazzo, J. D. (1972). *Wechsler's measurement and appraisal of adult intelligence* (5th ed.). New York: Oxford University Press.

Mayes, S. D., Calhoun, S. L., & Crowell, E. W. (1998). WISC-III profiles for children with and without learning disabilities. *Psychology in the Schools, 35*, 309–316.

McDermott, P. A., Fantuzzo, J. W., & Glutting, J. J. (1990). Just say no to subtest analysis: A critique on Wechsler theory and practice. *Journal of Psychoeducational Assessment, 8*, 290–302.

McDermott, P. A., Fantuzzo, J. W., Glutting, J. J., Watkins, M. W., & Baggaley, A. R. (1992). Illusions of meaning in the ipsative assessment of children's ability. *Journal of Special Education, 25*, 504–526.

Neisser, U. (Ed.). (1998). *The rising curve: Long-term gains in IQ and related measures.* Washington, DC: American Psychological Association.

Ochoa, S. H., Powell, M. P., & Robles-Pina, R. (1996). School psychologists' assessment practices with bilingual and limited-English-proficient students. *Journal of Psychoeducational Assessment, 14*, 250–275.

Parker, F. (1981). Ideas that shaped American schools. *Phi Delta Kappan, 62*, 314–319.

Phelps, L., Leguori, S., Nisewaner, J., & Parker, M. (1993). Practical interpretations of the WISC-III with language-disordered children. *Journal of Psychoeducational Assessment, 81*, 71–76.

Ponton, M., Zimmerman, I. L., & Woo-Sam, J. M. (1997). *WISC-III versus WIAT comparison for referred children.* Unpublished manuscript.

Prewett, P. N. (1995). A comparison of two screening tests (the Matrix Analogies and the Kaufman Brief Intelligence Test) with the WISC-III. *Psychological Assessment, 7*, 69–72.

Prewett, P. N., & Matavich, M. A. (1993). A comparison of referred students' performance on the WISC-III and the Stanford-Binet Intelligence Scale: Fourth Edition. *Journal of Psychoeducational Assessment, 81*, 142–148.

Prewett, P. N., & Matavich, M. A. (1994). A comparison of referred students' performance on the WISC-III and the Stanford-Binet Intelligence Scale: Fourth Edition. *Journal of Psychoeducational Assessment, 12,* 42–48.

Prifitera, A., & Dersh, J. (1993). Base rates of WISC-III diagnostic subtest patterns among normal, learning disabled, and ADHD samples. *Journal of Psychoeducational Assessment* [WISC-III Monograph], 43–55.

Prifitera, A., & Saklofske, D. (Eds.). (1998). *WISC-III clinical use and interpretation.* San Diego, CA: Academic Press.

The Psychological Corporation. (1991). *The WPPSI-R Writer.* San Antonio, TX: Author.

The Psychological Corporation. (1994a). *Scoring Assistant for the Wechsler Scales (SAWS).* San Antonio, TX: Author.

The Psychological Corporation. (1994b). *WISC-III Writer.* San Antonio, TX: Author.

Raven, J. C. (1938). *Progressive matrices.* London: Lewis.

Raviv, A., Rahmani, L., & Ber, H. (1986). Cognitive characteristics of learning-disabled and immature children as determined by the Wechsler Preschool and Primary Scale of Intelligence test. *Journal of Clinical Child Psychology, 15,* 241–247.

Reitan, R. M., & Wolfson, D. (1992). *Neuropsychological evaluation of older children.* South Tucson, AZ: Neuropsychology Press.

Reynolds, C. R., & Kaufman, A. S. (1990). Assessment of children's intelligence with the Wechsler Intelligence Scale for Children–Revised. In C. R. Reynolds & R. W. Kamphaus (Eds.), *Handbook of psychological and educational assessment of children: Intelligence and achievement* (pp. 127–165), New York: Guilford Press.

Reynolds, C. R., Sanchez, S., & Willson, V. L. (1996). Normative tables for calculating the WISC-III Performance and Full Scale IQs when Symbol Search is substituted for Coding. *Psychological Assessment, 8,* 378–382.

Ricco, C. A., Cohen, M. J., Hall, J., & Ross, C. M. (1997). The third and fourth factors of the WISC-III: What they don't measure. *Journal of Psychoeducational Assessment, 15,* 27–39.

Roid, G. H., & Gyurke, J. (1991). General-factor and specific variance in the WPPSI-R. *Journal of Psychoeducational Assessment, 9,* 209–223.

Roid, G. H., Prifitera, A., & Weiss, L. G. (1993). Replication of the WISC-III factor structure in an independent sample. In B. A. Bracken & R. S. McCallum (Eds.), *Journal of Psychoeducational Assessment monograph series, advances in psychoeducational assessment: Wechsler Intelligence Scale for Children–Third Edition* (pp. 6–21). Germantown, TN: Psychoeducational Corporation.

Roid, G. H., & Worall, W. (1997). Replication of the Wechsler Intelligence Scale for Children–Third Edition four-factor model in the Canadian normative sample. *Psychological Assessment, 9,* 512–515.

Rourke, B. P. (1998). Significance of Verbal-Performance discrepancies for subtypes of children with learning disabilities: Opportunities for the WISC-III. In A. Prifitera & D. Saklofske (Eds.), *WISC-III clinical use and interpretation* (pp. 139–156). San Diego, CA: Academic Press.

Rust, J. O., & Lindstrom, A. (1996). Concurrent validity of the WISC-III and Stanford Binet-IV. *Psychological Reports, 79,* 618–620.

Rust, J. O., & Yates, A. G. (1997). Concurrent validity of the WISC–Third Edition and the K-ABC. *Psychological Reports, 80,* 89–90.

Saklofske, D. H., Schwean, V. L., Yackulic, R. A., & Quinn, D. (1994). WISC-III and

SB:FE performance of children with attention deficit hyperactivity disorder. *Canadian Journal of School Psychology, 18,* 167–171.

Sandoval, J. (1984, April). *Verifying the WISC-R ACID profile.* Paper presented at the meeting of the National Association of School Psychologists, Philadelphia.

Sandoval, J. (1995). Review of the Wechsler Intelligence Scale for Children, Third Edition. In J. C. Conoley & J. C. Impara (Eds.), *The twelfth mental measurements yearbook* (pp. 1103–1104). Lincoln, NE: Buros Institute of Mental Measurements.

Sapp, G. L., Abbott, G., & Hinkley, R. (1997). Examination of the WISC-III with urban exceptional students. *Psychological Reports, 81,* 1163–1168.

Sattler, J. M. (1988). *Assessment of children* (3rd ed.) San Diego, CA: Author.

Sattler, J. M. (1992). *Assessment of children: WISC-III and WPPSI-R Supplement.* San Diego, CA: Author.

Schneider, W., & Shiffrin, R. M. (1977). Controlled and Automatic Human Information Processing: Detection, Search, and Attention. *Psychological Review, 84,* 1–66.

Schwean, V. L., & Saklofske, D. H. (1998). WISC-III assessment of children with attention deficit/hyperactivity disorder. In A. Prifitera & D. Saklofske (Eds.), *WISC-III clinical use and interpretation* (pp. 91–118). San Diego, CA: Academic Press.

Schwean, V. L., Saklofske, D. H., Yackulic, R. A., & Quinn, D. (1993). WISC-III performance of ADHD children. *Journal of Psychoeducational Assessment* [WISC-III Monograph], 56–70.

Seidman, L. J., Biederman, J., Faraone, S. V., & Weber, W. (1997). A pilot study of neuropsychological function in girls with ADHD. *Journal of the American Academy of Child and Adolescent Psychiatry, 36,* 366–373.

Silver, L. B. (Ed.). (1993). *Learning Disabilities. Child and Adolescent Psychiatric Clinics of North America, 2,* 181–353.

Slate, J. R. (1995). Discrepancies between IQ and index scores for a clinical sample of students: Useful diagnostic indicators? *Psychology in the Schools, 32,* 103–108.

Slate, J. R. (1998). Sex differences in WISC-III IQs: Time for separate norms? *Journal of Psychology, 132,* 677–679.

Slate, J. R., & Jones, C. H. (1995). Relationship of the WISC-III and WISC-R for students with specific learning disabilities and mental retardation. *Diagnostique, 21,* 9–17.

Sparrow, S. S. (1991, August). WISC-R and WISC-III: profiles of gifted boys. In A. Prifitera (Chair), *Clinical validity of the WISC-III.* Symposium conducted at the annual meeting of the American Psychological Association, San Francisco.

Sparrow, S. S., & Gurland, S. T. (1998). Assessment of gifted children with the WISC-III. In A. Prifitera & D. Saklofske (Eds.), *WISC-III clinical use and interpretation* (pp. 59–72). San Diego, CA: Academic Press.

Spruill, J. (1998). Assessment of mental retardation with the WISC-III. In A. Prifitera & D. Saklofske (Eds.), *WISC-III clinical use and interpretation* (pp. 73–90). San Diego, CA: Academic Press.

Sternberg, R. J. (1982). Lies we live by: Misapplication of test in identifying the gifted. *Gifted Child Quarterly, 26,* 157–161.

Sternberg, S. (1966). High-Speed Scanning in Human Memory. *Science, 153,* 652–654.

Stott, L. H., & Ball, R. S. (1965). Infant and preschool mental tests: Review and evaluation. *Monographs of the Society for Research in Child Development, 30* (3, Whole No. 101).

Tellegen, A., & Briggs, P. F. (1967). Old wine in new skins: Grouping Wechsler subtests into new scales. *Journal of Consulting Psychology, 31*, 499–506.

Terman, L. M. (1916). *The measurement of intelligence.* Boston: Houghton Mifflin.

Terman, L. M., & Merrill, M. A. (1937). *Measuring intelligence.* Boston: Houghton Mifflin.

Terman, L. M., & Merrill, M. A. (1960). *Stanford-Binet Intelligence Scale.* Boston: Houghton Mifflin.

Tiholov, T. T., Zawallich, A., & Janzen, H. L. (1996). Diagnosis based on the WISC-III processing speed factor. *Canadian Journal of School Psychology, 12*, 23–34.

Tyerman, M. J. (1986). Gifted children and their identification: Learning ability not intelligence. *Gifted Education International, 4*, 81–84.

U.S. Department of Education. (1994). *Sixteenth annual report to Congress on the implementation of the Education of Individuals with Disabilities Act.* Washington, DC: Author.

Vance, B., & Fuller, G. B. (1995). Relation of scores on WISC-III and WRAT-3 for a sample of referred children and youth. *Psychological Reports, 76*, 371–374.

Ward, S. B., Ward, T. J., Hatt, C. V., Young, D. L., & Mollner, N. R. (1995). The incidence and utility of the ACID, ACIDS, and SCAD profiles in a referred population. *Psychology in the Schools, 32*, 267–276.

Watkins, M. W. (1996). Diagnostic utility of the WISC-III developmental index as a predictor of learning disabilities. *Journal of Learning Disabilities, 29*, 305–312.

Watkins, M. W., Kush, J. C., & Glutting, J. J. (1997a). Discriminant and predictive validity of the WISC-III ACID profile among children with learning disabilities. *Psychology in the Schools, 34*, 309–319.

Watkins, M. W., Kush, J. C., & Glutting, J. J. (1997b). Prevalence and diagnostic utility of the WISC-III SCAD profile among children with learning disabilities. *School Psychology Quarterly, 12*, 235–248.

Wechsler, D. (1939). *Measurement of adult intelligence.* Baltimore: Williams & Wilkins.

Wechsler, D. (1944). *The measurement of adult intelligence* (3rd ed.). Baltimore: Williams & Wilkins.

Wechsler, D. (1949). *Manual for the Wechsler Intelligence Scale for Children.* San Antonio, TX: The Psychological Corporation.

Wechsler, D. (1955). *Manual for the Wechsler Adult Intelligence Scale (WAIS).* San Antonio, TX: The Psychological Corporation.

Wechsler, D. (1974). *Manual for the Wechsler Preschool and Primary Scale of Intelligence (WPPSI).* New York: The Psychological Corporation.

Wechsler, D. (1981). *Manual for the Wechsler Adult Intelligence Scale–Revised (WAIS-R).* San Antonio, TX: The Psychological Corporation.

Wechsler, D. (1989). *Manual for the Wechsler Preschool and Primary Scale of Intelligence–Revised (WPPSI-R).* San Antonio, TX: The Psychological Corporation.

Wechsler, D. (1991). *Manual for the Wechsler Intelligence Scale for Children–Third Edition (WISC-III).* San Antonio, TX: The Psychological Corporation.

Wechsler, D. (1997). *Wechsler Adult Intelligence Scale–Third Edition (WAIS-III) administration and scoring manual.* San Antonio, TX: The Psychological Corporation.

Weiss, G., & Hechtman, L. (1993). *Hyperactive children grown up.* New York: Guilford Press.

Weiss, L. G. (1995). WISC-III IQs: New norms raise queries. *Assessment Focus, 1*, 5–6.

Wilson, M. S., & Reschly, D. J. (1996). Assessment in school psychology training and practice. *School Psychology Review, 25*, 9–23.

Wislar, J., Hal, C. W., Bolen, L. M, & Webster, R. E. (1993, April). *Concurrent validity of the WISC-III and the Woodcock-Johnson Psycho-Educational Test Battery–Revised.* Paper presented at the meeting of the National Association of School Psychologists, Washington, DC.

Woodcock, R. W. (1990). Theoretical foundations of the WJ-R measures of cognitive ability. *Journal of Psychoeducational Assessment, 8,* 231–258.

Woodrich, D. L., & Barry, C. T. (1991). A survey of school psychologists' practices for identifying mentally retarded students. *Psychology in the Schools, 28,* 165–171.

Zimmerman, I. L., & Woo-Sam, J. M. (1972). Research with the WISC, 1960–1970. *Journal of Clinical Psychology Monograph Supplement, 33,* 1–44.

Zimmerman, I. L., & Woo-Sam, J. M. (1973). *Clinical interpretation of the Wechsler Adult Intelligence Scale.* New York: Grune & Stratton.

Zimmerman, I. L., & Woo-Sam, J. M. (1990, April). *The interchangeability of major measures of intelligence.* Paper presented at the meeting of the Western Psychological Association, Los Angeles.

Zimmerman, I. L., & Woo-Sam, J. M. (1997). Review of the criterion-related validity of the WISC-III: The first five years. *Perceptual and Motor Skills, 85,* 531–546.

Annotated Bibliography

Bracken, B. A., & McCallum R. S. (Eds.). (1993). *Wechsler Intelligence Scale for Children: Third Edition*. Brandon, VT: Clinical Psychology Publishing.

A series of articles explores the WISC-III's psychometric properties, its use with exceptional samples, and reviews of the test. Issues of factor structure, diagnostic subtest patterns, and fairness of testing are reviewed. Populations examined include deaf, language impaired, attention-deficit hyperactivity disorder, emotionally disturbed, reading disabled, and others. Reviews include the perspectives of theorists, practitioners, and psychometricians.

Cooper, S. (1995). The clinical use and interpretation of the Wechsler Intelligence Scale for Children–Third Edition. Springfield, IL: Charles C. Thomas.

This book presents conceptual approaches to using the WISC-III in the context of research that has been conducted with the test. A variety of frameworks are provided for clinical use and interpretation of the WISC-III. Topics include development of the WISC-III, reliability and validity, writing the psychological report, bias and the Wechsler scales, and reviews of the test.

Flynn, J. R. (1998). WAIS-III and WISC-III: US IQ gains 1972 to 1995; how to compensate for obsolete norms. *Perceptual and Motor Skills, 86,* 1231–1239.

Flynn compares the IQ gains from (a) the WISC-R to WISC-III revision, to (b) those of the WAIS-R to WAIS-III revision. Important differences in samples are noted. The negligible differences between a sample tested on both the WISC-III and WAIS-III are also presented. Various explanations for the results are discussed.

Gyurke, J. S. (1991). The assessment of preschool children with the Wechsler Preschool and Primary Scale of Intelligence–Revised. In B. A. Bracken (Ed.), *The psychoeducational assessment of preschool children* (pp. 86–106). Boston: Allyn & Bacon.

This chapter provides a description of the WPPSI-R, including each of its individual subtests. It also evaluates psychometric qualities of the test, including reliability and validity. A brief section on interpretation of the WPPSI-R is presented.

Kaufman, A. S. (1994). *Intelligent testing with the WISC-III*. New York: Wiley.

This book covers several topics relevant to the WISC-III and the WPPSI-R. The third and fourth factors (Freedom from Distractibility and Processing Speed) on the WISC-III are reviewed in depth through multiple explanations and interpretations. A theoretical understanding of scales and tasks (especially from Horn's theory) is presented, along with many hypothesized explanations for Verbal > Performance and Performance > Verbal profiles. Numerous case reports illustrate how to combine and present complex test data and how to apply the philosophy of intelligent testing.

Kaufman, A. S., & Lichtenberger, E. O. (1998). Intellectual assessment. In A. S. Bellack & M. Hersen (Series Eds.) & C. R. Reynolds (Vol. Ed.), *Comprehensive clinical psychology: Vol. 4. Assessment* (pp. 187–238). New York: Pergamon.

This chapter reviews several measures of intelligence with a focus on the Wechsler scales. It provides an overview of the WPPSI-R and WISC-III, their standardization properties, and the research available on the tests. A brief guide to analysis of WISC-III data is introduced. The chapter also discusses how clinicians may integrate various cognitive instruments with the Wechsler scales to obtain a more comprehensive picture of client functioning.

McGrew, K. S., & Flanagan, D. P. (1998). *The Intelligence Test Desk Reference (ITDR): Gf-Gc cross-battery assessment.* Boston: Allyn & Bacon.

This book provides information about the Fluid and Crystallized (Gf-Gc) Intelligence theory. It presents information on various tests of intelligence, including the WPPSI-R and WISC-III. The authors spell out how practitioners can conduct assessments that tap a broader range of abilities than any single cognitive test can. Suggestions help practitioners combine Wechsler subtests with other batterys' subtests to measure abilities from the Gf-Gc theory.

Prifitera, A., & Saklofske, D. (Eds.). (1998). *WISC-III clinical use and interpretation.* San Diego, CA: Academic Press.

This book contains a collection of recent research information and in-depth clinical perspectives on the WISC-III. Topics include research relevant to the use of the WISC-III for groups such as gifted, mentally retarded, ADHD, emotionally disturbed, language impaired, hearing impaired, and culturally diverse children. The book emphasizes the need to soundly justify one's interpretation of test results within the context of the individual's history.

Sattler, J. M. (1992). *Assessment of children: WISC-III and WPPSI-R supplement.* San Diego, CA: Author.

This supplement to Sattler's text provides information on the latest versions of the WPPSI and WISC. Basic technical information such as reliability and validity is reviewed, as well as statistical information such as intercorrelations between subtests and scales, and factor analyses. Values obtained on the WISC-III and WPPSI-R are compared to those obtained on the WISC-R and WPPSI, respectively. A checklist is provided for examiners to ensure proper administration of each subtest. Very brief information is provided on interpreting the tests. Strengths and weaknesses of the tests are reviewed. Supplementary tables are provided for calculating short form scores on the tests.

Truch, S. (1993). *The WISC-III companion: A guide to interpretation and educational intervention.* Austin, TX: Pro-Ed.

This book helps practitioners develop hypotheses concerning children's learning patterns on the basis of their WISC-III performance. Professionals in the field of school psychology, clinical psychology, and counseling psychology were the intended audience for the book, according to the author. The book reviews practical educational applications of the WISC-III profile.

Wechsler, D. (1989). *Wechsler Preschool and Primary Scale of Intelligence–Revised Edition (WPPSI-R) manual.* San Antonio, TX: The Psychological Corporation.

This manual, which is part of the WPPSI-R kit, provides a basic description of the WPPSI-R scales and subtests. Revisions from the previous version of the WPPSI are reviewed in a subtest-by-subtest manner. The manual details important information about administration and articulates the starting, discontinue, and timing rules for each WPPSI-R subtest. Examiners are provided a basic script and directions for how to administer each subtest in a standardized manner. Subtest norms tables appear in Table 25, and IQ tables appear in Table 27. The text reviews development of the norms and standardization procedures, and it discusses reliability and validity studies.

Wechsler, D. (1991). *Wechsler Intelligence Scale for Children—Third Edition (WISC-III) manual.* San Antonio, TX: The Psychological Corporation.

This manual, which is part of the WISC-III kit, provides a basic description of the WISC-III scales and subtests. Revisions from the WISC-R to the Third Edition are reviewed in a subtest-by-subtest manner. WISC-III examiners can gather important information about administration from this manual. For each WISC-III subtest the starting, discontinue, and timing rules are articulated. Examiners are provided a basic script and directions of how to administer each subtest in a standardized manner. Subtest norms tables appear in Table A.1, and IQ and Index Score tables appear in Tables A.2 through A.7. Supplementary tables for determining the size of differences needed for significance appear in Tables B.1 through B.7. The text reviews development of the norms and standardization procedures, and it discusses reliability and validity studies.

Index